CHILDREN OF THE STORM

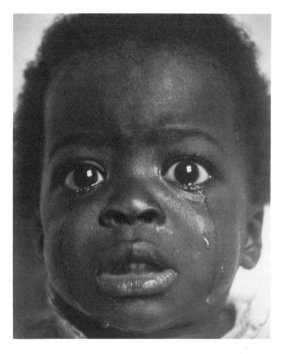

When the storms of life are raging, stand by me.
GOSPEL HYMN

To rid this nation of racism we must bring to the attention of our people the gravity and scope of this disease, explaining how it is manifested and how it is dangerously vitiating the strength of our nation and dividing it against itself.
1970 WHITE HOUSE CONFERENCE ON CHILDREN

Children of the Storm

Black Children and American Child Welfare

ANDREW BILLINGSLEY
Howard University

JEANNE M. GIOVANNONI
University of California, Los Angeles

HARCOURT BRACE JOVANOVICH, INC.
New York   Chicago   San Francisco   Atlanta

COVER   Photograph by Maury Englander for the Children's Aid Society, New York.

FRONTISPIECE   Reprinted from *Women, Heroes, and a Frog,* by Nina Leen by permission of W. W. Norton & Company Inc. Copyright © 1970 by Nina Leen.

CHAPTER OPENING PHOTOGRAPHS

1   Black child and brother. Photograph by Mike Levins.
2   Black students in Harlem receiving food during the Depression. Photograph by James Van DerZee.
3   Colored Orphan Asylum, Memphis, Tennessee, shortly after the Civil War. The Bettmann Archive.
4   Maryland House of Reformation for Colored Boys. From *Report of the Board of Managers, Maryland House of Reformation for Colored Boys,* 1915. Schomburg Collection, The New York Public Library, Astor, Lenox, and Tilden Foundation.
5   Page from the 1939 annual of the Children's Aid Society, New York. Courtesy of the Children's Aid Society, New York.
6   Members of the Child Placing and Adoption Committee of the State Charities Aid Association, New York, with Samuel A. Allen, State Department of Social Welfare.
7   Adoptive parents with their child and a staff member of the Spence-Chapin Adoption Agency. Courtesy of the Spence-Chapin Adoption Agency.
8   Council meeting at the Harlem-Dowling Agency, 1972. Photograph by Geri Davis.
9   Children looking from a window. Photograph by Henry Monroe.

© 1972 by Andrew Billingsley

Paperbound ISBN: 0-15-507271-4
Hardbound ISBN: 0-15-117340-0
Library of Congress Catalog Card Number: 72-75593

Printed in the United States of America

Foreword

Throughout the 1960's, with increasing frequency as well as intensity, white racism was cited as a fundamental element in American society. This trend reached its culmination in the 1967 Kerner Commission's report,* which came as a startling revelation to the majority of Americans. The prestige of a presidential commission, combined with the moderate composition of its membership, created sufficient credibility in the report for white America to admit what Black America had known all along: America is a racist society.

White America made lip-service admission, but not complete acknowledgment, of this fact, and the extent to which racism has permeated American social, political, and economic institutions has not been fully comprehended even to this day. Thus, despite the long series of additional exposés of racism in various aspects of American life, each new revelation has brought its own sense of shocked disbelief.

As Americans begin to inspect their society more thoroughly, they

* The National Advisory Commission on Civil Disorders was appointed by President Lyndon B. Johnson in 1966 and was headed by Governor Otto Kerner of Illinois.

find a continuous stream of evidence that racism pervades the social fabric in every seam and in every stitch. Whether it is in the brutal, dehumanizing mistreatment of Black prisoners, the systematic exclusion of Black citizens from the appointive processes of local government, or the omission or distortion of the historic role of Black people in American history textbooks, one finds that racism is so endemic as to be virtually total.

The value of this book is that it exposes, in a readable style and with perceptive insight and scholarly documentation, yet one more specific manifestation of the problem of racism in America. The authors focus on child welfare and find that the system is failing Black children and that that failure is both a manifestation and a result of racism. They cover thoroughly the policies and practices in child welfare as they relate to Black children.

Chapter 1 is a must. Besides providing an overview of the major themes of the book, it contains a useful discussion of the subtle nuances of racism that goes beyond a simplistic definition. The differences between overt and covert racism, between individual, collective, and institutional racism, and between attitudinal and behavioral racism are clearly delineated. The concluding chapter is also particularly noteworthy because it proposes reforms in child welfare that follow logically from the discussions in the book and cites up-to-date sources of new initiatives for Black leadership in child welfare reform.

From the authors' analysis, it is clear that the only viable alternative for child welfare reform depends on the exertion of strong Black leadership. This book, therefore, is a call to action in child welfare reform. It has my full endorsement.

MERVYN M. DYMALLY
State Senator
Watts, California

Preface

The racism that characterizes American society has had tragic effects upon Black children. It has given the Black child a history, a situation, and a set of problems that are qualitatively different from those of the white child. In a narrower context, American racism has placed Black children in an especially disadvantaged position in relation to American institutions, including the institution of child welfare. As for the child welfare system itself, societal racism has had extensive and intensive effects upon the organization, distribution, and delivery of services to Black children. Moreover, specific aspects of the welfare system complement this racism and serve as barriers to change. This book traces the past and present interplay of systemic and institutional racism and describes the resulting disadvantages to Black children in relation to child welfare. It is intended for all who care about the well-being of these children.

Chapter 1 establishes the conceptual framework of the book. We define and examine aspects of racism and consider the social systems context in which Black children live: the family, the Black community, and the broader society. We present material supporting our premise that poverty, discrimination, and a distinctive history have placed the Black child in a situation different from that of the white child.

The underlying philosophy of the present child welfare system is that *all* families *should* be able to function adequately without the assistance of society and that failure to perform the parental role without such assistance is indicative of individual pathology. Services to supplement or supplant parental role performance are thus geared in both quantity and kind to correct assumedly rare, accidental, individual cases of parental failure. Services designed to alleviate social and environmental stresses on families are virtually nonexistent in this country. While this philosophy has led to inadequate provision for the white child, it has resulted in a far greater disservice to the Black child. Poverty and racism have produced stresses on Black families different both qualitatively and quantitatively from those on white families; because of these stresses, Black children are apt to suffer regardless of the presence or absence of pathology in their parents.

In Chapters 2, 3, and 4, we place the relationship of Black children and American child welfare in historical perspective. Chapter 2 traces the historical development of child welfare services from colonial times to the late nineteenth century. We discuss the philosophical roots of the provision of services, the major transitions in the forms of service provided, and the evolution of the agencies, institutions, and systems of services. The forms of service that evolved were highly attenuated, and the child welfare system that developed was—and is —almost exclusively focused on placement of children away from their families; services to children in their own homes were not (and are not) extended to any significant degree. As a result, the system serves all children inadequately. But the omission of in-home services is especially crucial to Black children, for they are burdened with many special problems which require much more than placement for solution. Moreover, the systems that developed in America were voluntary and religious—characteristics that led to the systematic and deliberate exclusion of Black children from the developing child welfare institutions.

Chapter 3 examines a segment of American history that has been almost entirely ignored. In the latter part of the nineteenth century, Black people made highly creative and courageous efforts in developing an extensive and intricate network of social welfare services. Black child welfare leaders provided an array of services for their children, including day-care services, small group homes for children, and services for migrant adolescents.

Chapter 4 concludes the historical perspective with an examination of twentieth-century child welfare up to the present. We outline the major changes that have occurred within the system in general as well as those specific to Black children and trace the gradual admission of Black children into the established systems of services. The distribution of services is still inequitable; in this chapter we discuss the institutional forces and practices which contribute to these inequities.

Chapters 5, 6, and 7 analyze specific efforts which have been made since the late 1930's to extend child welfare services to Black children. Each of these efforts can be considered a battle against institutional racism, and as such should be of interest to all who are concerned with the impact of institutional racism on service systems. We examine these battles in order to elucidate the courses of action, both fruitful and ineffective, barriers to change, and the implications for future planning, reforms, and application.

Chapter 5 is based on empirical data drawn from a study conducted by the Child Welfare League of America in 1944 on behalf of Black children in three major cities—New York, Philadelphia, and Cleveland. This study deals with efforts—exasperatingly unsuccessful —engendered within the child welfare system at the community level.

In Chapter 6 we turn to a nationwide effort: the National Urban League Foster Care and Adoptions Project, which was carried on in more than thirty cities between 1953 and 1959. This project was begun outside the established system by an organization of Black people. We analyze the philosophical bases of the project, the various strategies employed in eliciting change on behalf of Black children, and the major manifestations of resistance to change. The chapter concludes with an examination of the Adopt-A-Child Project in New York City, which was an outgrowth of the National Urban League effort: a specific community-wide effort by Black social workers to improve conditions for Black children.

In Chapter 7 our emphasis shifts to efforts toward change made by individual organizations. The discussion is based on research we conducted on adoption agencies in four cities—Los Angeles, New York, Chicago, and Philadelphia—agencies which in 1968 and 1969 were serving the largest numbers of Black children in those cities. Our study was sponsored by the National Urban League and the

Metropolitan Applied Research Center in New York City. The data we present and analyze are concerned with the origins of change within these agencies, the strategies employed in bringing about organizational reform, the innovative structures and practices employed, the levels of success achieved, and the persistent barriers to further progress.

The problems are all too clear. But what are possible solutions? In Chapter 8 we propose a more diversified system of child welfare services. We recommend that services to Black children be extended through a system that provides fully developed public and private agencies, giving service without regard to race, but that also includes agencies directly under the control of Black people and operated specifically for Black children. Such a plan calls for both the creation of new agencies and the deliberate reorganization of many existing agencies and practices. Fundamental to this reorganization are the yielding of control over direction and the administration of services, at all levels, to the Black community, and the revision and innovation of practices and procedures, with specific and deliberate reference to Black children and their situations. Many existing practices are dysfunctional for Black-specific innovations and changes if they are ultimately to benefit Black children.

The book concludes with a consideration of major social-policy issues and directions which transcend the field of child welfare but which are of desperate urgency to the welfare of Black children.

ANDREW BILLINGSLEY
JEANNE M. GIOVANNONI

ACKNOWLEDGMENTS

The authors gratefully acknowledge the assistance of some of the many people and institutions that so generously provided data, counsel, and comments during the development of the book. Drs. Dunmore, Morisey, and Walker as well as Mrs. Billingsley read the complete draft and offered a great many suggestions that were very useful in revising the manuscript.

Amy Tate Billingsley, Washington, D.C.

Ethel Branham, Department of Adoptions, County of Los Angeles

Loyce W. Bynum, the Spence-Chapin Adoption Service

Kenneth B. Clark, Metropolitan Applied Research Center

Sarah S. Collins, formerly of the Women's Christian Alliance

Ruth A. Davis, formerly of the University of California, Berkeley

Janice M. Dickson, Center for the Study of Higher Education, University of California

Division of Adoption Services, Bureau of Child Welfare, New York City Department of Social Services

Sydney Duncan, Homes for Black Children

Charlotte J. Dunmore, School of Social Work, Simmons College

Jane D. Edwards, the Spence-Chapin Adoption Service

Benjamin Finley, Afro-American Family and Community Services

Marge Fleming, Department of Adoptions, County of Los Angeles

Mollie Ginyard, Department of Adoptions, County of Los Angeles

Morris Grant, Boston Urban League

Marilyn C. Greene, Howard University

Jyl Hagler, Howard University

Walter A. Heath, Department of Adoptions, County of Los Angeles

Donna B. Hess, Department of Social Welfare, Sacramento, California

Nelson Jackson, National Association of Social Workers

William S. Jackson, School of Social Work, Atlanta University

Wetonah B. Jones, Children's Service, Incorporated

Florence Kreech, Louise Wise Services

Hylan Lewis, Metropolitan Applied Research Center

Jeweldean Jones Londa, National Urban League

Doris McKelvey, Louise Wise Services

Patricia G. Morisey, School of Social Service, Fordham University

Albert J. Neely, Children's Division, Cook County Department of Public Aid

Sister Mary Patricia, formerly of the New York Foundling Hospital

Willie V. Small, Children's Service, Incorporated

Joseph H. Smith, Harlem-Dowling Children's Service

A. Lenora Taitt, National Urban
League
Helen S. Tinsley, formerly of the
University of California, Los An-
geles
Walter Walker, University of Chi-
cago
Martin Warren, Department of So-
cial Welfare, Sacramento, Cali-
fornia

Kenneth W. Watson, Chicago Child
Care Society
Betti S. Whaley, National Urban
League
Ann V. White, Women's Christian
Alliance
Eloise C. Whitten, Detroit Urban
League and Homes for Black
Children
Women's Christian Alliance

Contents

CHILDREN OF THE STORM

1 Black children and white child welfare

The system of child welfare services in this country is failing Black children. It is our thesis that the failure is a manifest result of racism; that racism has pervaded the development of the system of services; and that racism persists in its present operation. This book is, in effect, an attempt to analyze the manifestations and effects of racism in a major American social institution—the institution of child welfare services.

Our analysis is divided into three parts. In Part One we survey the effects of racism on the historical development of child welfare in this country, from the beginning to the present day. In Part Two we study the efforts to change the child welfare system that took place between the 1930's and the present. Part Three is devoted to a discussion of changes that should be made to reform our present system.

As we shall see in the chapters that follow, racism manifests itself in the present system of services in three major ways: (1) the kinds of services developed are not sufficient to the special situation of Black children; (2) within the system of services that has developed, Black children are not treated equitably; and (3) efforts to change the system have been incomplete and abortive. All three reflect the fact that the services were never developed for Black children. Rather, they were developed by white people for white children, and are maintained and controlled by white people. All three manifestations will persist, we maintain, as long as the most profound manifestation of racism—white domination and control—continues to characterize the system. The last chapter of this book is therefore devoted to a plan for restructuring the child welfare system in a manner that would entail full and equal Black participation and control.

It will be best to begin with some definitions.

CHILD WELFARE

Ideally, "child welfare" should encompass every effort made by a nation on behalf of its children, including its educational system, its medical services, its parks and recreational facilities, even its roads and highways. But the term is more usefully defined as meaning the limited array of social services provided for children by the society. "Child welfare" refers, then, to a limited array of services overwhelmingly focused on the placement of children away from their parents and administered largely through social agencies by professional social workers.

Child welfare, in its broader and ideal sense, should be concerned with the general welfare of all children. This has never really been true of the child welfare endeavors in this country. Like other American social welfare endeavors, child welfare efforts have been predicated on the belief that institutionalized services need be extended to only a small segment of the population, because individuals can ordinarily be expected to preform the functions of these services for themselves. In the case of children, the American society expects that children's fundamental needs for survival, sustenance, and socialization will be met through functions performed by their parents. Only when their parents fail them—and it is expected that not many parents will so fail—does it become necessary for society, through special institutionalized services, to assume responsibility for meeting these needs. This narrow concept of child welfare is the system's definition, its historical basis, and its major failure.

WHAT CHILD WELFARE SHOULD BE

Because our own conception of a more adequate system of child welfare for Black children is central to this book, it should be set forth in brief terms at the outset. We shall discuss it fully in Part Three.

In our view, if a system of child welfare services is to serve Black children adequately, it must abandon the residual approach in which child welfare programs are designed and operated primarily to rescue unfortunate children whose parents have failed them and who have thus fallen through the cracks of an otherwise well-functioning social order. The programs must be based instead on the fact that the present social order is not functioning properly. Furthermore, in its attempt to improve the well-being of all of the nation's children, the system must be able to harness the total resources of society. Child welfare must be oriented toward prevention of child-care problems as well as toward curative and corrective measures; it must focus on preserving and enhancing family life for children rather than on rescuing children from families that are considered malfunctioning. These are the more general features of our concept of child welfare.

A system designed to serve Black children must have not only an historical perspective and a social perspective, but a Black perspective. The Black child must be the central focus of the system rather than the incidental or accidental recipient of services designed and operated by and for other people. What this means is that child welfare services must be based on the historical experience out of which Black children have emerged and within which they are still enmeshed. The hard realities of these conditions—their destructive and constructive features, their uniquenesses, their similarities with those of other people —cannot be ignored or assumed. The social perspective requires that the network of relationships between Black children and the various levels of social reality in which they exist be fully understood. Black children cannot be effectively helped to healthy, functioning lives if they are viewed in isolation or in a limited context. They must be seen as members of Black families and Black communities in all their variety and complexity; and the relationships between the larger, white society and the Black community must be explicitly recognized, analyzed, and changed. Moreover, it is vital to consider the ways in which the various major and dominant systems of the larger society work together to ignore, enhance, or obstruct the well-being of Black children. For example, child welfare is usually considered a subsystem of the welfare system. It is not conceived of as an integral part of the political system, the economic system, and the law enforcement system. Consequently, the potential inherent within these systems for the good and the ill of Black children is not generally appreciated. Finally, the Black perspective requires that the system be analyzed from the *standpoint* of Black people. A set of child welfare measures must not only be designed for Black children, it must also reflect the views, the feelings, the aspirations and the satisfactions of Black people. This requires a striking departure from the present operation of child welfare programs, which are largely designed, administered, and evaluated according to the perspective of white people. Ours, then, is an argument for recognizing, honoring, and enhancing the cultural pluralism of society, in order to enhance the well-being of Black children.

The Situation of Black Children

Our own concept of the situation of Black children is sketched in the accompanying diagram (fig. 1). Black families are the most intimate, intricate, and functional social reality these children know. The misguided notion that Black children do, can, or should exist apart from Black families permeates most concepts of child welfare today. In our opinion the distinction usually made between child welfare and family welfare cannot enhance the well-being of Black children, but rather the reverse. We also consider the Black community and its variously strong and weak social networks extremely important to the well-being of the children. As will be seen in later chapters, a positive concept of the Black community has been absent in past and present efforts to reform child welfare.

Finally, the welfare of Black children cannot be satisfactorily enhanced as long as the larger society, white-oriented and white-controlled, is ignored. The malfunctioning of the political system with respect to Black people—their levels of participation, power, and rewards—is an excellent measure of the well-being of Black children. The manner in which the nation's economic system malfunctions for Black people is much more a cause of the difficulties Black children face than any weaknesses or malfunctioning within their families or communities. Indeed, the malfunctions of Black families and Black

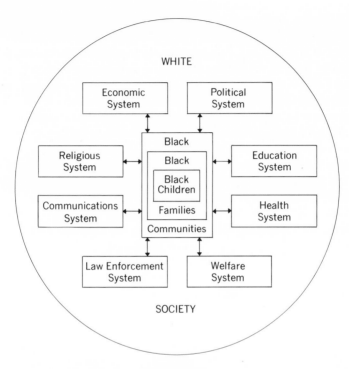

FIGURE 1

communities are largely due to the malfunctioning of the larger society. None of the institutions of the larger society work as well for Black people as they do for white people. They were not designed to do so. This is true of all the major institutions without exception. Of course, there is some variation; some institutions function worse for Black people than do others. But whether we think of education, health services, the communications media, religion, law enforcement, or any other dominant system of the larger society, we see white racism at work. It is this force more than any other which makes Black children, Black families, and Black communities specially vulnerable to the vicissitudes of life; and it is the major cause of the widespread and continuing poverty within the Black community. The combination of racism and poverty caused and maintained by the institutions of the larger society is, we contend, primarily responsible for the stormy past, present, and future of Black children in need.

RACISM

Racism is a social force deeply imbedded in the fabric of the society in which we live. It is the systematic oppression, subjugation, and control of one racial group by another dominant or more powerful racial group, made possible by the manner in which the society is structured. In this society, racism emanates from white institutions, white cultural values, and white people. The victims of racism in this society are Black people and other oppressed racial and ethnic minorities.

Let us examine this conception more closely, in order to clarify its nature, its complexity, its pervasiveness, and its consequences.

Racism, in our view, is reflected in a set of attitudes and/or behaviors exhibited by members of a dominant racial group (in our society, white people) toward members of another racial group (Black people) which are negative, unfavorable, and detrimental to the well-being of the latter and functional for the well-being of the former. In our society, it is the systematic negation, exploitation, and oppression of Black people and other racial minorities. There is no systematic oppression of white people by Black people in this society. The society is not structured for this, nor do Black people have the power, the values, or the interest to systematically oppress white people.

Attitudinal racism exists when one racial group thinks or believes that another is inferior. *Behavioral* racism exists when one group excludes, oppresses, or persecutes another, or serves it less well. Racist attitudes and behaviors may be held and exhibited by individuals, shared in groups, or embodied in the policies and procedures of organizations and institutions. They may be covert or they may be manifested out in the open. Thus, the mildest form of racism is individual, attitudinal, and covert. At the other extreme is institutional, procedural, overt racism, where the normal operations of the health, education, welfare, and other institutions of society fail to serve one racial group as well as they do the dominant racial group.

Let us consider briefly several basic manifestations of racism in this society.

Negative Conception of Black People

The first element in white racism is a negative conception and evaluation of Black people. The genesis of this abhorrence of Blackness and adulation of whiteness lies in the "Anglo-conformist doctrine"—that it is desirable to conform to the standards and values of the Anglo-American culture—which is still dominant in the United States. (Gordon, 1964) "Black people are inferior," "Black is a condition to be overcome," "Some of my friends just happen to be Black," "We don't serve Black children, we serve children period," are some of the most obvious verbal manifestations of this negative conception of Black people and Blackness. But whatever the expressions, the essential and underlying dynamic of racism is the belief that white people are somehow brighter, prettier, more responsible, and more law-abiding than Black people. These "illusions of white grandeur" constitute one of the most subtle and pervasive aspects of white racism; they are often completely internalized by white people, and Black people have also internalized these illusions to a great extent. (Billingsley, 1968) "I don't want anything all Black," a Black executive of an agency with a white board of directors recently observed. "Even my black Cadillac has white-wall tires." The notion that all Blackness must be legitimated by a bit of whiteness is an extension of the negative conception of Blackness that is evident in the structuring of social institutions. For years the official policy of the Child Welfare League of America was to discourage the formation of all-Black agencies in Black communities. It insisted on a bit of whiteness on the board, on the staff, and among the clientele in order to legitimize the agency as one serving not only Black people, but all people in need. To the credit of C.W.L.A., that policy was changed in 1968.

The underlying illusion of "white grandeur" also masquerades as a commitment to racial integration; however, there is a deep and basic difference between a system where integration is only a token and a system that permits and encourages the full participation of Black people in building their own institutions and strengthening the fabric of their community life.

Exclusion from Participation and Control

A second element in white racism is the tendency on the part of white people to exclude Black people from adequate participation in the creation and control of the institutions that affect the lives and well-being of Black people. Adequate Black participation means proportional representation in the policy-making bodies that govern the institutional life of the whole society, and majority control over the policies and operations of those institutions that operate primarily in, or for the members of, the Black community. This element of racism has resulted in the systematic exclusion of Black people from substantial participation in the design and execution of programs of child welfare. A related factor at work here is the paternalistic view that white people know what is best for everybody.

Exclusion from Rewards, Supports, and Services

The third element of white racism is the exclusion or partial exclusion of Black people from the rewards, supports, and services of white-dominated institutions. In child welfare, as we shall see, services have been deliberately closed off to Black children and families throughout the nation's history. More recently, this type of deliberate exclusion has been less prevalent; but less obvious and pervasive forms of exclusion still exist.

To sum up, then, racism is a social force which results in the systematic oppression of one racial group by another. In our society it is reflected in a set of attitudes embodying a negative evaluation by white people of Black people, and a corollary belief in the superiority of white people. These attitudes prompt behavior that results in the oppression, exploitation, and negation of Black people. Chief among the behavioral manifestations of racism at the institutional level are the exclusion of Black people from control and participation in society's major institutions and a consequent denial to them of the rewards these institutions offer. It is this type and level of racism that is of paramount concern in the analysis of child welfare in relation to Black children; for it is the racism in the institutional fabric of society that sets the disadvantaged life conditions for Black children and at the same time precludes the alleviation and remedy of these conditions. Let us consider now child welfare's major failures in serving Black children adequately, and the forms and types of racism to which these failures are linked. Here we shall speak in broad terms; our case is documented in the chapters that follow.

THE IRRELEVANCE OF PRESENT CHILD WELFARE SERVICES

The kinds of child welfare services that have come to be institutionalized in the United States are almost exclusively focused on the care of children away from their parents through some sort of substitute parental care. Services to enhance the welfare of children living with their own families have been only minimally developed and do not constitute any significant portion of the total child welfare effort. This characteristic of the current child welfare system can be traced to the antique American belief that poverty is the result of personal inadequacies, a belief that influenced the provision of all social welfare services, not only child welfare. If individual inadequacy is the cause of poverty (as the American belief runs), then a poor family is an inadequate family, and there is little value in maintaining it as a unit. As a result, child welfare has not made a heavy investment in maintaining families, but in maintaining children away from their families. A corollary to this belief in individual inadequacy as the source of poverty has been the belief that "adequate" families will themselves provide all that is necessary for the welfare of children, and that services to supplement the parental role are unnecessary on any major institutionalized scale. "Adequate" parents are expected to provide everything their children require and to purchase the supplemental services that would enhance their children's welfare. The burden on those who cannot purchase such services falls ultimately on the children. How does this failure to provide for poor children represent a special assault on Black children? To be sure, poor Black children share with poor white children the two misfortunes of being poor and being children in a society which abhors the poor and which has no formal definition of children's rights. This middle-class-oriented society shows its hostility toward the poor in a number of ways. For example, the national Congress finds it exceedingly difficult to appropriate even modest sums for the construction and maintenance of decent low-income public housing while appropriating billions of dollars to subsidize middle- and upper-income housing developments, particularly since World War II. And then, in the states and local communities, private and public interests representing the nonpoor often erect further obstacles. In California, for example, and at least six other states, a public referendum is required before units of low-income public housing can be constructed, even when there are federal funds available for that purpose; and the referenda more often fail than not. No such referenda are required for construction of highways, colleges and universities, hospitals, or law enforcement projects. And in April, 1971, the United States Supreme Court under Chief Justice Burger gave legal sanction to this practice.

Like the poor, children are in a disadvantaged position in America.

While we consider ourselves a child-centered society, we are more likely to treat children as pets than as people. Adults, usually those very well advanced in age, make most of the decisions affecting this society. Most of their decisions are made according to their own interests, needs, and perspectives, without considering the standpoint of children. This nation claims that it has been victimized by the "Dr. Spock revolution"; however, its institutions, programs, and policies governing child welfare are amazingly adult-centered. Children are still largely to be seen and not heard, and certainly not heard *from* in the planning of programs and services for them. The 1970 White House Conference on Children made the first halting steps on a national level to consult with children themselves about child welfare services. It also went a long way toward articulating these basic rights. Asserting that children should have the "inalienable rights" to life, liberty, and the pursuit of happiness, the Conference stated further: "Other basic rights and needs are unique to children, including parental care, a secure home, proper nutrition, mental and physical health, moral guidance, reasonable limits on conduct and education and training commensurate with natural talents and ability." (*White House Conference on Children*, 1971, p. 389) In our view, children should also have the right to participate in the development of programs designed to secure for them these other rights. But it is clear that in the Black community, neither adults nor children enjoy these more basic guarantees and protections.

The failure of society to address itself to the problems of poor children is a special failure in relation to Black children because disproportionate numbers of them are born into poverty. Black children constitute approximately 15 percent of the nation's children, but nearly 40 percent of the nation's poor children. The persistence and pervasiveness of poverty as a condition of Black life in this country is the direct result of the exclusion of Black people from the rewards of the economic system and their exploitation by that system. This inextricable link between racism and poverty places special obstacles in the path of poor children who are not white.

Not only are disproportionate numbers of Black children born into poverty, but the ravages of poverty among them are even greater than they are among white children. The most fundamental threat of poverty is the threat to life itself. The chances of poor babies being born alive and of surviving their first year are not as good as those of babies who are not poor. But even among poor babies, the chances of

Black babies are not as good as those of white babies. Data on infant mortality consistently confirm that not only do Black babies die at a higher rate, even among the poor, but more of them die from causes that are usually preventable through adequate medical care.

The racist dimension of infant mortality can be seen very clearly in the West, where American Indian and Mexican-American populations are highly concentrated. There the single best index of the infant mortality rate in a given county is the percentage of Indians or Mexican-Americans living there. But everywhere in the country, whatever the region and whatever the socioeconomic level of their parents, white babies have a better chance of living beyond their first birthday than their multicolored neighbors.

In the South, Mississippi, Alabama, Georgia, Florida, Louisiana, South Carolina, North Carolina, and Virginia have the highest overall infant mortality rates, the highest infant mortality rates for Blacks, and the greatest discrepancy between infant deaths of Blacks and of whites. The Black rates in this region often are twice as high as the rates among white babies.

Outside the South, the Black infant mortality rates are still considerably higher than those for whites in all the states except Hawaii, Idaho, and Maine, where the Black rates are higher, but only slightly so. (Hunt, 1967, pp. 1–12) As for the northern urban areas, residence in a defined poverty area of the city increases the death rate for both white and Black babies. (Hunt, 1967, pp. 1–12) The increase in poverty areas over nonpoverty areas is roughly the same for both white and Black babies. Of course, a higher proportion of Black babies live in poverty areas than white babies do, which helps to account for the fact that the infant death rates are higher among Black babies than among white babies. But this is only part of the explanation. In northern *nonpoverty* areas the infant death rates for Black babies are considerably higher than the rates for their white counterparts living in similar (and often the very same) neighborhoods. Furthermore, the difference between racial groups within each type of area is greater than the overall difference in death rates between poverty and nonpoverty areas. Thus, the racial dimension exceeds the poverty dimension as a cause of infant deaths.

Finally, for one category of infant mortality, the deaths of children between the ages of one month and eleven months, the racial differential is greater by far in the nonpoverty areas than in the poverty areas. In short, the difference in death rates for white and Black babies is just as great among those who live in nonpoverty areas as among those who live in poverty areas. Poor and rich alike, Black children die faster. This is the effect of racism on infant mortality in the United States. And in many areas of the country—in Minnesota as well as Mississippi and North Carolina—the white infant mortality rate is decreasing while the rate for Black babies is on the *increase*. (Hunt, 1967, pp. 4–7)

In the United States each year thousands of children die before they reach their first birthday; in 1969 twenty-two out of every one thousand babies born here died before age one. The infant mortality rate for Black babies is more than twice as high as that for the nation as a whole. (*Monthly Vital Statistics*, 1969, p. 5) The overall infant mortality rate in the United States, though it has declined over the past few years, is still among the highest in the Western World, and —shamefully—ranks twenty-second among the countries of the entire world. Most of the countries of western Europe have a better record of caring for their children than the United States. So do Taiwan, Japan, and the Crown Colony of Hong Kong. (*United Nations Demographic Yearbook*, 1966, pp. 185–92; countries not reporting total population omitted)

Once a Black baby has managed to reach the age of one, his chances are still worse than those of white children. In the past few years the nation has received the "jarring" information that there are hungry children in its midst; however, for Blacks, Indians, Chicanos, and white Appalachians, hunger and malnutrition have been a part of daily life. What this means can be understood from the study *Hunger U.S.A.,* the 1967 report of the Citizens Board of Inquiry into Hunger and Malnutrition in the United States.

Infant mortality and malnutrition—death and hunger—are very fundamental manifestations of the physical deprivation faced by Black children. Yet societal and governmental attention has only reluctantly been focused on them. It has been more comfortable to think about the "cultural deprivation" of the children. "Cultural deprivation" not only suggests a matter of less urgency, but places the focus of the problem with the children. However, at least some of those working with programs for "culturally deprived" children have had to acknowledge the all too prevalent signs of physical deprivation. One of the more important findings of the Headstart program—intended to overcome cultural deprivation— has been that many of the children are so malnourished and have such extreme iron deficiencies that they are physically unable to concentrate in school.

Infant mortality and hunger are not the only hazards that racism and poverty inflict on the early life of Black children. Many of the Black children who manage to survive their first year do not live to reach adulthood; the death rate for Black children between one and fourteen years of age is twice as high as for white children. The suffering of their parents is another assault on Black children. The maternal mortality rate among Blacks is more than four times the rate among whites. The parents are more than twice as likely to suffer unemployment, and are nearly three times as likely to be living in deteriorated and dilapidated housing. Black mothers are more than four times as likely to be living without their husbands as a result of death, separation, or divorce; and even when there are two parents, the mother is much more likely to have to work in order to maintain an adequate family income.

These facts, and their direct relevance for child welfare services, have not gone unnoticed in the child welfare literature. Kadushin, in his recent textbook, notes them all and concludes that "all these factors contribute to the fact that the non-white child is much more likely than the white child to need child welfare services." (1967, p. 59) But in reviewing the history and present array of child welfare services, and the kinds of services that have been developed, we have little success in finding services which address themselves to the kinds of problems confronting children in these kinds of circumstances. Child welfare services in this country are almost entirely devoted to the placement of children away from their parents. Is separation from their parents the prime need of children ravaged by poverty?

Racism and the Black Family

The systematic negation of Black people—one element of racism—is nowhere more evident than in the all-too-pervasive white beliefs about Black families and about the relationship of Black family life to poverty. The fact that this system of beliefs has in fact invaded official policy formulations of the institutions which should be providing for Black children is a most important cause of the present failure of child welfare in this country.

It is several years since the Moynihan Report concluded that the structure of family life in the Black community constituted a "tangle of pathology . . . capable of perpetuating itself without assistance from the white world," and that "at the heart of the deterioration of the fabric of Negro society is the deterioration of the Negro family. It is the fundamental *source* of the weakness of the Negro community at the present time." (U.S. Department of Labor, Office of Planning and Research, 1965, pp. 47, 5; emphasis ours) It is this "analysis" of the relationship between Black families and white society which reverses the true tangle of pathology afflicting Black people. The family is a creature of society. And the greatest problems facing Black families are those which emanate from the white society. Perhaps not surprisingly, the Moynihan analysis, which placed the blame for Black people's difficulties on the family unit, was eagerly received by the American reading public as a key to understanding Black people. It also gave rise to similar "analyses" by other white students of the Black family. Despite their incorrectness, these views of Black family life are held by many people, and ramifications of such views are all too obvious in the present child welfare system.

The 1970 United States Census showed that most Black children live with both their parents. The proportion of Black children growing up in these favorable circumstances ranges from 60 to 95 percent, depending on such factors as geography and economic status. This simple fact, well known within the Black community, has been true with minor variations for a hundred years, ever since the end of slavery. And yet, much of child welfare theory, planning, and programs, and almost all child welfare institutions are predicated on the assumption that children will be living apart from their parents. When Black children are given any special theoretical attention at all, and where they are considered as having any parents at all (that is, not primarily in need of homes), they are considered as having only one parent, namely a mother. A cursory examination of the literature and of actual practice will show the pervasiveness of this orientation in child welfare.

A corollary result of this racist view of the Black family is that a great portion of the attention to Black children is focused on the instances of unwed motherhood and female-headed families. To be sure, relatively large numbers of Black children spend some portion of their growing-up years outside the conventional American-European family model. But this is not their major problem nor the major problem for their families and communities. And growing up in a conventional two-parent home is not the solution to the problems Black children face. Fortunate though the circumstance is, it is not sufficient in itself to ward off the more crippling problems faced by Black children, their families, and their communities: the oppression of Black people by white people and institutions, the exclusion of Black people from the rewards of white society, and white society's negative reactions to Black people, Blackness, and the Black experience. Of the twin evils of our time, racism and poverty, racism ranks first and poverty second as causes of the difficulties Black children face. Neither of these maladies is caused within the Black community. Both are generated, operated, and perpetuated by the white community and the institutions it dominates.

If a major misconception in child welfare has been that Black children have no parents, or at best only one, another and perhaps even more crippling mistake has been the assumption that a major problem within the Black community is parental inadequacy whatever the number of parents. It follows from this misconception that the inadequate parents need to be treated and cured of their inadequacy, or else the children need to be removed and placed with more adequate parents. It is for this reason that child welfare services for Black children in every large metropolitan area consist in large part of "rescuing" them from these inadequate parents and herding them into large, impersonal institutions or shelters until they can be placed in more adequate homes. These adequate homes are, according to child welfare ideology, hard to find within the Black community because of the "pervasive internal pathology." An important corrective to this view of Black families in relation to child care is Robert Hill's study, "Strengths of Black Families," presented at the July 1971 Annual Conference of the National Urban League.

This basically racist ideation concerning the Black family is intimately entwined with the irrelevance of the system of child welfare services. What else could be expected when a Black family is considered nonexistent or inferior, and a *poor* Black family doubly inadequate?

FAILURE TO SERVE BLACK CHILDREN WITHIN EXISTING SERVICES

While we believe that the kinds of services that exist are insufficient for Black children and devote our final chapter to recommendations for change, the greater portion of our book is necessarily devoted to an examination of the treatment of Black children within those services that have developed. First, while we maintain that a vast array of new services must be developed, focusing on the worth of the Black family unit, we do not question that there are and will continue to be thousands of Black children who are in need of placement with families not their own. What is and will be happening to those children is then a matter of great importance. Second, the present treatment of Black children within the existing services is discriminatory and inequitable, a fact that we shall document in detail. If the new services are conceived, designed, controlled, and administered as are the present ones, the same inequities, the same discrimination, and the same ineffectiveness in meeting the needs of Black children shall prevail. Thus it is necessary to understand first of all what is wrong in the present system.

PART ONE

2

The development
of child welfare
in America

In this chapter we shall trace the evolution of child welfare services from colonial times to the late nineteenth century. We will examine first the early American beliefs that influenced both the kinds of services developed and the manner in which they were organized and administered. Next we will explore the principal types of care that emerged—from the indenture system and the almshouse to the orphanage and the "free" foster home—and the manner in which Black children were treated in the system. We will examine the early practice of "outdoor relief," or services to the poor in their own homes, and consider the reasons why such services have never become a major part of American welfare (and child welfare) efforts.

PHILOSOPHICAL ORIGINS OF AMERICAN CHILD WELFARE

The philosophy and beliefs brought to America by the English colonists meshed with factors inherent in the colonization of a new land to shape the nature of child care in this country far beyond the colonial period. This constellation of factors has not only strongly influenced the development of child welfare in America, but even today has direct implications for the situation of Black children in child welfare.

The first of these factors was the concept of poverty in the New World. Given the potential wealth due to the abundance of natural resources of the new country, coupled with the potential mobility of individuals in a less rigid class structure than prevailed in England, the belief was engendered that no man need be poor, save for his own indolence and depravity. Moreover, according to the dominant religious beliefs, industriousness and thrift were of fundamental value to the human soul, and the spirit of idleness was inherently detrimental. Thus, though Anglo-Americans imported the English Poor Laws, they did not import the philosophy in which the laws had been rooted— public assumption of responsibility for the poor.

The basic philosophical leanings of the Anglo-American settlers shaped the nature of child welfare in this country in several ways. First, if there was to be no poverty, there need be little emphasis on public provision for the poor, including poor children. As a corollary, the care of children was properly the concern of private citizens and groups. Second, the conviction that poverty was a result of one's own inadequacies inextricably tied provision for poor children to individual reform. Thus, our social reforms of the nineteenth century were movements not so much of reform *for* the poor as reform *of* the poor. Perhaps the most basic reflection of this concept in our child welfare services has been the emphasis on care of children away from their parents. The thinking has been: if poor children are in need of care because of the poverty of their parents, and their parents' poverty is in turn due to their personal indolence, then leaving children with such people will only spawn another generation of poor indolents. Finally, since provision for poor children was not to come from public coffers—not even with the notion of reforming them—and since even reform costs money, the inevitable result was that child welfare had to be supported by the wealthy, directed by them, and controlled by them.

The second factor that shaped the development of child welfare services was integral to the colonists' pursuit of a new country—the desire for religious autonomy. Persecution by the state in the mother country and persecution by one another in the New World led each group to a fierce protection of its religious rights. As is typical, each religious group saw its continuance and vitality in the early indoctrination of the young. Quite logically, then, each religious group had an enormous stake in seeing to it that children not adequately cared for by their parents were placed under its dominion. The sectarian roots of the child welfare system were thus deeply and early imbedded. And this sectarianism firmly reinforced the philosophical preference for private over public provision.

The third factor which would have long-term effects on child welfare was that the early settlers were predominantly English and almost exclusively Anglo-Saxon. Although people of other nationalities came to this part of North America, the nation that emerged was engendered in the English colonies and founded in the name of the English King by people of English culture, tradition, values, language, and morality. Thus from the beginning a high potential for deeply ethnocentric policies was present. In nineteenth-century child welfare, for example, if a child was not Anglo-Saxon, then conformity to the standards and values of the Anglo-American culture was an important part of his "reform." Some of the most notable child welfare reformers of the nineteenth and twentieth centuries, exposed for the first time to people of different cultures, sadly confused the ravages of poverty with inherent and cultural depravity. In doing so they not only reinforced the belief in individual responsibility for poverty, but added to it the concept of ethnic group responsibility.

This idea became another reason to remove children from their families, for poor "Italian organ-grinder" or "German rag-picker" parents could hardly be expected to bring up other than indolents like themselves, and "culturally deprived" ones at that. The implications of this Anglo-conformist frame of mind were even more critical for Black children and their families.

The final factor stemming from colonial times that influenced the development of child welfare was, of course, slavery. In one sense it might be said that until 1865 slavery was the major child welfare institution for Black children in this country, since that social institution had under its mantle the largest numbers of Black children. Black historian and social scientist W. E. B. Du Bois has noted the peculiar ways in which slavery performed social welfare functions: "In contrast with free white laborers, the Negroes were protected by a certain primitive sort of old-age pension, job insurance, and sickness insurance; that is they must be supported in some fashion, when they were too old to work; they must have attention in sickness, for they represented capital; and they could never be among the unemployed." (1935, p. 9) But the very existence of slavery meant that child welfare institutions could develop in this country without concern for the majority of Black children; this factor alone ensured an inherently racist child welfare system.

Slavery affected not only Black children, but also white children, for the persistence of slavery as an institution even retarded reforms for white children. In a sense slavery acted as a kind of social barometer—whatever abuses existed in the treatment of white children could be rationalized by the notion that they were treated better than Black slaves. Slavery was particularly effective in retarding improvements in the indenture system and weakening efforts at child labor reforms. As Grace Abbott, social welfare historian, has noted: "In a society in which slaves and indentured servants were used and the supply of free workers was inadequate, the employment of children was not challenged and apprenticeship seemed to have certain advantages; among them the fact that apprentices lived in the master's family." (1938a, p. 191) This situation affected attempts at reform in behalf of Black children. An unspoken value system had been established in relation to the provision of children's services: no white child shall be any worse off than any Black child; no Black child shall be any better off than any white child. This attitude is reflected today among those who oppose system reforms or changes that are specific to Black children, for they say, "The system works badly for all children."

Thus, misconceptions about the poor, certain religious beliefs, Anglo-Saxon domination, and slavery influenced the development of social welfare in this nation. The system came to rely heavily on private philanthropy, accepted religious sectarianism, and thoroughly reflected English traditions and values. The philosophy that linked poverty with personal inadequacy was quite compatible with the practice of slavery in the eighteenth century and early nineteenth century; it works equally well with present-day racism.

The perception of mankind as being made up of adequate and inadequate beings, or superior and inferior ones, is consonant with a belief that the superior know what is best for the inferior. Thus, in the social institutions provided for the American poor, including child welfare, the approach has never been based on the rights of the poor as human beings. Rather, assistance to the poor has been based on their needs *as judged by others*. Neither the rights of the poor nor the rights of children, regardless of economic status, have been established in this country. While this denial of rights affects all children, it places the Black child in a particularly precarious position. The history of American child welfare shows that to be a child and poor is to be doubly disadvantaged; to be a child and poor and Black is truly triple jeopardy. When, as in our racist society, children have needs but no rights, Black children are the most likely to have their needs totally overlooked and denied.

ORIGINS OF THE FORMS OF CHILD WELFARE SERVICES

Care for poor children in America began with the imported traditions of personal almsgiving and private, primarily religious, charity which had their roots in the feudal society of the Middle Ages. Also conveyed to America was the principle of public responsibility for the poor that had been established by the English Poor Laws of 1601, which provided for tax-supported assistance to the needy. The basic structure of the Poor Law system was the starting point for America's welfare services, so it is worth our examination. The structure had three main elements: provision for paupers in their own homes, or "outdoor relief"; contractual arrangements with private individuals, which included "farming out" and indenture; and institutional aggregate care, provided mainly in workhouses and almshouses. In the colonial period there was no provision specifically geared to children; they were served within the adult welfare structure or not at all.

Outdoor relief, or aid to poor families in their own homes, did not develop fully in America; by the nineteenth century it had become only a stingy dole provided by some local communities and private individuals. Through the nineteenth century little in the way of social services was available to poor children who remained with their poor families; financial assistance to families who stayed together was largely a twentieth-century development. Thus, the two major forms of care on which this nation initially relied were contractual arrangements with private individuals, or indenture, and institutional care, or almshouses.

Indenture and the Almshouse

Indenture was a system in which one person could buy or contract the labor of another for a specified period of time, usually five to ten years. After that time, the indentured individual was, theoretically, a free agent.

In colonial times and in the first decades of the new nation, indenture was a primary means of caring for poor children. As Grace Abbott notes,

> Young apprentices were among the earliest settlers in the United States. Large numbers of children recruited from the almshouse populations and the poor of London were sent to Virginia in the seventeenth century under apprenticeship contracts. While the purpose was cloaked in words of Christian charity the real reason for the professed interest of the Virginia Company of London in the future of the poor children of England is not difficult to understand. Workmen were greatly needed in the new country, and young children who worked during their minority without pay were cheap and useful. As in England, the idea of trade-training and self-support for poor children was combined or confused in the minds of colonial leaders. (1938a, p. 89.)

There were some free Black children as well as English in the indenture system. There is evidence, however, that some colonial communities saw fit to make the indenture of Blacks paupers more harsh. Special provisions were sometimes drawn up making slavery the punishment for Afro-Americans who fell into pauperhood. Du Bois has recorded such a special provision passed in 1726 in Pennsylvania. (Du Bois, 1967, pp. 413–14)

Another form of care for paupers, the almshouse, came increasingly into use following the Revolutionary War. The almshouses, almost all deplorable places, housed all who could not care for themselves; this included, of course, orphans who were too young to be useful as well as young children whose parents were not able to support them. In the latter case the parents were also housed in the almshouse. In the early decades of the nineteenth century (and possibly later), some free Black children were to be found in the almshouses. (Thurston, 1930, p. 160; Du Bois, 1967, p. 270)

These major systems of providing for the poor (and poor children)—indenture and the almshouse—persisted throughout the nineteenth century. However, their importance in the care of poor children gradually gave way to two parallel forms of care. In the first half of the nineteenth century, a major reform on behalf of children was the establishment of orphanages, an alternative kind of institution to the almshouse. In the latter half of the century, very much as a result of the abolition of slavery, the indenture method was supplanted by another form of placement of poor children with private families, the "free" foster home.

From the Almshouse to the Orphanage

The major child welfare effort of the first half of the nineteenth century was the establishment of the orphanage, which was somewhat of a misnomer from the start, since many of the children taken into them were not orphans but poor children whose families could not maintain them. It was an effort essentially directed toward young children, an alternative to the kind of institutional care given in the almshouse. Indenture persisted throughout this time, and in fact was a complement to the orphanage system because most children graduated from the orphanages into an indentured position.

While Black children had been included in the almshouses, they were specifically excluded as a matter of policy from most of the orphanages established before the Civil War. It is not surprising that one of the major responses to this exclusion of Black children came from The Society of Friends, a religious group that was then involved in the Abolitionist Movement. In 1822 they established the Philadelphia Association for the Care of Colored Children; similar institutions were later founded by Friends in other northern cities, including Providence (1835) and New York (1836). (Folks, 1907, p. 56–60)

The position of the poor Black child in the pre-Civil War North and his relationship to the child-care reformists of the early nineteenth century are made clear in the following description of the founding of that first "colored" orphanage in New York in 1836, the Association for the Benefit of Colored Orphans:

> One chilly spring day when Miss Anna Shotwell and her stepniece, Miss Martha Murray, were walking along Cherry Street, near where the base of the Brooklyn Bridge now stands, they saw two miserable looking little Negro children huddling on the steps of a dilapidated house. Inquiries revealed that the children were orphans, being kept—"cared for" were scarcely the proper words to describe their state—by a woman in the neighborhood. The woman was too poor herself to continue this help for long, and it seemed that the next step for the little waifs was the Almshouse.

There were, at that time, three orphanages in New York City for white children, as well as the Long Island Farms, a public institution for white orphans. But for the Negro orphan there was only the public Almshouse. The discrimination against these unfortunate children was a matter of great concern to Miss Shotwell and Miss Murray. Being Quakers, they shared the strong feelings of that group that all men, women and children were equal and should have equal rights in society. Nor was it enough for them simply to deplore this situation. They wanted to do something about it. Emptying their purses, they instructed the woman to keep the two children for a few days until some plan could be made for their future care. . . .

When the two women returned to Cherry Street a few days later, they found not two, but six orphans. That the number of their charges could triple in a few days made Miss Shotwell and Miss Murray realize that their personal benevolence was not going to be equal to the problem. At this point the idea of an asylum for Negro children came into being, and work to bring it into effect was started. [Leonard, 1956, pp. 1–2]

Misses Shotwell and Murray hoped to save these children from the "real dangers" of the almshouse; for in the almshouses children were "surrounded by vicious influences and destitute of any schooling, with no incentive or any effort apparently put forth to instill into their susceptible minds principles of morality or religion." (Leonard, 1956, p. 2) Reflecting the reformist doctrines of the times, these women soon set eight years as the maximum age for admission to the asylum on the notion that "older orphans who had been longer subjected to the sordid life of the poorest classes of New York's population, would prove difficult to educate and would be a bad influence on the other children." (Leonard, 1956, p. 10)

Thus, one of the earliest child welfare efforts on behalf of Black children, although not governed by the exclusionary racist ideology of the day, was pervaded by the exclusionary reformist traditions that were the cornerstones of child care for white children. Children were to be saved from a life of sin by learning individually to conform to the "right" standards. However inappropriate this reformist philosphy may have been for white children, it was vastly more inappropriate for Black children. Whatever education, religion, discipline, and an acceptance of popular morality might do for his soul, they could not change the color of the Black child's skin; and that was the source of his problems. Because he was Black, he would have to live along the docks and wharves and in dark alleys—on Nigger Hill in Boston, in Little Africa in Cincinnati; because he was Black, however well he learned his lessons in the orphanage school for the colored, he would be refused admission to some states and denied the ballot in most others. And because he was Black, his life would constantly be endangered, not only on the docks and wharves, but sometimes even within the refuge of the orphanage itself: in 1838 white mobs burned the shelter for colored orphans in Philadelphia, and the Colored Orphan Asylum in New York was broken into and set afire by five hundred white men and women during the Draft Riot of 1863.

The founders of the Association for Colored Orphans, like other people of the time, subscribed to the doctrine of individual responsibility for poverty. One wonders how they could apply this fully to the Black child. All too obviously, the Black child was being born into a society that discriminated against him. This fact could hardly be ascribed to his individual responsibility, and it could hardly be overcome through his individual reform. Yet this was the best that child welfare had to offer: the best that could be done for Black children was to treat them as if they were white. The minutes of the Association for Colored Orphans recorded its dedication to the principle that the Negro child should have the same care and training as the white child. "It was the desire of all interested to establish this [orphanage] on the basis of enlarged Christian charity, without sectarianism or party spirit, and entirely independent of the exciting questions [abolition] that have lately agitated the public mind in relation to the colored race." (Leonard, 1956, p. 4)

Independence from the questions that had "lately agitated the public mind" seemed to the institution's founders to be necessary for its survival. The Quakers had long taken a stand against slavery; they had been leaders in the abolitionist movement that brought an end to slavery in New York in 1827, less than a decade before the founding of the asylum. But it was thought, and probably wisely so, that there must be no connection between the abolitionist movement and the orphanage, as this would surely jeopardize the availability of funds to run the orphanage. Toward this end, the Board of the orphanage recorded this principle of operation: "All are convinced that the interests of the institution should not be endangered by mingling them with exciting topics, and feeling how much depended on the wisdom and discretion of the Managers, nothing has been done in their associated capacity, which referred to any other subject than the welfare of the orphans." (Leonard, 1956, p. 4)

In the caution that was necessary for the orphanage's survival we see another important element that shaped the character of child welfare services for Black children. Heavy reliance upon private philanthropy was synonymous with a reliance upon wealth—and most of the wealthy were white, Anglo-Saxon, and not without personal stakes in the social and political developments of the times. This fact about the system meant that any efforts made on behalf of Black children were going to have to be made attractive to a white donor's eye. The "colored orphan" was at best an unpopular cause. Furthermore, he had to compete for the donor's dollar with all of the more attractive causes. Thus, Miss Shotwell and Miss Murray had to soft-pedal their deep convictions about "matters pertaining to the colored race."

Since an orphanage was basically a white institution, developed by the more affluent white people for poor white children, we must raise a deeper question here than simply the matter of who ran the orphanage. We must ask whether Black leaders of the pre-Civil War era would have developed the same kinds of institutions and solutions if they had been able to control the destiny of their people. *Richness* and *poorness* were white European concepts, and American methods of "dealing with the poor" were white methods. Afro-Americans were not bound by these concepts; they might well have created far different types of solutions. Harriet Tubman risked her life many times to free Black slave children; given the necessary funds, would she have shut them up in a dreary asylum because their parents were destitute or had died? It is impossible to measure the loss of Black creativity to the whole of American society due to racist oppression. The loss to the child welfare field is certainly cruelly ironic: the Black child was to be cared for within a system not only not created for him, but created for the least loved of his white brethren, the poor child.

The fact that the original orphanages were deliberately racially segregated institutions is not often mentioned today. Indeed many of the best child welfare textbooks, especially those written in the last two decades, contain nary a mention of the "colored orphan asylums," and not one word concerning the discriminatory practices of the other institutions which made the colored asylums necessary. Unlike more recent books, which claim to deal with "all" children, earlier books were quite open in their exclusive concern with white children. For example, a classic volume by Homer Folks, one of the foremost child welfare leaders of the century, includes this description of the origins of Girard College in Philadelphia: "Stephen Girard died in 1831, leaving property for the establishment of a college for orphans. Evidently he had both charitable and educational objects in mind, for in his will he specified 'as many poor *white* male orphans between the ages of six and ten years as the said income shall be adequate to maintain shall be introduced into the college as soon as possible.'" (Folks, 1907, p. 57; emphasis ours) While Mr. Folks goes on to praise Girard College as "the largest and most important endowed children's institution in the United States, and probably in the world," he takes issue with one characteristic of the college. His criticism consists of questioning "whether its founder did wisely in yoking together free education and free maintenance." (Folks, 1907, p. 59) No criticism whatsoever is made by Folks of the discriminatory clause in the will. In fact, it took one hundred and thirty-four years, and a group of young Black people willing to risk their lives in a direct-action compaign during 1965, before anyone took Mr. Girard to task on that score.

From the Almshouse to the Penitentiary

The growth of orphanages was not the only facet of the era of almshouse reform. The gradual emptying of the almshouses took place through the efforts of a variety of reformers—each with his own special category of people to be saved from the ravages and inhumanity of the catch-all almshouses.

The most winning argument for the almshouse as the best method to deal with destitute people had been that it was the cheapest way to care for the poor. (Thurston, 1930, p. 23) In view of the American dislike of the poor, those who intended to rescue any of the almshouse inhabitants would find it necessary, in attempting to enlist financial aid, to distract attention from their despicable poorness and focus the donors' eyes on some other characteristic that might be shared by the nonpoor. Thus they asked for aid for systems of care directed toward characteristics other than pauperism. A process of deviance definition began. Instead of one kind of social deviance—"poverty"—being defined, now there were many. As the almshouses were emptied, their inhabitants left not as the "poor people" but as the "insane," the "lame," the "blind," or the "orphaned," carrying new deviance definitions. This process of definition had far-reaching effects, as we shall see.

One of the new deviance definitions was the nineteenth-century version of "juvenile delinquent." The evolution of care for children so labeled shows some striking parallels to the beginnings of care for "dependent children." The first orphanages were established to rescue children from the evil influences of the almshouse. The first institution for juvenile deliquents, the New York House of Refuge, was established in 1825 by the Society for the Prevention of Pauperism in order to rescue children from the evil influences of the jail and penitentiary. The aims and approach of the society may be inferred from its remarks on Bellevue Prison: "Here is one great school of vice and desperation; with confirmed and unrepentent criminals we place these novices in guilt—these unfortunate children from ten to fourteen years of age, who from neglect of parents, from idleness or misfortune, have been doomed to the penitentiary by condemnation of the law. . . . is this the place for reform?" (Folks, 1907, p. 199–200)

While all deviance definitions carry with them a connotation of social devaluation, some carry more than others. Depending on how one's deviance is defined and the extent of social devaluation attached to it, one will be treated better or worse by society. The institution that ministers to a particular form of deviance will be rewarded or punished by society according to the extent of social devaluation placed on the deviance it tends. The societal resources accorded the various systems of care and the elements within each will be apportioned on this basis. This is no less true of child welfare than it is of any other social system. In child care today, this stratified approach based on deviance definition is nowhere better epitomized than in the distinction made between "dependent" and "delinquent" children. ("Dependent" is the twentieth-century label that has supplanted "orphan.") These labels stem from the two very separate systems of child care that evolved during the nineteenth century. Care for destitute older youths is still divided into these two systems.

Entry into one or the other system is dependent upon the definition of a youth's deviance. Once labeled "delinquent" and placed in the less socially desirable system (that for delinquents), it is unlikely that he can cross back again into the "dependent child" category, and the more desirable system.

That Black children are and were more readily shunted to the less desirable system can be concluded from a little thought. Now, as then, because he is Black, the Black child is more likely than the white child to be poor. Because he is poor, he is more likely to be in need of care outside his family. But because he is Black, he is, today as in 1830, less likely to be cared for in the same manner as the white child. In 1830 the Black child in the almshouse had less chance of getting out because there was no orphanage that would take him. Thus, he was more likely to be considered a "pauper," rather than the more highly valued deviant the "orphan." Today, because he is less likely to have a foster home or adoptive home available to him, he is more apt to be cared for in a reform school. He is thus more likely to be labeled a "delinquent" because that is the system of child welfare that is most available to him. The Black child today suffers along with the white child at the mercy of a system that was designed not to benefit children, but to dispose of poor people. The Black child suffers more, however. The system was originally designed with his deliberate exclusion at its very core. It could hardly be expected that as he has gradually been admitted into the total system his entry would be equal in all aspects.

From Indenture to the Free Foster Home

The principal innovation in the care of poor children during the first half of the nineteenth century was, as we have seen, the shift in institutional aggregate care from the almshouse to the orphanage. In the second half of the century the major shift was in the area of individual contractual arrangements—from the indenture system to the free foster home.

Nowadays we tend to think of foster homes as an alternative to orphanages. This was not the case in the nineteenth century: the foster home was necessary as a place to go *after* the orphanage. The indenture system had performed this function while it lasted, for Black children as well as white. In fact, one of the reasons why the Colored Orphan Asylum in New York had an upper age limit of eight years at admission was "the need to prepare the children for indenture, usually at the age of twelve." (Leonard, 1956, p. 11) Article XIV of the bylaws of the institution provided that

> All indenture shall be properly executed according to the law, and no child shall be bound out until twelve years of age, and able to read, write, and cipher unless peculiar circumstances

render a variation from their rule expedient. Children shall be apprenticed either as farmers, domestics, or to obtain trades as may be considered conducive to their welfare. Each child, on being bound out shall be furnished with a Bible, in which the name and residence of one of the Correspondence Committee shall be placed; . . . The Committee shall ascertain that the family or persons to whom a child is bound, will exercise a Christian care over him. [Leonard, 1956, pp. 11–12]

The period of indenture varied, but in most cases it was about seven years; that is, until age eighteen or nineteen. Most of the placements were near New York City, so that the members of the Board might visit occasionally to see to the children's welfare. Other orphanages for Black children followed a similar pattern of child care.

The development of the free foster home for children was stimulated by the abolition of slavery. When, in fact, children of African descent were no longer being bought and sold, discomfort arose in the child welfare movement with the fact that children of European descent were still being sent into a state of serfdom through indenture. The first children to benefit from this discomfort were almost exclusively white.

Two key figures are credited with the eventual institutionalization of the free foster home—Charles Loring Brace and Martin Van Arsdale. Brace is credited with being the pioneer, commencing his work in New York City in 1853. Van Arsdale's work began later, in 1882 in Illinois.

The free foster home began as a form of indenture; it did not make use of a contract, but in all other ways there was a strong resemblance between the two forms of care. The child placed in a foster home was expected to work for the foster family and the placement was expected to last until the child reached adulthood. The child worked for his keep; no money was paid to the foster family. Unlike the indentured child, the foster child was "free" to leave, though such "freedom" was certainly questionable for a twelve-year-old who had been transported some thousand or so miles from his unsavory home in New York City for placement on a salubrious farm in Michigan.

The free foster home was the major non-institutional form of placement until well into the first half of the twentieth century. The State Children's Home Society of Illinois, founded in 1882 by Martin Van

Arsdale, was duplicated in thirty-four other states by 1920, and the New York Children's Aid Society, founded by Charles Loring Brace in 1853, became the prototype for private child-placement agencies in the East. The Brace and Van Arsdale efforts, like those of virtually all their imitators, excluded Black children.

The free foster home was ultimately to be replaced during the first half of the twentieth century by the foster boarding home—that is, a foster-home arrangement in which the foster parents are paid for the expense of caring for children. The gradual shift from the free foster home to the foster boarding home—and from the orphanage to the foster boarding home—will be detailed in Chapter 4. Here we shall only say that the development of the foster-home form of care and its eventual replacement of institutional care in orphanages were eventually beneficial to Black children. The foster-care system, despite its exclusionary beginnings, has been more open to Black children than the institutional system of care.

Adoption

The arrangement between adoptive parents and children differs considerably from that between foster parents and children. In adopting, the legal relationship is identical to that between the biological parent and child; in foster care no legal tie is established. As a legal institution, adoption is of comparatively recent origin. There was no provision for it in English common law, and, in fact, adoption was not authorized by statute in Great Britain until 1926. Of course, informal adoption has been practiced from the beginning in this country. Many children, including foster children and indentured children, were taken in permanently by families and often shared the family name, and, if there was any, the inheritance, but this occurred beyond the province of the law, and no legally binding parent-child relationship was established through such arrangements. The earliest adoption laws are described by Grace Abbott as being intended "merely to provide evidence of the legal transfer of a child by the natural parents to the adopting parents, and provision for a public record of the transfer, *similar to the registration of deeds,* was all that was considered necessary." (1938b, p. 172; emphasis ours) The adoption law of the State of Texas, passed in 1850, is an example of this earlier kind of legislation. It illustrates clearly that the essential and basic benefit of adoption was the benefit to the parents:

> *Law of the State of Texas, 1850, Chapter 39, Section 1.* Be it enacted by the legislature of the State of Texas, That any person wishing to adopt another as his or her legal heir, may do so by filing in the office of the Clerk of the County Court . . . a statement in writing, by him or her signed and duly authenticated or acknowledged, as deeds are required to be, which statement shall recite in substance, that he or she adopts the person named therein as his or her legal heir, and the same shall be admitted to record in said office.
>
> *Section 2.* Be it further enacted, That such statement in writing, signed and authenticated, or acknowledged and recorded as aforementioned, shall entitle the party so adopted to all the rights and privileges, both in law and in equity, of a legal heir of the party so adopting him or her. Provided, however, that if the party adopting such person have, at the time of such adoption, or shall thereafter have a child or children, begotten in lawful wedlock, such adopted child or children shall in no case inherit more than one-fourth of the estate of the party adopting him or her which can be disposed of by will. [Abbott, 1938b, p. 172]

Such adoption, known as adoption by deed, was pretty much a matter between the private parties, and the only legal matter involved was transfer of the rights to control of the child, a matter simply handled by a clerk, as with the paperwork in the transfer of any piece of property.

The Massachusetts Law of 1851, considered the first modern "adoption" law, made the matter somewhat more complicated. Written consent of the natural parents or guardian of the child was required; the level of the public official involved was raised to that of probate judge, and such judge was charged with determining if the adoption was "fit and proper." The Massachusetts law became the model for that in a number of other states. Adoption by deed, however, persisted in several states well into this century.

The establishment of adoption as a child welfare institution, and as a major element in the array of child welfare services, did not occur until the twentieth century was well along. But its intent to benefit the adopting parents rather than the children has been a persistent characteristic of adoption as a child welfare service.

Services to Children in Their Own Home

Child welfare services in the United States have focused narrowly on the placement of children away from their families. Few services have been developed for children living with their parents, and none have commanded the funds and energy devoted to placement services. The system of outdoor relief of the English Poor Laws, essentially the financial maintenance of people in their own homes, was the last form of care for the poor to be developed on any major scale. It was not really until the 1920's and 1930's that public financial assistance to families reached proportions of any consequence.

Before the close of the nineteenth century, however, charitable organizations had begun to provide services for families (and children) in their own homes. The Charity Organization Societies, formally established in the 1880's, had as their primary function the giving of alms and commodities, but they also gave many kinds of personal services and assistance to needy families. No less than the child welfare institutions, these organizations accepted the philosophy of individual responsibility for poverty, and all that they gave was heavily peppered with efforts at personal reform. Many other organizations aimed at helping the poor evolved in the 1880's and 1890's as part of the Settlement House Movement. Hull House, established by Jane Addams in 1889, was probably the most famous of these. The settlement workers differed from those in the charity organizations in their approach to the poor; they focused on the neighborhoods and subcommunities near the settlement houses and, more importantly, stressed social problems rather than individual reform. Personal services to families were, however, an integral part of the work. A notable contribution to child welfare made by settlement houses was the establishment of day-care centers. In fact, of the two-hundred-odd day-care centers in the United States by the turn of the century, the vast majority were connected with settlement houses.

One type of service that was eventually to focus directly on children at home did develop in the late nineteenth century. This was the protective service concerned with families where the parents had either neglected the children or had physically abused them. The private organizations that spearheaded the protective services movement originated in the 1870's and 1880's. These were the various local Societies for the Prevention of Cruelty to Children and the Humane Associations. It underscores the position of children in this country that these types of organizations had existed for the protection of animals before they were established to protect children. Such organizations, until the 1920's or so, focused on rescuing children— rescuing them from their abusive parents or employers and removing them to another family or to institutions. Gradually, however, these agencies more and more sought to help families to improve the care of their children, and to maintain the family unit, rather than removing the children from their homes.

How did Black children fare in these movements? The weight of the evidence is that Blacks rarely benefited from the charity organizations. (Richmond and Hall, 1913) In *The Philadelphia Negro*, Du Bois analyzes the extent of racial discrimination in Philadelphia's charitable agencies during the 1890's. He found that the agencies fell into four groups: charitable agencies exclusively for Blacks; those exclusively for whites; those that professed not to discriminate, but did in some cases; and those that made no statements, but usually were discriminating. He estimated that about half the agencies in Philadelphia were open to Negroes. Interestingly, the kind of service being given in part explained the relatively open or closed nature of the agency: "In the different kinds of charities, however, some disproportion is noticeable. Of direct almsgiving, the most questionable and least organized kind of charity, the Negroes probably receive their just proportion, as a study of the great distributing societies clearly shows. On the other hand protective, rescue and reformatory work is not applied to any great extent among them." (Du Bois, 1967, pp. 357–58)

The settlement houses, neighborhood-based as they were, followed whatever pattern of residential segregation existed in the giving of services.

BLACK CHILDREN IN THE POST-CIVIL WAR PERIOD

What did the sudden and unplanned-for emancipation of four million Black slaves mean to the child welfare movement in this country? It was possible for Henry Thurston to write, as late as 1930, "Moreover in this country and in our own lifetime we have had experience with children brought up as slaves. The care of dependent Negro children is one of the major problems of child care in the United States which is yet to be solved. It is partly, at least, because of the background of slavery that the solution of the problem is still in its first stages as compared with the progress made in caring for the white dependent child." (p. 1) But though Thurston saw that they presented a major child welfare problem, his book gives only fleeting attention to Black children. Even Grace Abbott, in her landmark volumes, *The Child and the State,* makes only scattered references to Black children and their treatment under the law. Why is the Emancipation Proclamation, which drastically changed the legal status of millions of Black children, left out of a survey of relations between children and the state? Should not the Emancipation Proclamation be considered a piece of child labor legislation? Perhaps the reason why it has not been so treated is that it involved directly only Black children. What is in fact usually reported about the end of slavery, as we noted earlier, is that it benefited white children by bringing about the demise of the indenture system.

Although emancipation meant little to the child welfare movement, it meant a great deal to the children. One of the first things it meant was more extensive poverty. Du Bois commented upon this relationship: "Emancipation and pauperism must ever go hand in hand; when a group of persons have been for generations prohibited from self-support, and self-initiative in any line, there is bound to be a large number of them who, when thrown upon their own resources, will be found incapable of competing in the race of life." (Du Bois, 1967, p. 269) In *Black Reconstruction,* written in 1934, he concludes that the extreme poverty of the freed Black people was a direct result of the workings of the economic system of the country. His earlier quote, however, represents a line of thinking compatible with beliefs about individual responsibility of the poor for their status. Even within the framework of individual reform upon which the work of the child welfare reformers of the day was predicated, one would think there would have been some major and dramatic recognition among these reformers in the post-Civil War period that a new group of potential paupers had now to be reckoned with. However inappropriate the individual reform measures of the child savers of the day might have been in dealing with the massive social and economic dislocations that attended emancipation, their response was meager and sporadic. And so it was to remain well into the twentieth century.

The racism that played a part in this failure was most compatible with a dominating social ideology of the time, that of Social Darwinism. Formulated by Herbert Spencer, this philosophy transposed the survival-of-the-fittest doctrine onto society, proclaiming that social intervention on behalf of the poor constituted an interference with nature and the evolution of the socially adaptable. Such an idea easily incorporated, and reinforced, the beliefs that the poor, and the Black, were "unfit." One of the major child welfare reformers of the nineteenth century, Charles Loring Brace, founder of the free foster home movement, espoused just such a philosophy. The failure of the child welfare institutions of the day to mount a special and specific effort on behalf of the millions of Black children caught in this great social upheaval stemmed in part, then, from a very direct and fundamental form of racism.

The philosophy of the child welfare system and the operation of the system were not suited to the situation of Black children. The belief in individual responsibility for poverty did not provide for an understanding of the massive socially and environmentally engendered poverty that followed emancipation. Thus, an organized response was not forthcoming. Even the response by the federal government, the Freedmen's Bureau, which was quite apart from the welfare system, was too little, too late, too shortlived, and too halting to deal with the problem effectively. This philosophy, coupled with the basic ethnocentrism in the system, compounded the problem. The system of services and institutions that had developed was primarily concerned with saving poor white children. The fact that these services developed primarily in the urban North made it unlikely that there would be much concern for southern Black children. Even in the North, while there were thousands of poor Black children in need of services, the fact was that in terms of numbers, Black children did not constitute the largest, most visible problem group—European immigrant children did. The major child welfare institutions of the country developed during a period when the proportion of Afro-Americans in the nation's population actually decreased, due to the massive European immigration. In 1830, the United States census reported Black people to comprise 18.1 percent of the population. By 1890 this figure had fallen, to 11.9 percent, and most of this decrease was reflected in the northern cities. (Bennett, 1964) As later chapters will discuss, the responsiveness of the child welfare system to Black children came about largely through the pressure of their increased numbers due to successive waves of northern migration.

Some religious groups other than the Quakers did make an effort to extend services to Black children and, after the Civil War, opened many orphanages for them. For example, the Episcopal Diocese of

Philadelphia established the House of Saint Michael and All Angels for Colored Cripples in 1887, and the House of the Holy Child in 1889. In New York City the Roman Catholic Church first took note of the Black population with the establishment of Saint Benedict's, the Moor Church for the Colored in 1883. In 1886 the parish house of this church was converted into a home "to rescue the children of destitute or dissolute colored people from evil influences, to shelter and nurture such, and give them such instruction as shall counteract their tendencies to vice and irreligion and shall fit them to earn their own living in the various branches of industry." (Jacoby, 1941, p. 230) The parish house soon became too small for all of the "dissolute colored," and a more formal institution was opened in Rye, New York. When that institution was on the brink of financial disaster, receiving no subsidy from state or city, it was incorporated as a branch of the Mission of the Immaculate Virgin in 1898, since, in the words of the Archbishop, "the fact that these children are colored should be no reason why charitable Catholics should not aid them when they are destitute." (Jacoby, 1941, p. 241) In such ways, sectarianism and segregation found a happy union in the child welfare movement.

While the child welfare system of the late nineteenth century essentially failed in relation to Black children, some efforts on their behalf came from other sources. Two major developments beyond the welfare system, had they been nurtured and sustained, might have drastically changed the situation of Black children in this country. One was the ill-fated federal agency called the Freedmen's Bureau. The other, which we shall discuss in Chapter 3, was the rapid growth of social service organizations within the Afro-American community.

The Freedmen's Bureau

The Freedmen's Bureau, which Du Bois has referred to as "the most extraordinary and far-reaching institution of social uplift that America ever attempted," (Du Bois, 1935, p. 219) was established by an act of Congress in March, 1865. The passage of the bill came after over a year of debate in the House and Senate as to what the nature of the Bureau should be; the Bureau which was finally established was a compromise of several points of view as to how the newly freed slaves and the white war refugees were to be assisted. Much of the debate centered on how permanent and comprehensive such an operation should be. An alternative bill had proposed the establishment of a permanent and independent government department, a Department of Freedmen and Abandoned Lands. Those who advocated such a department saw the task of planning for freedmen as one requiring long-range and radical measures. In part, those who opposed a permanent establishment, while not unsympathetic to the plight of the freedmen, based their opposition on just the kind of thinking that had characterized the provision of social welfare in the past. They believed that, once given freedom and the vote, former slaves would find their way into the economic mainstream through hard work, industriousness, and thrift. One legislator expressed the following view in his opposition to the establishment of such a department: "I am opposed to the whole theory of the Freedmen's Bureau. I would make them free under the law. I would protect them in the courts of justice; if necessary, I would give them the rights of suffrage, and let loyal slaves vote their rebel masters down and reconstruct the seceded states; but I wish to have no system of guardianship and pupilage and overseership over these Negroes." (Du Bois, 1935, p. 222)

In many ways, the whole concept of the Freedmen's Bureau, in whatever form it took, ran counter to the prevailing views on social welfare provision, especially in that it was an arm of the federal government. Relief of the poor had always been undertaken by private charities or local levels of government. The Freedmen's Bureau, even in its limited form, went far beyond temporary relief of the poor, and was for its day, and for a long time to come, a model of comprehensive social welfare planning. Du Bois has listed "the twelve labors of Hercules" that faced the Freedmen's Bureau:

> to make as rapidly as possible a general survey of conditions and needs in every state and locality; to relieve immediate hunger and distress; to appoint state commissioners and upward of 900 Bureau officials to put the laborers to work at a regular wage; to transport laborers, teachers and officials; to furnish land for the peasant; to open schools, to pay bounties to the soldiers and their families, to establish hospitals and guard health; to administer justice between master and man; to answer continuous and persistent criticism, North and South, black and white; to find funds to pay for all this. [1935, p. 225]

It had to be a combination of the present Departments of Labor; Justice; and Health, Education and Welfare; and a Veterans Administration to boot. Ahead of its time, bitterly opposed by the South and by many in the North, the Bureau was continually underfinanced and undermined; it lasted only until 1871. Yet during its existence it undertook many commendable tasks, and some had lasting benefits. Most notable among its achievements was the establishment of several Black institutions of higher education—Howard, Fisk, and Atlanta universities.

The underlying conceptions and assumptions of the Freedmen's Bureau rendered it a far more advanced instrument of child welfare than existed at the time. Intended, in part, to prevent and eliminate poverty, the Freedmen's Bureau represented a vastly different approach to children. In effect, the provision of land, work, and direct relief served poor Black children within their families, for it was a means of strengthening and keeping those families together. This approach was quite different from that taken by the established child welfare agencies and organizations of the nineteenth century. Short-lasting and inadequate though this endeavor was, it was, in a way, a revolutionary development in child welfare.

Some of the traditional approaches, such as the establishment of orphanages, were also employed by the Freedmen's Bureau. However, reliance on these measures as a primary mode of caring for needy children became greater as the work of the Bureau began to deteriorate due to lack of support. A theme of the attacks leveled at the Freedmen's Bureau was the idea that its work simply encouraged the natural slothfulness of the Black race, and continuance of the work would produce a people totally dependent on the government for sustenance. Influenced by this thinking and bedeviled by a lack of resources, some administrators of the Freedmen's Bureau began to lapse into the more traditional means of caring for poor Black children—indenture, orphanages, and former slave holders. In Georgia, for example, a General Tillson of the U.S. Army ordered that the Bureau was no longer to remove young children from their former masters if the children had no visible means of support. Older children who were not supported by their parents were indentured. The imginative and visionary approach to the poor and to poor children began to deteriorate even before the end of the Freedmen's Bureau, and with its abolition came to a complete halt. Poor, free Black children in the South were left in an even worse position than their poor, free northern brothers.

3 Black alternatives after the civil war

From the beginning of United States history, as we have seen, Black children have been at least partially excluded from welfare services. Fortunately, Black children were not totally dependent upon the institutions of the broader society; they have always been able to rely on their own people.

The long struggle on the part of the Black community to provide for those of its children whose parents could not adequately care for them is one of the strong features of the Black experience in this country. These self-help efforts have never been adequately chronicled; indeed, they have been virtually ignored in child welfare literature. Black self-help efforts not only should be included in the literature but should influence the planning and implementation of child welfare programs in the Black community.

As W. E. B. Du Bois observed in 1898,

> Probably no portion of the people of the country more quickly respond to charitable appeals of all sorts than do the colored

people. They have few charitable societies but they give much
money, work and time to charitable deeds among their fellows:
they have few orphan asylums, but a large number of children
are adopted by private families, often when the adopting
family can ill afford it; there are not many old folks' homes,
but many old people find shelter and support among families
to whom they are not related. [p. 3]

The capacity and readiness of Black families to open their homes to
children and others in need of special care is both traditional and
current. In spite of almost overwhelming oppression and the absence
of adequate or even rudimentary resources, Black families have shown
a spirit of benevolence which deserves to be appreciated and supported in the more general approaches to child welfare today.

This historical spirit of concern, charity, and benevolence has manifested itself in a variety of ways. In Africa the socioeconomic context
in which most Black people lived was "tribal socialism"; patterns of
mutual concern and sharing, even in situations of great scarcity, were
highly developed. Du Bois observed that "of charity as such, there
was no need among Africans, since all shared the common fund of
land and food." (1909, p. 10) Moreover, the systems of kinship ties
and lineage rights provided for the care of children left in need of
parents. Depending on the society, the father's brother or the mother's
oldest living brother was automatically charged with responsibility
for the orphan.

During the period of slavery in America, the principal arrangement
for Black children without parents was adoption again. "Among the
slaves," Du Bois has observed, "the charitable work was chiefly in the
line of adopting children and caring for the sick. The habit of adoption is still widespread and beneficent." (1909, p. 11)

After slavery, once the Freedmen's Bureau had collapsed, the
fledgling Black communities were ignored by the larger society and
were forced to provide for the needs of their dependent children without the social resources available for the care of other children. Therefore, most of the benevolent work was of an informal, neighbor-to-
neighbor nature and as a result was not recorded. But, thanks to the
pioneering social research of Du Bois and his students at Atlanta
University, some of the more formalized social welfare efforts among
Black people have been documented. Five major sources of aid to
children and families emerged among Black people during the late
nineteenth century: the Black churches; Black schools and colleges;

Black lodges; Black women's clubs; and Black individual philanthropy. We shall discuss each of the sources of aid before turning our attention to the actual child welfare services provided.

SOURCES OF AID WITHIN THE BLACK COMMUNITY

Churches

The Black church has had a tremendous role in meeting the social welfare needs of Black families. The white community, including the professional community of child welfare experts and planners, does not generally appreciate this historical fact, nor does it recognize the extraordinary potential of this institution today. As Du Bois has said, "The Negro Church is the only social institution of the Negroes which started in the forest [of Africa] and survived slavery; under the leadership of the priest and medicine man, afterward of the Christian pastor, the Church preserved in itself the remanents of African tribal life and became after emancipation the center of Negro social life. It is natural, therefore, that charitable and rescue work among Negroes should first be found in the churches and reach there its greatest development." (1909, p. 16) As we shall see shortly, many of the institutions for Black children were established and supported in the late nineteenth century by Black church organizations.

Schools

Schools constituted the most important tool in community efforts at social betterment after slavery. Once they were established (usually through the efforts of church organizations) they in turn provided a multiplicity of social welfare and child welfare functions. In a study titled "Self Help in Negro Education" (in Du Bois, 1898), R. R. Wright illustrates the commitment that the Black community, especially the Black church, exhibited toward education. He notes that the African Methodist Episcopal Church supported twenty schools with 202 teachers and 5,700 pupils. Furthermore, he found school property valued at over a million dollars. The schools had an annual income of $150,000 contributed by 300,000 people. Altogether he

found that "since 1844, they have raised $3,000,000 for education."
(p. 29) Another Black denomination, the African Methodist Episcopal Zion Church, had established (by 1906) twelve schools with 150
teachers and 3,000 students. Their school property was valued at over
$300,000 and they raised about $100,000 annually. Overall, they had
raised over $1.1 million for education. A third denomination, the
Colored Methodist Episcopal Church (which in later years has
changed its name to Christian Methodist Episcopal Church), had established six schools. Finally, Wright found, the Baptist churches had
established 120 schools run entirely by Black people and worth in
assets about $700,000. They had 613 teachers and 8,644 students.
"During the past forty years," Wright concluded, "Negro Baptists
have contributed $6,000,000 to their own education." (p. 30)

But even with the contributions of the churches, a great share of
the cost of these schools had to be borne by the students and their
families. Wright noted: "Negro students have paid in nine years
$5,187,269 in cash and work to 74 institutions or 44.6 percent of the
entire running expenses." He further observed that "Negroes have
contributed at least $15,000,000 to education through their churches,"
and concluded, "It is probably true that the Negroes pay possibly a
larger percentage of the cost of their schools than any other group of
poor people in America." (p. 30)

This commitment to and investment in schools by the newly eman-
cipated Black citizens resulted in a sharp decrease in the Black illiteracy rate. Wright observed: "The history of civilization does not show
one other instance of a wholly illiterate race in the nation reducing its
illiteracy by half in a single generation." (p. 30)

But the Black schools did not confine themselves to the simple,
although important, teaching of academic subjects. They served a
variety of valuable social welfare functions for the communities. One
observer reported: "The work which these schools are doing for their
communities falls generally under four or five heads: (a) religious
work of the Y.M.C.A., (b) Sunday school work and preaching in the
churches, (c) social work, such as is done by women's clubs, the
visiting of homes, almshouses, jails, etc., (d) educational work, such
as making addresses, conducting teachers' institutes, organizing school
improvement leagues, holding night schools for working girls, holding
farmers' conferences, etc., and (e) contributing to and directing the
amusements of their communities." (Du Bois, 1898, p. 31) In short,
Black schools were, therefore, genuine community institutions, per-

forming child-welfare-oriented services among a variety of other functions.

Black institutions of higher learning also performed many social service functions within the Black community. In addition to sponsoring research and annual conferences for the study of Negro problems, Atlanta University also housed a free kindergarten association, established a fifty-unit traveling library system, and conducted a series of extension lectures for the community. Hampton Institute sponsored visits by its members to poor people in their cabins and in jails, poorhouses, and workhouses; it also sponsored three night schools, two settlement houses, and a series of annual social-betterment conferences. Penn School, in South Carolina, sponsored a variety of social service activities, including home visits, training of nurses, temperance work, women's meetings, and amusement for the community. Atlanta Baptist College conducted neighborhood settlement work.

Secret Organizations

In addition to the charitable efforts of churches and schools, much community work was done by lodges and other secret organizations. The chief Black lodges—the Masons, the Odd Fellows, and the Knights of Pythias—always engaged in a great deal of benevolent work along with their purely social and business functions.

Research reports received by Dr. Du Bois attest to these activities. Here is one from South Bend, Indiana: "Our city, as you may know, is small. We have about seven or eight hundred colored families. Two secret societies: Masons and Knights of Pythias with women's auxiliaries. These organizations are a wonderful help to our city. They have done and are still doing much good work, socially and financially, for the betterment of our people." From Texarkana, Texas: "Aside from the secret organizations here in Texarkana among Negroes, all of which care for their members in sickness and death, paying sick benefits and a small death claim, there are no organizations here doing a strictly philanthropic work." From Charlotte, North Carolina: "We have any number of insurance organizations which give sick benefits, run wholly by the colored people, at least five or six operating here in the city. All of the above mentioned, in some way, do a little charity and social work for the uplift of our people." (Du Bois, 1909, pp. 36–37)

Women's Clubs

Still another mechanism for benevolence in the Black community was the women's clubs, which engaged in a broad spectrum of social work. An honorary President of the National Association of Colored Women's Clubs once stated (rather radically to some modern ears): "That organization is the first step in nation making, and that a nation can rise in the scale no higher than its womanhood, are principles which have come to be looked upon by the sociologists and all students of the development of humanity as self-evident truth; hence it seems quite natural to speak of one in connection with the other, i.e. organization and women." (Du Bois, 1909, p. 47) Social work was a central feature of these clubs. "The value and extent of the local work speaks for itself in the number of hospitals, homes for orphans and the aged, reformatories, kindergartens, day nurseries and other much-needed institutions, which through the heroic efforts of the noble and self-sacrificing women that constitute these clubs, have been established." (Du Bois, 1909, pp. 47–48)

Unlike the other self-help efforts we have described, the women's club movement developed mainly in the North. The National Association of Colored Women was founded in Washington, D.C., in 1896 and, for the next few years, held most of its national conferences in northern cities.

Individual Philanthropy

Finally, we must pay some attention to the role of individual Black philanthropists, if only to establish their historical existence. Du Bois (1909, pp. 39–41) described seventeen of these individuals. Two vignettes will suffice to illustrate the presence of individual philanthropy in the Black community.

Thomy Lafon, who was born in 1810 in New Orleans, apparently to free parents, was a lifelong bachelor. Somehow he became educated and in his youth was a schoolteacher. Later he operated a small dry-goods store; still later he started lending money at "advantageous" rates, and thus had accumulated a fortune by the time of his death in 1893. His estate was appraised at $413,000. His will provided amply for his relatives and friends, but left the bulk of his estate to various charities. The Lafon Asylum, an orphanage for boys which he had established earlier, was provided a lump sum for its continual support. Moreover, he left $10,000 to the Charity Hospital of New Orleans, $3,000 to the Charity Hospital Ambulance Department, $5,000 to Lafon's Old Folks Home, $5,000 to the Little Sisters of the Poor, and $2,000 to the Catholic Institution for Indigent Orphans.

All these and other bequests were doubled by his executors when they discovered that he had underestimated the true value of his holdings by half. (pp. 40–41)

Another Black philanthropist was George Washington, born in slavery, who died in Illinois in 1868. Nothing else is known of his life except that he died rich. He willed all his fortune for the purpose of the education of "young colored men and women of the State of Illinois." Unfortunately, after what was described as the "speculations of the white trustees and endless litigation," the funds were reduced to $22,000 in 1909. At that time, Washington's estate had supported twenty Black youths through higher education, and five were enrolled in Fisk University. (pp. 39–40)

CHILD WELFARE SERVICES WITHIN THE BLACK COMMUNITY

Child welfare services within the Black community developed as part of a broad spectrum of Black social services, ranging from literary and art clubs to hospitals, old people's homes, libraries, and Y.M.C.A.'s. Among the services directly for children were orphanages, homes for the aged and for children, day nurseries and kindergartens, and homes for working girls.

Orphanages

Many of the orphanages for Black children in the late nineteenth century, particularly in northern cities such as New York and Philadelphia, were sponsored by white people. Du Bois and his researchers divided these white-sponsored orphanages into three categories according to the quality of care offered. One group of institutions provided grossly inadequate care, "appear[ed] very cold and business-like, and seem[ed] to regard their chief function to be the training of servants." A second type of institution was "a little more humane," but seemed intent on turning little Black children into conforming Christians. However, a third type of institution, such as the Leonard Street [Children's] Home in Atlanta, Georgia, was conducted "not like a charity but like a loving human home." (1909, p. 78)

Among those homes for children organized and managed by Black people, some were sponsored by white organizations. An example was the Laing Orphan's Home for Colored Children in Mt. Pleasant, South Carolina, run by the local Black schoolteacher and sponsored by the Society of Friends in the North. A Black children's home in Richmond, Virginia, was supported jointly by the Society of Friends and the city's Black churches.

Some orphanages for Blacks were supported by the limited resources of the Black community. Many of these orphanages were organized by single individuals and initially resembled large boarding homes more than they did formal institutions. The founder of the Reed Home and School established in 1884 in Covington, Georgia, described its origin:

> While a student at Atlanta University I grew more anxious to finish my course in school that I might go out and be of some service to my people. The thing that most inclined my heart and made me more determined than ever before was something that I saw while a student. . . .
>
> There is a street that cuts through the campus of the Atlanta university and a bridge across the street was being dug out by chain gang hands. One cold icy morning, I was crossing the bridge and heard a pitiful scream below. I looked down and there stood a poor little boy of about nine or ten years old, with the lash being applied to his back. There was no one to say a word of comfort to this dear little fellow. It pressed my heart and caused me to weep bitterly. When school was dismissed, I hastened to my room for I didn't want to see anyone. I at once pleaded with the Lord and asked him for strength to complete my course, that I might go out to save one boy from the chain gang.
>
> In July, 1883, I began teaching school in Covington, Georgia. . . . In June, 1884, I set up housekeeping for the purpose of caring for one little girl. I made most of my furniture of dry goods boxes, and now and then a friend gave me a plate, a cup and saucer or some little piece necessary for housekeeping, and we did our cooking in ovens and frying pans on the fireplace, as we had no stove. I set up housekeep-

ing in one room, and lived in this room until there were five
little ones in the family. [Du Bois, 1909, p. 82]

This Afro-American woman's motivation is in sharp contrast to
that expressed by her contemporary white reformers. The white
reformers' intentions were to save children from vice and corruption.
This woman expressed a wish to save them from the ravages of a
cruel environment. The environment these Black children faced
threatened their lives; the child welfare task in relation to them was
quite as much a matter of life saving as of soul saving. This is not to
say that all Black people who started orphanages were imbued with
this same philosophy, for many were not. Some were motivated by
simple profit, as were some white people; and many were imbued with
the reformist traditions of the day. Yet, there were clear examples of
a very different kind of philosophy toward the care of children in
need. One statement by this same Black woman reflects her orientation toward the needs of her people: "At the beginning I took only
girls, but now I have a large number of boys as well as girls. It makes
the work doubly hard, but the boys must be cared for. We need men
in the race, and it is very necessary that we take greater interest in the
boys than we have before, so that there shall be better homes and
better citizens. When I took the first boy into the family, I felt now I
had kept by agreement with the Lord." (Du Bois, 1909, p. 84)

Many intrepid and inspired individuals, such as the woman described above, somehow managed to provide for children in need
without any substantial aid from others. They existed through their
own and the children's labors, and from payments by the children's
parents. Elizabeth McDonald, the founder of a Black orphanage in
Chicago, reported:

> For fifteen years, I have been engaged in the rescue work, in
> this state and in other states. . . . Seeing that in the prisons
> the larger majority were colored according to population;
> knowing that we have always had prisons and dungeons, and
> people have been burned at the stake and have been hanged
> by the neck and nothing seemingly to have done any good in
> regards to reforming one that has fallen, experience in my
> work has taught me that it would be easier to prevent crime
> than to reform hardened criminals. . . . On October 3, 1907,
> we established the Louise Juvenile Home for dependent and
> neglected children in my own private home, in which we care

for fifty-six children and two mothers. . . . Our home is industrial. The children are taught washing, ironing, cooking,
sewing (such as plain sewing), embroidering, hemstitching,
etc. . . . Our work was supposed to be supported by charitable donations, but we have failed absolutely along that line,
and the most support we have is my lecturing and my evan-
gelistic work; the parents pay $1.00 to $1.50 and $2.00 for their
children, sometimes. [Du Bois, 1909, p. 80]

Often these small institutions, very dependent upon the leadership
of one person, failed to survive after the death of that individual.
Others, however, found their way to firm financial standing through
private donations, and some through acquisition of public monies.
The Reverend D. J. Jenkins, who established an orphanage in Charles-
ton, South Carolina, in 1891, wrote: "The City Council has been
very much impressed with the work of the Jenkins Orphanage and
Industrial School for Colored Children; their interest is manifested by
what they appropriate annually. They appropriated $200 in 1897;
$250 in 1898; $300 in 1899; $300 in 1900; $300 in 1901; $500 in
1904; $1,000 in 1905; $1,000 in 1906; and $1,000 in 1907." (Du
Bois, 1909, p. 79) The Jenkins Orphanage is still in operation today.
Other orphanages established by Black individuals included the
Amanda Smith Industrial Orphan Home in Illinois, The North Georgia
Industrial Orphanage, The Weaver Orphan Home for Colored Children
at Hampton, Virginia, and the Garred Orphanage in Columbia, South
Carolina. Some were quite formal institutions, with boards of trustees
and hired directors. They were financed in a variety of ways: the
Home for Destitute Negro Children in New Castle, Pennsylvania, was
supported by the State Federation of Colored Women's Clubs; and a
number of orphanages were established by Black fraternal societies,
including the Masonic Home in Rock Island, Illinois, and the Masonic
Orphans' Home in Bennetsville, North Carolina. Still others were
funded primarily through public monies and donations from Black
individuals and organizations. One of the latter was the Carrie Steele
Orphanage in Atlanta, which in 1908 had ninety-seven inmates and
an income of "$2,200 ($100 from Negroes directly; the balance from
taxes on both races)." (Du Bois, 1909, p. 86) Finally, there were
those which were principally the result of endowments by Black
philanthropists, like the Lafon Asylum in New Orleans.

Institutions for Both Children and the Aged

A number of institutions designed to serve both the aged and children, especially very young children, were established by Afro-American individuals and organizations. There were several in Tennessee, notably the Old Ladies and Orphans' Home and Old Folks and Orphans' Home in Memphis, and the Masonic Widows and Orphans' Home in Nashville. In Kansas City an Old Folks and Orphan's Home was established by Samuel Eason around 1894, and Liner's Harvest Home, established in New Orleans by Edward Liner in 1886, cared for men, women, and children. As with the orphanages, some of these combined homes were on fairly sound financial footing. Others, however, eked out a bare subsistence: "The Colored Old Folks and Orphans' Home of Mobile, Alabama, was organized for $4,000 cash. It contains two acres of land, with fourteen pecan trees. The college has nine rooms, running water, and $120 is earned from pecans and pears. They have a cow and chickens, and own other real estate." (Du Bois, 1909, p. 72)

By the end of the nineteenth century there had been established, primarily through the efforts of Black individuals and organizations, a number of institutions for Black children in need of care. In view of the severe financial hardships under which many operated, these institutions could not have been the most pleasant places, at least in a material sense. But whatever their defects, these institutions were to remain the primary source of institutional care for Black children until well into the next century.

Day Nurseries and Kindergartens

The efforts of Afro-Americans on behalf of their children were not limited to charity services and institutional aggregate care. There were very notable efforts to establish services designed to enrich the lives of children, not simply to find a place for them. Such services have never been well developed in the formal child welfare system of this country.

Principal among these services were day nurseries and kindergartens. Ordinarily, kindergartens are considered a part of the educational system. We discuss them here, however, because racial discrimination in many of the nation's school systems excluded Black children from kindergartens, even when they were admitted to the later grades. A special effort, therefore, was necessary on the part of Black people to see that their children were provided with kindergartens.

The Atlanta University monograph contains detailed information on the day nurseries and kindergartens established at the turn of the century. Of day nurseries the report states: "The Day Nursery is a widespread and crying need among Negroes. There ought to be not only several in each city and town, but also in county districts. It is a potent field for philanthropic enterprise." (Du Bois, 1909, p. 119) At least ten day nurseries described in the Atlanta University survey were under the sponsorship of Afro-American organizations, and there were interracial enterprises in Columbus, Ohio, and in Washington, D.C. The nursery in Columbus

> was inaugurated by the Womens Educational and Industrial Union, a corporation of Christian women (white) on February 4th, 1901. Realizing the necessity of some assistance from the colored people in carrying on this work, on April 19, 1901, an auxiliary board of managers was organized among them, consisting of four members, who worked in conjunction with the white board. Owing to the rapid growth of the institution the auxiliary board was increased in 1902 to twelve members. . . . As the necessity for more room and increased facilities for doing the work became evident it was decided by the board to purchase larger quarters which they did by securing the present quarters—a seven room brick house. [DuBois, 1909, p. 120]

This was a rare institution in its time; not only was it a day nursery for Black children, but it was one of the few child welfare institutions of any kind that was directed by an interracial board. Most of the white child welfare organizations that served Black children did not establish interracial boards for several decades.

One of the most successful day nurseries established by a Black group was the Women's Union Day Nursery in Philadelphia, which was opened in November, 1898. This nursery cared for children twelve hours a day, from 6:30 A.M. to 6:30 P.M., at a charge of five cents to working parents. In Lexington, Kentucky, a Black women's organization, the Women's Improvement Club, began a day nursery in a four-room cottage, and women of the Baptist Church in Pittsburgh, Pennsylvania, opened a day nursery which also provided temporary residential care for Black children who had come under the jurisdiction of the Juvenile Court. Several other day nurseries were established in various parts of the country. But there were never enough.

Among the kindergartens established at the turn of the century, perhaps the largest was the Gate City Free Kindergarten Association of Atlanta, Georgia. The initial efforts of the organizers had faltered, but by 1905 over 200 children were in attendance at the Association's five kindergartens. They were operated entirely through funds raised by the organization; they received no aid from the state, although it was the practice at the time for the state to support kindergartens for white children. A similar effort in Columbus, Georgia, begun by a Black organization, was eventually taken over by the city. Kindergartens were also established in connection with some interracial social settlements for Black people, a notable one being the Colored Social Settlements in Washington, D.C.

Homes for Black Working Girls

Another type of social institution established by Afro-American efforts was the home for working girls. In the early twentieth century many such homes were opened in northern cities to accommodate girls who had recently migrated from the South. As with the kindergartens, this type of facility cannot be considered a child welfare service *per se;* but many of the girls were indeed children, not nearly out of their teens, and many of these homes also cared for children born to the girls and women. Notable among these homes were the Phillis Wheatly Home in Chicago, the Harriet Tubman House in Boston, established by the Black women of the Woman's Christian Temperance Union, and an interracial effort, the National Association for the Protection of Colored Women, which operated houses in New York, Philadelphia, Baltimore, Norfolk, and Washington. The Phillis Wheatly Home gives an idea of the functions performed by these institutions:

> The Home is established to solve the problem of befriending
> the colored girls and women who come into this great city
> seeking work, often without relatives, friends or money. . . .
> of the hundred or so homes established here for working girls
> not one of them offers shelter to our girls. . . . we determined to do something toward helping the stranger girls and

women especially as well as those in our own midst. . . .
we opened the home May 31, 1908, and have never been without an inmate a single day. We have housed thirty girls and
have secured employment for over one hundred, and have given
encouragement, sympathy, and in a few cases financial aid to
many more. . . . A home of this kind ought to be in every
large city, and notices of same given wide publicity in every
town and city throughout the country, in order to safeguard
our women and girls. [Du Bois, 1909, p. 100]

A vast number of such homes were established by Black women's
organizations during the early decades of the twentieth century. One,
the Women's Christian Alliance, later became a child welfare social
agency and will be discussed at length in Chapter 5. But many of these
homes, like the industrial schools, were little more than employment
agencies and training schools for servants. Nonetheless, the establishment of homes for working girls was an example of the Afro-American responsiveness to the problems of their young people.

THOUGHTS ON BLACK SERVICES FOR BLACK CHILDREN

In this chapter we have tried to show the efforts Black people made to
provide for needy Black children in the face of an inadequate and
discriminatory child welfare system. Private charities and private
services for poor children, orphanages, day care centers, kindergartens, and working girls' homes were part of a movement toward
community provision of child welfare services that continued well into
the twentieth century. Until the 1950's, this movement was not only
the major source of services for Black children, but, in many areas, it
was the only source of services.

In those cruel and fateful years just after emancipation, when
Black people were largely deserted by the wider society, it was both
necessary and possible for them to draw on the inner resources of their
communities and their relationships, and the ancient spirit of benevolence reaching back to Africa, in order to provide a modicum of care
and protection to the needy in their midst, especially the elderly and
the children. But whether these Black agencies were developed because white people would not, or because of community preference,
and whether they were struggling successes or struggling failures, they
were always up against a hostile and indifferent society, and often up
against hostility within the Black community.

In *The Philadelphia Negro,* Du Bois called attention to the disapproval within the Black community:

> Much of the need for separate Negro institutions has in the last decade disappeared, by reason of the opening of the doors of the public institutions to colored people. There are many Negroes who on this account strongly oppose efforts which they fear will tend to delay further progress in these lines. On the other hand, thoughtful men see that invaluable training and discipline is coming to the race through these institutions and organizations, and they encourage the formation of them. [1967, p. 233]

The Douglass Memorial Hospital and Training School in Philadelphia, founded by a Black physician, Dr. N. F. Mossel, was a good example of the situation Black people often found and find themselves in with respect to the operation of Black institutions:

> For years nearly every hospital in Philadelphia has sought to exclude Negro women from the course in nurse-training, and no Negro physician could have the advantage of hospital practice. This led to a movement for a Negro hospital; such a movement, however, was condemned by the whites as an unnecessary addition to a bewildering number of charitable institutions; [and] by many of the best Negroes as a concession to prejudice and a drawing of the color line. Nevertheless the promoters insisted that colored nurses were inefficient and needed training, that colored physicians needed a hospital, and that colored patients wished one. Consequently the Douglass Hospital has been established and its success seems to warrant the effort. [Du Bois, 1967, p. 230]

Du Bois added in a footnote that after the hospital was opened, Black nurses had less trouble getting into white institutions and that "one colored physician has been appointed intern in a large hospital."

One of the important functions of Black agencies, then as now, is to amass and utilize the strength within the Black community in order to move beyond the historic reliance on the white community, which has so often proved to be unreliable. Another function is to provide the experience and the demonstration, to both the white and the Black communities, of Black competence. Still another function is to create fuller opportunities for Black people, which in turn are often reflected in companion white institutions.

4 Child welfare in the twentieth century

The system of child welfare services which had evolved by 1900 in America has undergone modifications in this century. However, the principal modifications have been in the means of providing and administering the services; the services themselves have remained heavily focused on the placement of children away from their parents. The major child welfare institutions have been modified by a gradual extension of services to Black children. The distribution of services remains inequitable, however, and the best that can be said of child welfare efforts for Black children in the twentieth century is that there has been a shift from total exclusion to partial inclusion.

In this chapter, we shall look at the changes that have come about in the philosophical bases for the provision of care, the shifts in emphasis in the forms and provision of care, and the gradual change in the position of Black children in the system that has evolved.

CHANGING IDEAS OF PROVISION FOR THE POOR

The twentieth century has seen a major change in American ideas about poverty. The national belief that the fundamental causes of poverty are rooted in the poor remains, but there is now an expectation that there will be poverty, largely because there is now an expectation of unemployment.

At the end of the nineteenth century, public provision for the poor was made largely through the almshouse system. Outdoor relief, or financial and material assistance to people in their own homes, was the province of private charities. The first advances that were made in extending public money to the poor outside the almshouses benefited two groups whose poverty was considered a result of unemployability, not of individual inadequacy. The first group was men injured in industrial accidents; the second was families—mothers and children—deprived of a wage earner (usually by death). Such public provision did not extend beyond the state level and was never nationwide. By 1930, however, several states did have some provision for injured workmen, under the Workmen's Compensation laws, and families deprived of a wage earner were assisted in several states through the Mother's Aid programs. Both these programs were directed toward groups whose unemployability was due to characteristics resident in them, albeit characteristics to which no "blame" was attached. During the depression of the 1930's, the other kind of unemployability came to be acknowledged—the kind that is due to factors in the economy, factors external to individuals and not restricted to any particular groups. Such unemployability was first provided for through the Social Security Act of 1935. Provision for this type of unemployment was established on a far different basis than that for unemployability due to individual characteristics, since it was based on a system of social insurance. That is, the potential beneficiaries contribute money through a mandatory tax on their earnings during the time that they are wage earners; when the hazard against which they are insured befalls them, they collect payments. The Social Security Act of 1935, with its subsequent amendments, had as its philosophical basis a recognition that individuals may become poor because they cannot find work, even though they are willing to work. As well as protection against the hazards of short-term unemployment, it established protection against unemployability due to old age, and later against physical disability and against the death of the wage earner. The Social Security Act was the first official refutation of the colonial belief that there would be no poverty in the New World.

But what of those who are poor but have not been wage earners or attached to a wage earner; those who are poor because they receive low wages even though they are employed; and those who are poor because their Social Security payments are not enough to survive on? There are separate public assistance programs under the Social Security Act for alleviation of these kinds of poverty; they show the pervasive influence of all of the colonial and nineteenth-century beliefs about poverty. In Chapter 2 we discussed the spread of the almshouse method of care for the poor. The Yates Report of 1824, which had been very influential in that spread, described categories of "permanent paupers" all too reminiscent of the present categories in the public assistance programs. The classes of "permanent paupers" delineated in the Yates report were "idiots and lunatics," "blind," "extremely aged and infirm," "lame," "in such a confirmed state of ill health as to be totally incapable of labor," and "children." (Thurston, 1930, p. 121) After a hundred years, the first public assistance programs established under the Social Security Act were Aid to the Blind, Old-Age Assistance, and Aid to Families with Dependent Children. It was not until 1950 that provision began to be made for the other classes noted in the Yates report—the "idiots, lunatics, lame, and those in a confirmed state of ill health"—through the Aid to the Permanently and Totally Disabled programs. Indeed, the concept of individual responsibility for poverty continues to underlie public provision for the poor: the poor do not have rights; they are aided only on a basis of need—and on the reason for the need.

Aid to Families with Dependent Children is often thought of as a program for children who are in need. It is not. It is only a program which provides for certain children, who are in need because of certain characteristics of their families, especially their fathers. "Dependent" children, as defined in the 1935 Social Security Act, are essentially children who are in need because their fathers are dead, disabled, or have deserted them.* Under such a public assistance pro-

---

* The term "dependent" is given many meanings. In A.F.D.C., it simply refers to children who are still minors, and who can be expected to depend on their parents for financial support. In child welfare and social welfare, "dependent" has various and vague definitions. Basically, it refers to one not providing himself or being provided with the basic necessities within the usual,

gram, not only do children not have rights, their need is not really taken into consideration. Basically, Aid to Families with Dependent Children is a program for certain categories of unemployables who happen to have children. Children, of course, do constitute a class of unemployable individuals; they are unemployable due to their age, just as old people are. But they are one class of unemployables for whom there is no public assumption of responsibility. Children are aided on the basis of the unemployability of their parents. And they are never given so much financial assistance as would deter their parents from going to work. As of 1971, there is no program in the United States to provide for children because they are children or because they are in need.

National expectations concerning poverty, the shift toward public responsibility, and public-supported income-maintenance programs have combined with two other forces to shape the present child welfare system. These two forces—bureaucratization and professionalization—have tended to sharpen the placement focus of child welfare and to widen the separation between child welfare services and services to children in their own homes.

The Effects of Bureaucratization

The gradual recognition of public responsibility for the poor was accompanied by a similar shift to public services in child welfare. One effect was an increase in the size of public child welfare operations.

---

expected channels. Thus, in the case of economic "dependency" in adults, the meaning is "depending on others for financial support." In the case of child welfare, "dependent" children are those who must rely on persons other than their parents for financial support *or* parental care.

The important conceptual distinction between the states of poverty and dependency is almost universally ignored. A child born to a poor woman married to a poor man is a poor child. A child born to a poor woman without a husband is a poor child. In either case the poverty, not the marital status of the parents, conditions the economic status of the child. The potential difficulties of rearing a child without a husband, or a helpmate, on the other hand, might have a stronger bearing on the child's becoming dependent upon others, including social agencies, for care. So might poverty itself. Nonetheless, they are distinctly separable states. The obvious fallacy betrayed here is the common use of a variety of statistics on illegitimacy, dependency, and poverty, which are then interpreted in a causal relationship, with poverty considered the result, not the cause.

Privately administered agencies also grew, as public money was increasingly made available to them. Bureaucratization was an inevitable consequence of these increases in size.

By "bureaucracy" we mean a highly organized system of agencies with multilevel authority, extremely specialized functions, elaborate rules governing eligibility, and rigid jurisdictional division. The effects of bureaucracy can be seen most vividly at the county or city level where services are dispensed, but they extend through all levels of government, and all levels of private charitable organizations as well. We have already noted that by 1900, child welfare services—the orphanages and foster homes—had already been split off from the various organizations that were working with families and children in their own homes. Thus, when the large bureaucracies came into being, they were simply superimposed on an already disarticulated system. The inevitable division of labor that accompanies bureaucratization has increased the disarticulation. Agencies are funded on a basis of the functions they perform, and within the agencies, functions are still further subdivided. In short, services have been organized by function; they have not been organized with children in mind. This rigid division of labor has had negative consequences for children and for their families.

In itself, the shift from private to public auspices has had positive implications for Black children. Black children inevitably fare better where the givers of service are publicly accountable. When, in fact, bureaucratic mechanisms such as the withholding of funds have been employed to the benefit of Black children, services have been opened to them. Publicly financed and administered agencies were the first to extend services to Black children to any significant degree, and in the 1960's the likelihood of Black children receiving any kind of service was greater in public agencies than in private ones. Two factors, however, have prevented discrimination against Black children from being eliminated in the public sphere. Publicly supported agencies are very sensitive to political power, ultimately being under the influence of elected officials and their appointees. To the extent that Black people continue to be denied full participation in the political arena, their influence over elected officials and publicly supported services, including child welfare services, is similarly limited. The other factor is the orientation toward need, rather than right, than persists in child welfare services. When it can always be said that they are getting what they "need," all that is necessary is to redefine their "needs" to fit what they are being given. Once something is defined as a *right*—education is possibly their only recognized right at present—legal recourse on behalf of Black children can be—and has been—much more extensively employed.

The Effects of Professionalization

The professionalization of social work has failed to advance the child welfare field much beyond the nineteenth century, and in some ways has been influential in perpetuating the split between services to children in their own homes and placement services. A prime cause of this unhappy situation is the underlying philosophical and theoretical base of professional social casework—that of Freudian psychoanalytic belief. From the perspective of social services, the Freudian doctrine of individual psychopathology as the root of human suffering differs very little from the nineteenth-century doctrine of individual responsibility for poverty. In effect, the earlier influence of Calvin was little disturbed by the followers of Freud. While the nineteenth-century reformers earnestly and sincerely believed that the way to both celestial and earthly happiness was through spiritual and moral personal growth, the twentieth-century social caseworkers just as earnestly and sincerely have believed that similar goals are to be achieved through insight into one's personal psychological functioning. Not unlike the nineteenth-century reformer, the social caseworker thinks that the client's primary function is to attain such insight. In time, social service has come to be synonymous with this psychological service. Such an orientation can hardy be expected to encourage services of an environmental nature, including either financial assistance or the provision of services for the poor which they could not purchase. As the rendering of more purely psychological service has become established as the most prestigious work to be done, the prestige itself has tended to increase the separation of this kind of service from those services tinged with an environmental component. Thus, placement-oriented child welfare, rendering fundamental and environmental services—provision of a place to live—became increasingly split off from agencies rendering the purely psychological services, including those agencies serving families and children in their own homes.

Apart from the barrier to development of in-home environmental services and the additional disarticulation of the system of services, professionalization has had more direct influences on child welfare, which on balance cannot be considered positive from the standpoint of Black children. Consider, for example, the very firmly held professional standards for adoptive parents. In the professional view, adoptive homes should have two parents who are married to each other, have never been married before, and have been married for a certain length of time; the wife must not work; there must be no other children, and there must be sufficient room for the child; and the parents must pay a fee ranging from a few hundred dollars to a few thousand. Surely these professional standards were not designed with Black children of Black families in mind; they cannot be considered conducive to their being given the service of adoption.

Professional casework theories have reinforced a belief in the "rightness" of the existing systems of services, and have perpetuated the "need" rather than "rights" approach to services. Just as Freudian psychology has reinforced the belief that the individual is the chief source of social problems, so it gives an elaborate explanation of how each form of pathology should be treated. Thus, for every form of deviance that was so carefully defined in setting up the institutions that have come to replace the almshouse, there is now a full theoretical explanation—often referred to in social work as the "knowledge base" —of why that particular form of institution is just right for correcting that particular form of deviance. The fact that the institutions and the systems of services were there first, and that the twentieth-century explanations came a little later, has not deterred the professionals. This teleological approach has made it difficult for caseworkers to perceive the malfunctioning of the system for Black children, and has even permitted rationalizations for outright discrimination against them. Such a rationalization occurs in adoption agencies. In addition to the standards we mentioned earlier, prospective parents who wish a child must meet certain standards of psychological functioning in adult life. Similarly, children can be denied adoption because they have had certain life experiences which might render them psychologically unfit. The fact that such determinations are highly subjective and judgmental precludes any exact determination of other factors, such as racial discrimination, which may also be playing a part in the refusal of service. More fundamentally, however, just as the nineteenth-century reformist belief system had no room for the fact that Black children were born into a specifically hostile white environment, neither does the Freudian belief system provide for recognition of the special environmental circumstances of Black children. As in the nineteenth century, the philosophical underpinnings of child welfare in the twentieth century fail to consider the situation of Black children and perpetuate an indirect form of racism toward them.

In summary, twentieth-century child welfare has been influenced by developments in the broader society and in the broader field of social welfare. The financing and the administration of services have been modified, but new kinds of services for children have not been developed. The twentieth-century modification in the expectation of poverty brought a shift in responsibility for relief of destitution from private to public auspices and from the almshouse to cash payments to people in their own homes. The effect on child welfare has been a similar shift in auspices and an increase in the scope of activity, with an accompanying bureaucratization and professionalization of social work. But these changes have had little effect in changing the kinds of services given to children.

The Twentieth-Century Idea: Families Should Stay Together

In the nineteenth century, separating poor children from their poor parents was deemed a worthy endeavor. The underlying philosophy of the twentieth century dictates that children should not be separated from their parents for reasons of poverty alone.

This principle was enunciated at the first Conference on the Care of Dependent Children called by the President of the United States in 1909. As the official proceedings stated:

> Home life is the highest and finest product of civilization. It is the great modeling force of mind and of character. Children should not be deprived of it except for urgent and compelling reasons. Children of parents of worthy character, suffering from temporary misfortune, and children of reasonable and efficient mothers, who are without the support of the normal breadwinner, should as a rule be kept with their parents, such aid being given as may be necessary to maintain suitable homes for the rearing of the children. The aid should be given by such methods and from such sources as may be determined by the general relief policy of each community, preferably in the form of private charity rather than of public relief. Except in unusual circumstances, the home should not be broken up for

reasons of poverty, but only for considerations of inefficiency or immorality. [pp. 9–10]

The Twentieth-Century Practice: Take the Children Away from Their Parents

In the sixty years that have followed the 1909 conference, the major child welfare effort has been directed toward children for whom separation from parents is deemed appropriate, those separated for "considerations of inefficiency and immorality." Thus in 1962, a committee of the Child Welfare League of America, assigned the task of formulating standards for services to children in their own homes, had to report as follows: "It was anticipated at that time that it might be difficult for the child welfare field to develop a statement of standards for this service, primarily because its major efforts had been concentrated on services for children outside their own homes, and because child welfare agencies had had relatively limited experience in offering the service." (Turitz, 1968, p. 66)

Statistics issued by the U.S. Department of Health, Education and Welfare for the year 1969 further illustrate the persistence of the heavy reliance on placement services. (*Child Welfare Statistics,* 1969) In that year, 694,000 children were reported as receiving child welfare services from public agencies; 56 percent of these children were living away from their parents and relatives. Among the 216,000 children receiving services from private agencies, the proportion was even greater: 76 percent of the children served were living away from their families. The actual character of the services rendered to the children living with their own families is not clear. The vast majority of these children were in families receiving A.F.D.C., and presumably the major service given was some form of counseling to the parents. However, whether such services attached to an A.F.D.C. check really constitute "child welfare services" is questionable: several states did not report A.F.D.C. services at all in their accounts of "child welfare services" rendered. The numbers of children at home who received more tangible kinds of service, for example day care and homemaker service, were relatively few indeed: 20,300 children were in families receiving the services of a homemaker, and 22,600 children had day-care services purchased for them. As such statistics show, the principle that children should not be removed from their parents because of poverty has not been implemented to any significant extent through the development of service to poor families and poor children living with them.

TWENTIETH-CENTURY CHANGES IN CHILD-PLACEMENT RESOURCES

The Foster Boarding Home

The 1909 conference also maintained that children who had to be removed from their parents were best cared for in a family setting rather than in an institution. However, it was not until the 1920's that foster homes for children began to replace orphanages or institutions to any extent. At the same time, the use of free foster homes declined in favor of the boarding home. Under the free foster home system, as developed by Brace and Van Arsdale, families who took in children were not compensated in any way for their efforts or for money spent on the child—except, of course, through whatever work the children themselves performed. In foster boarding homes, the foster parents are still not paid for their efforts, but they do receive payments that are intended only to cover the cost of keeping the child. Foster parents were first paid for the cost of keeping the child by Charles Birtwell of the Boston Children's Aid Society, around the turn of the century; the later increase of public money in the child welfare field gradually caused the demise of the free foster home and the ascendancy of the foster boarding home.

The shift from institutions to foster homes has been sweeping. In 1923, 64.2 percent of the children receiving care from institutions and agencies were in residential institutions; in 1933, the figure dropped to 48 percent. In 1969, about 18 percent of the children in placement were in institutions. About 67 percent of the children were in foster homes. And 13 percent were in homes where they had been legally adopted. (*Children Under Institutional Care, 1927,* p. 18, 1935, p. 9; *Child Welfare Statistics,* 1969, p. 1)

Adoption

As an informal social institution, adoption has probably existed in America from the beginning of the nation; as a legal institution, it began in the deeding laws of the mid-nineteenth century. As a child welfare service—one administered by a child welfare agency—adoption is a twentieth-century development, and one principally of the last thirty years. It gradually evolved from the participation of child welfare personnel in investigating adoptions which had been arranged by independent parties (parties independent of any child welfare agency) to see that they conformed to the local statutes on adoption. (We refer here only to adoptions contracted by persons unrelated to each other; adoptions among relatives transcend child welfare.) Beginning in the 1920's, child welfare agencies were gradually established to provide adoption services, and agencies primarily concerned with other forms of child placement, principally foster care, began to develop adoption services as well. Since World War II, agencies have come to arrange larger and larger proportions of the total number of adoptions each year, and adoption arranged by private unrelated parties have correspondingly decreased. In 1970 approximately two-thirds of all adoptions by unrelated persons were arranged through child welfare agencies.

The first adoption agencies, in the 1920's, were not intended to benefit children primarily. They were established to provide children for couples unable to have their own children. Thus adoption, unlike other forms of substitute parental care, did not originate as a resource for dependent children, and especially not for poor children. In fact, until the last decade or so, most of the children adopted through agencies were not "poor children"; they were illegitimate babies born to white middle- and upper-income women. As a child welfare service, adoption is still enigmatic.

These general features of the development of adoption as a child welfare service have direct implications for Black children. First, the primary intended recipient of the service was the adopting parent. In a social climate where Black adults were denied rights to protection and privileges under the most fundamental laws, there was little likelihood that the services and the privileges of adoption would be extended to Black adults (and thus secondarily to Black children). Second, since adoption itself was considered neither a right nor a need of any child, the chances of recognizing the rights and needs of Black children to a permanent home were minimal. Finally, since adoption was not considered a primary mode of caring for dependent children, especially poor children, adoption agencies were not considered an element in the system of services for them. The voluntary nature of the earliest adoption agencies must be underscored here, since they were voluntary in the strictest sense—they defined their function, and its scope, and its limitations. All of these factors made adoption the least likely of all child welfare services to be extended to Black children. In fact, this has proven to be just the case. It is partly for this reason that we have elected in Part Three of this book to examine in detail the efforts at change for Black children in the area of adoption.

BLACK CHILDREN IN TWENTIETH-CENTURY CHILD WELFARE

How have Black children fared in the system of child welfare services in the twentieth century? Up to the end of World War I, Black children were largely ignored by the established child welfare system, as they had been since the Civil War. Spurred by Black pressure for equality and by the migrations of southern Black people during and after World War I, the system began to take some notice of them in the 1920's and 1930's. A third phase in the extension of child welfare services to Black children began at the end of World War II, in response to the same situational influence—northern migration and the increasing political influence of Black people.

1900 to 1920: The Persistence of Nineteenth-Century Exclusion

In 1909, the first Conference on the Care of Dependent Children was called by President Theodore Roosevelt. The conference has been hailed as a landmark in child welfare history, in many ways marking the discovery of children in America. Two Black men participated: Dr. Booker T. Washington, President of Tuskegee Institute, and Mr. Richard Carroll, manager of the South Carolina Industrial Home for Destitute and Dependent Colored Children. Both of these men were southern and both verbalized acceptance of segregation. Their selection as the sole Black participants among the hundreds at this historic White House conference was not accidental; it was fully representative of the view of Black people held by the callers of the conference.

The limitation of Black participation to these two men implies either that the white people who arranged the conference were ignorant of the efforts being made by other Black people for children, or a deliberate rejection of such people. The Atlanta University conference was held that same year, on "Efforts for Social Betterment among

Negro Americans." Apparently none of the hundreds of Black people who attended the Atlanta conference were invited to the White House conference. The white participants at the conference were mostly directors of orphanges and children's agencies, who were engaged in direct child welfare services to children. The parallel group among Afro-American people was ignored, with the single exception of Mr. Carroll. Dr. Washington had become by then the official spokesman for Black people at most White House functions. He was invited not because of any particular knowledge about children; he would have been invited had it been a conference on the welfare of farmers, hodcarriers, or the aged.

None of the white participants at the conference mentioned Black children in their papers. The only information about Black children and their welfare was that presented by the two Black participants. Mr. Carroll began his talk by saying, "I have been here two days, and I have been thinking of the fact of the colored man being a problem. . . . I wrote it [his speech] before I came here; if I had it to write over again, I should say something else." (Conference on the Care of Dependent Children, 1909, p. 136) We shall never know what he might have said, as the chairman interrupted, saying there would have to be a ruling of the conference if he was to address the gathering on any matter other than his announced topic; Mr. Carroll read his paper. His paper dealt chiefly with the continuing necessity for industrially oriented institutions for Black homeless children, such as the type of which he was manager.

Dr. Washington's address was mainly concerned with decrying the migration of Black people to urban centers, especially northern urban centers, which he always saw as a major mistake. His paper, which could be taken as representing the official white view of Black children at that time, may be summarized as follows. Black children were (1) southern, (2) not the responsibility of the white child-caring system and (3) somehow being adequately cared for, in some mysterious but nonspecific way, through the benevolence of their own people.

It was not an accurate view, and it was one which left the childcaring systems of the nation ill-prepared for the rapid changes in the status of Black adults and children over the next few years. That it was not a complete view is clear from remarks by Dr. Washington himself just two years later in an address at the Chicago Child Welfare Exhibit in 1912. At Chicago, Dr. Washington chose to discuss the alarmingly high death rates of Black children in several northern cities (not at that time mentioning the even higher rates in the southern states). He stated:

> In making a comparison between the death rate of colored children in large cities of the North, I find this to be true: In the city of Washington the number of deaths in a year per thousand of population is twenty-six; in Baltimore, twenty-eight; in Philadelphia, thirty; in New York, twenty-eight; in the City of Chicago I am glad to congratulate you on the fact that you have a death rate of only twenty-one among the colored children. [1912, pp. 238–39]

The view of the Black dependent child which held sway in 1909 changed over the next twenty years. A major impetus to the change was the massive migration of Black people during World War I, which, like the war itself, was accompanied by dramatic changes in American race relations. The principal changes occurred within the Black community itself. More and more the Black community, especially in the large northern cities, saw the creation of organizations that were not at all secret, but rather increasingly vocal, and dedicated to the achievement of freedom and equality for Black people. One such organization, the National Urban League, which originated in 1910 specifically to deal with the problems of urban Black people, eventually took a prominent role in pressing for the rights of Black children in the distribution of child welfare services. The first executive director, George Edmund Hayes, was the first Black graduate of the New York School of Social Work. Such events were to have an impact on the child caring systems of the country, particularly in the urban North.

World War I to World War II: The Beginning Recognition of Black Children

In the decade following the end of the First World War, the child welfare system's complacent obliviousness to the problems of Black children began to dissipate. There was little action on behalf of Black children, but there was a growing awareness of their presence.

Black Children in the Child-Placement System, 1923–1933

There was some change during the 1920's in the relation of Black children to the heart of child welfare services—the child-placement institutions and agencies. Census data from 1923 and 1933 give some picture of the modification.

While the 1923 Census gives no data summated by race, there is a listing of every child-care institution in the United States, which gives the admission policy of each with regard to race. Table 4–1 summarizes the data on child-caring institutions and their admission policies according to institutional auspices and geographical region.

In 1923 the child welfare system was relatively closed to Black

TABLE 4–1

Racial Admission Policies of Child-Caring Agencies by Region and Auspices, 1923 and 1933

Thirty-one Northern States, 1923

	Auspices					
	Public		Sectarian		Other Private	
Admission Policy	Number	Percent	Number	Percent	Number	Percent
All, or Black and white	85	76	85	16	94	21
Black only	2	2	16	3	17	4
All except Black	1	1	30	6	29	7
White only	24	21	390	75	297	68
Total	112	100	521	100	437	100

Thirty-one Northern States, 1933

	Auspices					
	Public		Sectarian		Other Private	
Admission Policy	Number	Percent	Number	Percent	Number	Percent
All, or Black and white	338	99	365	53	337	62
Black only	1	—	11	2	19	3
All except Black	1	—	29	4	10	2
White only	2	—	278	41	179	33
Total	342	100	683	100	545	100

Seventeen Southern States, 1923

Auspices

Admission Policy	Public Number	Public Percent	Sectarian Number	Sectarian Percent	Other Private Number	Other Private Percent
All, or Black and white	5	22	2	1	1	—
Black only	1	4	18	9	25	15
All except Black	2	9	17	8	9	6
White only	15	65	165	82	128	79
Total	23	100	202	100	163	100

Seventeen Southern States, 1933

Auspices

Admission Policy	Public Number	Public Percent	Sectarian Number	Sectarian Percent	Other Private Number	Other Private Percent
All, or Black and white	43	51	21	8	32	15
Black only	7	8	17	7	25	12
All except Black	—	—	11	4	5	2
White only	35	41	213	81	151	71
Total	85	100	262	100	213	100

SOURCE: "Children Under Institutional Care, 1923," 1927, pp. 48–138; and "Children Under Institutional Care, 1933," 1935, pp. 63–125.

children. In thirty-one northern states there were 1,070 agencies reporting. Thirty-five of these admitted Black children only, 264 admitted all races, and 60 of them accepted other nonwhite races, but excluded Black children. The vast majority, 711, admitted white children only. The policies with regard to other nonwhite children is testimony to the extreme race consciousness of the child welfare system. In California, for example, there were special institutions for Chinese children, Japanese children, and Indian children; there were also institutions which would admit white children and Japanese or Chinese, but excluded Black children and Indian children; still others accepted all but Chinese. In California, in fact, of 67 institutions reporting, only 9 stated they would accept "all children" without any racial restriction. The seventeen southern states had 388 institutions reporting in 1923. Of these, 44 were only for Black children, and 8 claimed to take in any child; 308 were only for white children, and 28 took children of other races (excluding Blacks).

By 1933, the situation had changed. Both the shift away from institutional care to foster boarding home care and the shift from private to public auspices had begun. The shift to boarding homes was more apparent in the care of Black children than of white. In 1933 only 34 percent of the Black children in care were in residential institutions, while 52 percent were in boarding homes, with the remainder being in free foster homes. The majority (59 percent) of white children were in residential institutions, while only 41 percent were in boarding or free foster homes.

Although this was the national picture in 1933, there were important regional differences. In the South a large proportion of Black children were in institutions. There were also regional differences in the relative distribution of services to Black children, differences which were not solely reflective of the percentage of Black children in the general population. Less than one-third of the Black children under care were reported as being in the South, and, in fact, some southern states with relatively large Black populations reported very few Black children under care. In the North itself the distribution of services was extremely uneven, a pattern that partly reflected the uneven Black population growth. (*Children Under Institutional Care, 1933,* 1935, p. 9) Over one-half of the Black children reported under care in the nation were in five northern states; each of these five states (New York, Pennsylvania, Ohio, Illinois, and Maryland) reported a larger number of Black children under care than did any sourthern state.

Nationwide, the number of public agencies tripled between 1923 and 1933. This was an increase in the one type of agency least likely to exclude Black children. In 1923 three-fourths of the northern public agencies had no policy of racial exclusion; on the other hand, three-fourths of the private agencies and the sectarian agencies were for white children only.

In the North, moreover, there was a change in policy among the private and sectarian agencies. By 1933, racial exclusion was the policy of only about a third of the sectarian agencies and about a fifth of all the other private agencies. In the South, the private agencies and the sectarian ones remained in 1933 almost entirely exclusively for white children.

In the South the growth of public agencies did not have as much impact on racial policies. Almost half the public agencies in the South

—35 out of 85—were for white children only in 1933. Only seven agencies were for Black children only. Little wonder, then, that there were more Black children under care in each of five northern states than in any southern state, in spite of the fact that the southern states had larger populations of Black children. It must be emphasized, of course, that we are dealing only with the expressed policies of the agencies reporting; the extent to which a "Black-and white" agency acted on its expressed policy and actually did care for Black children is quite another matter. It is very likely that many did not, as many do not today; otherwise we would not see the maldistribution of child welfare services to Black children which existed then and which persists today.

There was in the 1920's an unfortunate corollary to the growth of public services: the number of Black institutions for children did not increase. That is, the Black child-caring system, begun in the nineteenth century, ceased to expand beyond 1920. This happened in part because of the growing insistence among Black people that they should no longer be excluded from the major social institutions of the country, particularly agencies supported in part by Black people's taxes. The Black institutions, including child welfare agencies, came to be seen as incompatible with the goal of equality as manifested through integration.

In summary, after World War I, the position of Black children in the child welfare system began to change. The special hardships of Black children were beginning to be recognized, although no new services were developed to alleviate them. But the child welfare establishment did begin to extend some service to Black children, and policies of racial exclusion, so characteristic until that time, began to be changed.

This opening of services to Black children within the welfare establishment was concurrent with two major changes in the child welfare system. The first was the change in both forms of care and auspices. This fact has direct implications for those who would improve child welfare for Black children today. Then as now, improvements for Black children did not take place simply through improved treatment in the existing systems. The systems themselves—including the forms of services, the control of services, and the distribution of services— had to change dramatically. The same must happen today. The second major change which took place in the 1920's is also relevant today. For Black children, the shift to foster-home care also meant a direct involvement of the Black community in the care of their dependent children. Most institutions, then as now, were sponsored, controlled, and administered by white people. In essence Black children in such institutions were taken from the Black community, placed in white-dominated institutions, and in effect denied the resources of the Black community. Foster boarding homes altered this situation; while the placement agencies were controlled by white people, the vast majority of foster parents were Black. Thus, the development of the foster boarding home ultimately meant the active participation of Black adults—Black families—in the white child welfare system. It can be said that the extension of services to Black children has been directly related to the extent of participation by the Black community in their care. Black people's participation as foster parents, however, was not and is not accompanied by Black participation in control and administration. Such participation is urgently needed.

Black Children and Delinquency

As we pointed out in Chapter 2, the Black child was in the nineteenth century more apt to be labeled a delinquent child than an orphan (or as we say today, a "dependent child"). What happened to the institutions for delinquent children in the 1920's? The data in the 1923 and 1933 census reports illustrate not only the position of Black children in the delinquency sphere, but also the relationship between the delinquency sphere and the child welfare system, from the standpoint of Black children. Admittance to an institution for delinquents is often preceded by services which constitute alternatives to such institutionalization—probation and care as a dependent child. What were the relative numbers of "white" and "colored" children in such institutions who had received such services? In some states the difference was vast: "In Georgia 41.3 percent of the white children, but only 16.3 percent of the colored children had been on probation." (*Children Under Institutional Care, 1923,* 1927, p. 327) The national figures show only small differences in the percentages of white and Black children who had received alternative services, but in all regions the Black children consistently received them less often: "The [national] percentage of colored children who had been on probation was 37.1 as compared with the percentage of 43.1 for white children." (*Children Under Institutional Care, 1923,* 1927, p. 327)

This information is not complete for all children labeled as delinquent, and it is vastly incomplete for children of color. The reason is that these reports consider only children committed to institutions for juvenile delinquents, not those sent to penal institutions. In the relative disposition of children to institutions for juveniles and to adult penal institutions, the greatest discrimination against Black children is revealed. The 1923 census reported that only 20.4 percent of the white delinquent children (under age 18) had been sent to adult penal institutions; 50.6 percent of the black delinquent children were in adult penal institutions (*Children Under Institutional Care, 1923,* 1927, p. 304) It is not an overstatement to say that a major child-caring institution for Black and other nonwhite children was the prison.

Putting all of this information together, we can summarize the placement of Black children in the 1920's: they were largely excluded from child welfare institutions, less often received services prior to being labeled delinquent, and once so labeled, were much more likely to be sent to prison. In all sectors of the child-placement system, then, and whether labeled as dependent or delinquent, Black children were victims of racist and discriminatory practices.

The Situation of Black Children, 1930

Whatever Mr. Richard Carroll's private musings had been in 1909 on the "colored man as a problem," had he lived to attend the 1930 White House Conference on Child Health and Protection of Dependent and Neglected Children, he would not have had to think alone. By then the Black child *was* a "problem," and he was a *northern* problem. He was not the only problem, however. There was a special committee in Child Dependency as Affected by Race, Nationality, and Mass Migration. The introduction to the Committee's report reads:

> The dependent and neglected children of Negro, Puerto Rican, Mexican, and Indian families present special problems needing consideration, and while there is theoretical agreement among leaders in health and social welfare that the children of these groups should receive the . . . same standards of care as those given other children, their needs are in reality little understood by the general public, and in many communities are almost wholly ignored. [White House Conference, 1930, p. 278]

The papers presented contained valuable information, but the title under which they appeared might more appropriately have been simply "Child Dependency as Affected by Race." Child dependency had been markedly affected by both nationality and mass migration in 1909, but there was no special section with that heading. But then the nationalities and the mass migrations had been Italian, Irish, German, and Polish—all white. At least, however, the 1930 conference was more forthright than the 1960 White House Conference was to be. In 1930 there was, for example, a subcommittee on the Negro, chaired by Dr. Eugene Kinckle Jones, Executive Secretary of the National Urban League. In 1960 "Negroes," "Mexicans," and "Puerto Ricans" had disappeared. They had become "disadvantaged minorities."

All questionable nomenclature aside, the 1930 White House Conference gives us a valuable picture of the state of the nation's Black children. We have seen how they were related to the placement system of the country. Now let us see what other aid they were receiving from the larger society.

The principal spokesman for Black children at the 1930 conference was Dr. Ira De A. Reid, an official of the National Urban League and later Dean of the School of Social Work at Atlanta University. While Dr. Washington's paper at the 1909 conference is now of only historical interest, Dr. Reid's paper is tragically relevant today: the problems he cited in 1930 are the problems of Black children today; and the recommendations he made are still not acted upon. Dr. Reid detailed four areas where direct discrimination against Black parents had had direct implications for the welfare of Black children. These areas were income-maintenance programs, medical care, services to unwed mothers, and day-care services.

In discussing the income-maintenance program of the day, Mother's Aid, Dr. Reid made the following comments: "The only statute relating to mother's aid mentioning race or color as a factor conditioning the grant is found in Alaska." (White House Conference, 1930, p. 30) He then went on, however, to show how that particular income-maintenance system served to discriminate against Black mothers and children in fact, if not in the statute books. He noted that

> at present the development of Mother's Aid in the South, where there is a large dependent Negro population, is quite restricted. Three states, and those having exceedingly large Negro populations, Georgia, Alabama, and South Carolina, are without enabling acts; Mississippi and Kentucky passed their acts in 1928 and are operating in only a limited number

> of counties. . . . It is to be noted that among the 17 or 18
> states which have made little use of their Mother's Aid laws
> are those states having large Negro populations. [pp. 301–2,
> 303]

He then pointed out that in some states where the program was established, the system virtually denied the benefits of the program to Black people.

> In North Carolina, the only southern state having state super-
> vision, Mother's Aid is granted in 75 of its 100 counties. In
> the biennial report of the State Department of Charities and
> Public Welfare for 1924 to 1926 there were only 4 Negro
> families in the 246 (less than 2%) that had been aided. Dur-
> ing 1926 to 1928, 12 Negro families in a total of 542 recip-
> ients (2.2%) were aided. Negroes form approximately 29%
> of North Carolina's population. Although the North Carolina
> State Board of Charities and Public Welfare has supervision
> over Mother's Aid and is charged with making its administra-
> tion uniform throughout the State, all applications for aid
> must originate in the county of legal settlement. The state
> board can thus approve cases only after their approval by
> county officials. In the practical working out of the Mother's
> Aid in North Carolina, the impression still prevails among
> many county officials that all white mothers should be cared
> for before aid can be given Negro mothers. [p. 302]

He then reported similar abuses in Florida and Virginia. It was not possible to make a parallel analysis of the distribution of Mother's Aid in northern states, since the reports of aid given there made no mention of race. He did note, however, in three selected communities specially studied (Cook County, Illinois; Milwaukee, Wisconsin; and Detroit, Michigan) the underrepresentation of poor Black families among the recipients of the programs. (p. 303) It is apparent from the data Dr. Reid presented that Mother's Aid, the first major advance in income maintenance in this country, was not reaching Black people.

Dr. Reid also spoke of discrimination in relation to out-of-wedlock births. He cited the increase in the proportion of Black children born out of wedlock, as well as the magnitude of the difference in the ratio of Black and white illegitimacy. Unlike some more recent white observers, he did not point to this fact as the root of Black poverty; his concern was the tremendous paucity of services to the Black unwed mothers and their babies:

Children born out of wedlock add largely to the work of all agencies dealing with dependent children. How great an influence this is in pushing the Negro below the threshold of self-support can only be conjectured. *We do know, however, that it is much less influential* in causing poverty than in producing dependency.* For the unmarried Negro mother there is a special problem. Few are the facilities whereby she and her child may secure adequate care, fewer than those available to white mothers and children. . . . With approximately 20,000 Negro children born out of wedlock each year we have a special problem which demands the attention of society. The social problems attending illegitimacy are many. *Communities where other than municipal care is provided for Negro unmarried mothers and their babies are rare.* In New York the Katy Ferguson Home with a capacity for 16 mothers and 10 babies and the Salvation Army with accommodations for 6 Black mothers in its capacity of 38 offer some relief. The Florence Crittenden League provides information service, but has no provisions for housing them, as is true of similar institutions in many other sections of the country. . . . In Maryland, where there was one colored illegitimate birth to every 5 births, there was one illegitimate white birth in every 14. *Yet, with such a vast problem, the institutions and agencies available for the care of unmarried mothers and their children are rarest among the Negro group.* [pp. 299–301; emphasis ours]

The third area of discrimination which Dr. Reid covered was the deplorable lack of medical and health facilities for Black children and adults, the high infant mortality rate among Black infants (still a pressing problem), and higher rate among Black adults. Referring to both these situations, Dr. Reid remarked that

the diseases representing unfavorable sanitary conditions or low economic status, such as malaria, pellagra, pulmonary tuberculosis, typhoid and puerperal conditions show relatively higher death rates among Negroes. . . . Premature birth is the highest cause of infant mortality among Negroes, 253 for each 10,000 births; respiratory diseases are second, 247 for each 10,000 births; gastro-intestinal diseases third, 227 for each 10,000 births. [p. 290]

* See our footnote on page 65.

Finally, Dr. Reid discussed the scarcity of day-care resources. He demonstrated that the paucity of this service created a hardship which fell disproportionately on Black mothers and children. Then as now, Black women often had to work to augment family income: "The proportion of married women working away from home is three and one-half times as high among Negro women as among whites—a significant fact in relation to child dependency and neglect." (p. 303) In addition to the disproportionate burden placed on Black families by the general lack of day-care facilities, there was also enormous discrimination against Black children within the system of facilities that did exist:

> According to the National Foundation of Day Nurseries the problems of Negro day nurseries are not much different from those of any other group, with the exception that "the children are more likely to be undernourished and in need of special care and feeding to bring them up to normal."
>
> There is a distinct problem, however, in the extent of the day nursery care. There are fewer than 40 day nurseries for Negro children in the United States. Of this number, Philadelphia has 7, New York 6, and there are a number in Chicago. In the southern states there are very few. In southern cities a similar problem exists in the lack of kindergartens. [pp. 303–4]

Dr. Reid then gave a report on the existence of day-care facilities for Black children in eleven major northern cities. It was estimated that in these cities there were approximately 198,000 Black children under fourteen years of age, and 102,000 working Black mothers. The optimum day-care capacity of these cities at that time was 1,130. The fact that these were all proprietary services increased their unavailability; it screened out many children whose mothers could not pay even small fees.

It is notable that the four areas singled out for discussion by Dr. Reid were not directly concerned with the principal focus of child welfare—that of child placement. But they are matters which should be the concern of any truly enlightened child welfare system. As Dr. Reid's data validate, the failure to develop these kinds of services for *any* children was in 1930, as it is now, a form of particular discrimination against *Black* children, since their life situation especially demands such services.

In conclusion, Dr. Reid remarked:

> White and Negro social workers are agreed that every child, irrespective of race and religion, is entitled to those conditions which will enable him to develop to his full capacity physically, spiritually, and mentally. An analysis of the needs of dependent and neglected Negro children, therefore, leads to the conclusion that the needs of this group present one of the outstanding problems in the field of child welfare. [p. 310]

He recommended sixteen steps to correct this situation. Most concerned ending discriminatory practices in the systems of care already existing, and developing new services. Five of these recommendations are concerned with the infusion of Black leadership into all levels of the child-caring field. Three dealt with the need for Black child welfare workers:

> There is an increasing need for trained Negro social workers in all fields, particularly in the field of child welfare. . . . There is a need for more scholarships in approved schools of social work for the training of Negro men and women who desire to enter the field of social welfare. Agencies dealing with dependent and neglected Negro children should offer increasing opportunities for employment to trained Negro workers. [pp. 310–11]

Schools of social work, which are today amazed at the demands of Black students for increases in the enrollment of their brethren, might well consider the antiquity of the demand—and some forty years of unkept promises. Dr. Reid's final recommendation is another still being made today, and still not implemented: "It is desirable in every community that agencies should utilize the most effective methods for the care of Negro children, but it is hoped that the Negro population may have an ever increasing opportunity to share in such programs, both as laymen and professional workers." (p. 312)

The attention paid Black children, along with children of Puerto Rican and Mexican descent, at the 1930 White House Conference was considerably greater than that paid them at the Conference on the Care of Dependent Children of 1909. The principal change was not in terms of action; it was in the expectation expressed about their care. In 1930, it was becoming the expectation that these children were as much a responsibility of the child welfare establishment as were white children. In the 1930's, largely because of the continuing northern migration of Black people, Black children were finally becoming visible to the child welfare establishment, and gradual attempts were being made to incorporate them, somehow, into this system.

Black Children and Child Welfare Since World War II

Black children have been increasingly, although only partially, included in child welfare services since World War II. Three factors have been responsible. First is the increasing population shift of Black people from the rural South to the urban North. This shift has been accelerating greatly ever since the war. Thus a major impetus has been the simple presence of Black children.

The second factor is also situational: child welfare services, as we have repeatedly noted, have been for poor children, for "dependent" children. Since World War II, economic affluence among white people has steadily progressed, and there have been fewer and fewer white, poor children. This accelerated acquisition of wealth has not been true of Black people. Thus increasing proportions of poor children are Black children, and the system of child welfare service developed for poor, white, European immigrant children now has a potential clientele that is increasingly Black, Puerto Rican, and Mexican-American. The very survival of the system has come to mean service to this new clientele. As we shall see in the next chapter, some child welfare agencies, in the face of this change, actually have elected not to survive, or have changed their function to one more suitable to the affluent white clientele.

The third factor has been the change in the nation's ideological climate and legal climate. "Integration" has become the national goal; overt forms of racism and discrimination are becoming illegal. Child welfare, like the other social institutions in the country, has been imbued with this ideology. And like other social institutions in the country, it is failing to live up to the ideology.

Before we examine the evidence for our contention that child welfare is failing to live up to the ideology of integration, let us consider the ideology itself. Under pressure from both Black and white groups, child welfare agencies and institutions have been attempting for the last twenty-five years to develop an "integrated" system. But there was no "segregated" system to begin with. The problem has been one of *developing* services for Black children, not integrating services that already existed with the ones that existed for white children. In effect, "integration" has meant that agencies and institutions previously only for white children have said to Black children, "All right, now you can come in." But the effort has stopped there: it has not been complemented by any sustained effort to see that Black children do in fact get in. Thus the exclusion persists. The children continue to get no service at all.

Unfortunately, the idea that integration is a goal to be sought has hindered child welfare services to Black children for the last twenty-five years. It gave rise to the idea that the development of services specifically for Black children was an extension of segregation, an idea that made Black people stop working for separate services. Thus to some extent the pursuit of integration has denied Black children the resources of their own people and their organizations. Within the white child welfare system, efforts specifically for Black children have been similarly retarded. "Integrated" services have come to mean services for "all" children, without any adaptation specific to any one group of children. When the goal of integration has not been reached, when in fact Black children have failed to be included, the responsibility for the failure has been placed with the children, with their parents, and with their community.

This phenomenon is, of course, not unique to child welfare; most social institutions in this country, failing as they have to overcome the racism that is so much a part of them, also have their supporting mythologies which ultimately place the blame for the failure on Black people. Lerone Bennett, Black historian and writer, has referred to it as "the same old policy of giving a white disease a Black name." (1970, p. 38) In child welfare this process has had a very pernicious result: efforts to include Black children have in some instances simply ceased. A leading child welfare text, for example, in discussing the adoption of Black children, concludes that a number of characteristics of Black people make the extension of adoption services to Black children hopeless.

Black Children in Institutions, 1950–1960

In 1965 the Children's Bureau of the United States Welfare Administration issued a report by Seth Low analyzing trends in institutional care for children, based on comparative data from the 1950 and 1960 Census enumerations. While the report shows that the distribution of institutional services for Black children has remained much as it was in the nineteenth century, it also documents some definite changes. In Table 4–2 we present data for 1950 and 1960, for four specific types of institutions.

CORRECTIONAL INSTITUTIONS. In 1960, 54 percent of the nonwhite children in institutional care were in correctional institutions. These children (over 90 percent of whom were Black) also constituted 33 percent of the correctional-institution population. (Low, 1965, p. 38) Both the absolute number of nonwhite children in institutions and the relative number had risen since 1950. In 1950 only 49 percent of the institutionalized nonwhite children had been in correctional facilities, and these children had constituted only 26.4 percent of the correctional population. Moreover, of the various types of correctional institutions, nonwhite children were more frequently sent to penal facilities—jails, workhouses, and prisons—than were white youngsters. In both 1950 and 1960 approximately 20 percent of the nonwhite children in correctional facilities were in penal institutions, while this was so for only 7 percent of the white children. (Low, 1965, p. 38)

INSTITUTIONS FOR THE DISABLED. As for institutions for the mentally or physically disabled, nonwhite children constituted in 1950 a much larger proportion of the populations of tuberculosis hospitals and chronic-disease hospitals than of those for the blind, deaf, and physically handicapped. Nonwhite children constituted 40 percent of those in tuberculosis hospitals and 33 percent of those in chronic-disease institutions, but only 17 percent of those in institutions for the blind, 11 percent of those for the deaf, and 8 percent of those in institutions for other physical handicaps. (Low, 1965, p. 38) Since the latter two figures are lower than the proportion of nonwhite children in the general population it seems quite possible that a considerable number of nonwhite youngsters with these handicaps were going unserved. By 1960 both the white and the nonwhite populations in tuberculosis hospitals had declined, but the decline was much greater among white children. In chronic-disease hospitals, the proportion of nonwhite children had increased greatly by 1960, and in schools and homes for the physically disabled the nonwhite population rose much more than did the white.

Facilities for the mentally disabled can be divided into those for the retarded and those for the mentally ill. In 1950 nonwhite children

TABLE 4–2

Children Under Institutional Care by Race and Type of Institution, 1950 and 1960[a]

Type of Institution	1950 Nonwhite Number	Percent	1950 White Number	Percent	1960 Nonwhite Number	Percent	1960 White Number	Percent
Welfare	5,748	19	95,491	45	8,522	16	66,538	29
Correctional	14,973	49	41,691	20	28,730	54	58,593	25
Mental disabilities	5,343	18	51,945	25	11,279	21	81,542	36
Physical disabilities	4,254	14	21,337	10	4,751	9	22,616	10
Total	30,318	100	210,464	100	53,282	100	229,289	100

SOURCE: Low, 1965, p. 38.

were underrepresented (11 percent) in institutions and homes for the retarded; however, during the 1950's the increase in nonwhite children served was three times as great as the increase in white children. In facilities for emotionally and mentally disturbed children the situation was different: the proportion of nonwhite children in such institutions fell from 21 percent to 18 percent in 1960. (p. 38)

INSTITUTIONS FOR DEPENDENT CHILDREN. Between 1950 and 1960 there was a marked increase in the number of nonwhite children in institutions for dependent children, from 5,748 to 8,522. (Low, 1965, p. 38) The number of white children decreased at the same time. As a result, nonwhite children, who in 1950 constituted only 6 percent of the dependent-child institutional population, constituted 12 percent in 1960. This increase might seem to indicate that the civil rights legislation and agitation of the 1950's was actually beginning to bear fruit in dependency institutions. However, the gains are questionable. It may be that the situation of Black children is deteriorating. In 1950, children in dependency institutions constituted 19 percent of all nonwhite children in institutions; in 1960 this figure fell to 16 percent. The fact that the percentage of nonwhite institutionalized children in correctional facilities rose during this same period, actually strengthens the more negative interpretation of the change. In 1960 there were 2,800 *more* nonwhite children in jails and prisons than there were in dependency institutions. (p. 38)

For two reasons the data on dependency institutions do not give a full picture of the treatment of Black children. First, Black children are more likely to be placed in foster homes for dependent children than they are in institutions. If children in foster homes for dependency reasons were to be counted, the proportion of Black children under care for dependency reasons would no doubt increase significantly. Second, a high proportion of the institutional facilities available are under the auspices of the Roman Catholic Church. Thus, children receiving services from Catholic agencies are more likely to receive institutional care than are those served by Protestant, Jewish, public, or nonsectarian agencies. Since Black children are so predominantly of Protestant faiths they are much less likely to be cared for by Catholic institutions.

Keeping these limitations in mind, what generalizations can we draw from the information in the Low report? Low himself predicts that "As the status of the nonwhite population advances, the consequences for institutional care may appear in two directions simultaneously—

a relative reduction in the number of nonwhite children in types of institutions in which they have been 'overrepresented,' and a relative increase in other types which hitherto have been inadequately available to them." (p. 20) How likely is this prediction to be realized?

Quite probably the distribution of resources is going to change. The national nonwhite child population is increasing faster than the white child population, and the rise to affluence is far greater among the white population. Low describes the changing pattern as follows:

> Between 1950 and 1960 the white child population of the United States increased 21%; the white child population in institutions increased much less, only 9%. On the other hand, the non-white child population of the United States increased 43%, but the non-white child population in institutions increased much more, 69%. Expressed in terms of rates of institutionalization, *the rate for white children decreased* from 4.8 per 1,000 in 1950 to 4.0 in 1960. During this time *the non-white rate increased from 5.3 to 6.3.* [p. 9; emphasis ours]

We must note that Low rejects the notion that economic status is strongly related to rates of institutionalization: "Institutional care was much more directly linked with poverty in the early decades of this century than it is today, but some linkage undoubtedly remains." (p. 19) We, of course, argue that there is a very strong linkage, particularly in relation to institutions for dependency and delinquency. Thus, we anticipate that if the nonwhite child population continues to grow faster while the white population continues to get rich faster, the changes noted in 1960 with regard to institutions will only accelerate.

Distribution of Institutional Services for Black Children, 1950–1960

It can be predicted that the proportions of white and nonwhite children in the total institutional population will continue to change, but what can be said as to the future patterning of services within types of institutions? Let us look again at Table 4–2. First, during the 1950's the distribution of kinds of service changed much more among white children than among nonwhite children. *Among nonwhite children the distribution in types of institutions remained relatively constant: 49 percent to 54 percent in correctional facilities, 19 percent to 16 percent in dependency (welfare) institutions, 18 percent to 21 percent in mental institutions, and 14 percent to 9 percent in institutions for physical disabilities.* The distribution of services among white children was quite different, and while it was changing, it was changing *away* from the pattern for nonwhites. In 1950 about 45 percent, almost half of the institutionalized white children, were in dependency institutions; 25 percent were in mental institutions, principally those for the mentally retarded; about 20 percent were in correctional facilities, and 10 percent in institutions for the physically ill. *By 1960 the pattern had changed: instead of 25 percent there were 36 percent in mental institutions, again principally for the retarded; instead of 45 percent there were 29 percent in dependency institutions; instead of 20 percent there were 25 percent in correctional facilities; and there was an unchanging 10 percent in institutions for the physically disabled.*

The difference in patterning suggests that the linkage between institutionalization and poverty may be changing—but *only* for white children. Since there is a weaker correlation between mental retardation and economic status than between dependency and poverty, the changes among white children are in the expected direction, a direction which may eventually eliminate the association between institutionalization and poverty for white children. That is, white children may become increasingly scarce in the traditional areas of child welfare and in the field of correction. It is not simply affluence, however, that accounts for these differences in patterning, for some are literally centuries old. Insofar as the labeling systems reflect racial biases, the distribution of services will continue to reflect these biases. A prime example of this racial bias occurs in relation to the recent increase in drug use by white youth, and especially white middle-class youth. When drugs were considered primarily problems of "ghetto" youth, their use was considered a criminal offense. Now that drug use has extended to white middle-class youth, the laws—and consequently the labels—are being changed. Of course, when the laws and the labels change, so do the statistics.

Between 1950 and 1960, the patterning of institutional services among Black and other nonwhite children did not change much. It did not change much between 1850 and 1960, for that matter. The Black child's chance of "receiving care" from a correctional facility was still much greater than that of receiving any other type of care. However, it must be said that within the field of child welfare proper his chances of receiving some care, especially foster care, were a little better. In view of these small changes, the Black child of today might well reflect with his brothers of another era: "Well Lord, this child welfare business ain't what it ought to be, and it ain't what it's gonna be. But thank God it ain't what it wuz."

Distribution of Child Welfare Services, 1963

The best national statistics on child welfare services (as opposed to purely institutional services) in the early 1960's come from a special study by Helen Jeter published in 1963. Since it was based on a sampling of agencies, rather than the total population, it is vulnerable to whatever sampling errors may have occurred. Nonetheless it presents a picture of services to Black children that is quite consistent with expectation.

First Jeter notes the changing racial pattern of the children being served:

> The great majority of children receiving child welfare services, both from the public agencies and the voluntary agencies, are white children. Nevertheless, the proportion of nonwhite children is increasing.
>
> Seventy-three percent of the children served by public agencies and 84 percent of those served by voluntary agencies in 1961 were white. Twenty-four percent in the public agencies and 14 percent in the voluntary agencies were Negro children. Very small percentages of American Indian and other nonwhite children were served by both the public agencies and the voluntary agencies.
>
> The trend toward increasing proportions of nonwhite children in the public child welfare caseload is shown by comparisons with two earlier studies. In 1961 nonwhite children were 27 percent of the total, compared with 25 percent in 1959 and 14 percent in 1945 for a comparable group of States. In 1961, 24 percent were Negro, 2 percent American Indian and 1 percent other nonwhite.
>
> .   .   .
>
> The largest groups of nonwhite children in most States . . . were Negro. Eighty percent of the children receiving public child welfare services in the District of Columbia were Negro. Delaware had 51 percent Negro, Mississippi 49 percent, and Illinois 46 percent.
>
> . . . the several States, with few exceptions, increased between 1959 and 1961 the proportions of nonwhite children

among the children they served. Where decreases occurred
they were very slight or represented a change in agency
structure and program. . . .
. . . however, the States still vary widely in rates of services to nonwhite children in the population. The average
rate of service to nonwhite children for the United States was
10 per 1,000 nonwhite population under 21 years of age. . . .
Among the 9 States with the largest numbers of nonwhite
children in the population, New York, Mississippi, and North
Carolina served from 12 to 19 per 1,000 while Texas,
Georgia, and California served only 1 or 2. [pp. 129–33]

Although there were discrepancies in both public and private sectors
in the kinds of services being given Black and white children, these
discrepancies were much larger in the voluntary agencies. Jeter delineated four principal forms of service: services to children in their own
homes, or with relatives; foster-home services; adoptive services; and
institutional services. In the public agencies 48 percent of the white
children were in their own or a relative's home, and 45 percent of the
Black children were similarly situated. In the private sector 31 percent
of the white children served were in their own homes, and 25 percent
of the Black children. Among children served in public agencies 31
percent of the white and 41 percent of the Black children were in
foster homes. In the private sector this discrepancy was much greater:
27 percent of the white children were receiving foster-home services,
but 50 percent of the Black children were in foster homes. Institutional placements were being utilized for 13 percent of the white children in public agencies, and 9 percent of the Black children. In the
private sector 18 percent of the white children were in institutions
and 8 percent of the Black children. Finally, adoptive services varied:
in public agencies 8 percent of the white children and 5 percent of the
Black children were receiving adoptive home services; in voluntary
agencies 24 percent of the white children were in adoptive homes,
and 17 percent of the Black children. (pp. 3–12)

Three generalizations can be made from these data, which follow
the historical trends we have seen in earlier pages. First, public
agencies serve a larger proportion of Black children than do voluntary agencies. Second, there are inequities in the distribution of services in both sectors, but these are greater in the private agencies than
in the public. Third, among forms of placement, foster-home care is
more heavily relied upon for Black than for white children, consider-

ably more so in the private sector; conversely, both adoption and institutional placements are more frequently given to white than to Black children. That these racial inequities in the distribution of services are primarily attributable to the systems of services is attested to by Jeter, who notes that in both the public and private sectors, "The principal problems presented by non-white children did not differ greatly from the problems of white children." (p. 135) In the public sector the principal problem for both Black and white children was "neglect, abuse, or exploitation." In the private sector the principal problem was "parents not married to each other for both Black and white children, followed by neglect and abuse for both groups." In both the public and private sectors "emotional behavior problems" were reported for a considerably smaller proportion of Black children than white. Perhaps this reflects a greater prevalence of mental health among Black youngsters than among white ones, though one would be hard put to explain why that condition should exist. It seems much more likely that the difference is simply a reflection of racism in the systems' labeling of children, and in the distribution of institutional resources for children so labeled.

A major discrepancy is evident in the Jeter data with regard to the distribution of adoption services. The differences in distribution between Black and white children were not especially great in either the public or private sectors. But two pieces of information suggest that many, many more Black children are in need of adoption, or of some kind of permanent substitute homes, than are presently being served. In their 1959 study of adoption, Maas and Engler attempted to estimate the likelihood of adoption in the communities they studied. They used the idea of "proportion of children in care" (p. 280)—the idea that some indication of the likelihood of "need" for adoptive placement can be gleaned from the number of children in foster-home placement. Maas and Engler's findings give credence to the idea that many children in foster care do, in fact, need permanent substitute homes, *i.e.,* adoptive homes. Looking at the Jeter data in this way, we find that in both the public and private sectors Black children constitute a larger proportion of children in foster care than they do of children receiving adoptive services. This discrepancy would seem to be explained by the conclusion that foster homes are more available to them than adoptive homes. An added piece of data from Jeter corroborates this: Black children in both public and private sectors tend to remain in foster care longer than do white children. Jeter attributed this to the greater proportion of white children receiving adoption services, and thus remaining in foster care for less time. Among the children "growing up in foster care," then, a noted adverse circumstance of the child welfare system, a disproportionate number are Black.

Other data from the Jeter study also contribute to the idea that many Black children for whom adoptive services would be appropriate are not receiving them. The principal problem for *all* children receiving adoption services was, according to Jeter, "parents not married to each other." Compare the figures on adoption—in both public and private sectors—with the following data: in public agencies, 43 percent of the Black children and only 16 percent of the white were children of unmarried parents; in the private sector this was so for 58 percent of the Black children, but only 34 percent of the white. (Jeter, 1963, p. 11) While we do not for a moment suggest that all children of unmarried parents should be adopted, it seems obvious that one solution to the problems of these children—adoption—is not being offered on a racially equitable basis. We shall return to this subject in the next section of the book.

Black Children in Child Welfare in the Later 1960's

Curiously enough, it is easier to state exactly what the position of Black children was prior to the civil rights movement of the 1950's than it has been since. When racial exclusion in child-care facilities was legal and accepted, all records, official reports, statistics, etc., were kept by race. Unfortunately, legislation and practices related to civil rights institutionalized the belief that the Black child himself was better protected by the deletion of any reference to his race. Thus it is difficult today to state exactly what services are being received by Black children, and under what conditions. It is impossible, for example, to obtain a current national statistic on the number of Black children receiving foster care or day care or homemaker services. When *problems* are being counted—delinquency, illegitimacy, child abuse—the count is by race. It is only when *services* are being enumerated that the count is color blind. Presumably the assumption is that the problems accurately reflect social circumstances that exist—*i.e.,* the numbers and kinds of personal pathologies that exist. Services are not enumerated in this same manner, on the assumption that while personal pathologies are not distributed evenly across the population, services to correct those pathologies are! The practice of nonracial counts of services, originally intended to protect Black children, has in fact served primarily to protect the system.

SUMMARY

With this chapter we conclude our historical review of the services to Black children in this country. It must be concluded that the system of children's services still severely discriminates against and damages Black children. The failure to develop services to children of poor families and to children in their own homes causes increasing havoc among Black children. The pressing need for change—and for drastic change—is all too apparent.

In the next part of the book we shall examine some efforts at bringing about change in the child welfare field in the area of placement, and particularly adoptive placement. Let us now look at these efforts —both those that have had some small measure of success and those that have failed. Perhaps we will identify some more direct pathways to the better service of Black children.

PART TWO

Homes for Negro Children

Special to The Christian Science Monitor

NEW YORK, May 20—A service bureau for Negro children, designed to check delinquency through providing foster homes and thus handle what William Hodson, Public Welfare Commissioner, has called "the No. 1 child welfare problem of the city," has been opened at No. 154 East Forty-fifth Street and will experiment with the type of service that will probably be incorporated into the city's Welfare Department.

The Society has been providing foster home care for both white and Negro children for 15 years and, largely for this reason, it was selected to undertake the new project. Grants of money sufficiently large to pay expenses for Bureau services during the first year have been received from the Davison Fund, Inc., the Greater New York Fund, the Federation of Protestant Welfare Agencies and several private citizens.

CHRISTIAN
SCIENCE
MONITOR

Opens Bureau to Curb Juvenile Delinquency

AMSTERDAM
NEWS

The Children's Aid Society officially opened the Service Bureau for Negro Children Tuesday, a project designed to stem the wave of Negro child delinquency resulting from the acute shortage of foster home and institutional facilities, recently described by Welfare Commissioner Hodson as "the No. 1 child welfare problem of the city."

5 Early efforts for change within child welfare, 1937-1944

In Part One we examined the evolution of the child welfare system in this country and the position of Black children within that system. In this historical exploration we sought to establish that child welfare, a creature of its society like other social institutions, has had origins of a fundamentally racist nature. Two basic manifestations of this racism were established. One was the failure to develop services for children in their own homes, which was particularly disadvantageous for Black children. The second was the failure to include Black children in existing services.

Up to now we have been concerned with the totality of child welfare, and with national movements and trends. Beginning with Chapter 5, we narrow our focus considerably. Here we begin to analyze specific efforts to extend child placement services to Black children that have taken place over the last thirty years. This has been the period of partial inclusion—an inclusion that has been "partial" because the efforts to achieve it have also been partial. They have met with some success; they have met with considerably more failure.

Here we shall identify the commonalities in those efforts that have met with success, and those that have met with failure, and provide for the reader concrete and specific illustrations of each. While placement is not and never has been an adequate solution for Black children in need of care, it has often been the best the child welfare system has to offer, and thus deserves special analysis.

In this chapter we begin our analysis of efforts at change by examining a study conducted at the close of World War II—when Black children began to be a major focus of concern in child welfare. This study, which was conducted by the Child Welfare League of America and funded through American War-Community Services, focused on "recent changes in community facilities for the care of dependent and neglected Negro children." (p. ix) The study committee selected three cities for examination—New York, Philadelphia, and Cleveland. Each had had a relatively large Black population for many years, and each had a different pattern of organizing services for Black children, a variation which was representative of the different ways in which other cities had organized their services. Interracial teams of investigators in each of the three communities conducted interviews, reviewed documents and records, and produced a detailed report of the efforts at change that had taken place from 1937 to 1944. The report was published under the title *Child Care Facilities for Dependent and Neglected Negro Children in Three Cities: New York City, Philadelphia, Cleveland.*

One feature was common to all three cities. In each the war itself had brought an increase in the Black population, and this population increase was a major stimulus in the concern for Black children; and in all three cities, the pattern of distribution of services actually *magnified* the effects of the increased numbers of children.

Table 5–1 gives the population statistics presented for each of the three cities in the report. Even a cursory analysis of these figures raises questions in one's mind about one of the statements in the report that there was an increase in the Negro dependent-child population to the extent of "crisis proportions." That Black children were overrepresented in the dependent-child populations of all three cities is evident; but the general figures do not tell the whole story. The "crisis" in each city arose not from the migration of Black people, or from any other behavior of Black people, but from the fact that in each city the welfare system did not distribute Black children evenly across all elements; particular *forms* of service were closed to them, as were

TABLE 5-1

Distribution of Child Welfare Services to Black Children in New York City, Philadelphia, and Cleveland, 1940

	New York City	Philadelphia	Cleveland City	Cleveland County
General population				
Total	7,454,995	1,931,334	878,336	1,217,250
Black	458,444	250,880	84,504	87,145
Total under age nineteen	2,072,500	570,340	253,313	348,217
Black under age nineteen	133,351	83,439	27,295	27,805
Population of child welfare agencies				
Protestant agencies				
Total	5,500	4,200		
Black	2,000	1,850		
Roman Catholic agencies				
Total	12,000	4,500		
Black	1,000	120		
Jewish agencies				
Total	2,500	308		
Black	—	—		

Cleveland

Public   (*County Child Welfare*)

Religion	Black	White
Protestant	784	543
Roman Catholic	21	1,011
Jewish	—	19

Private   (*Humane Society*)

	Black	White
	129	1,044

SOURCE: "Child Care Facilities in Three Cities," 1945, pp. 11, 12, 39, 97, 107, 108, 165, 174, 183.

services under particular *auspices*. Thus in both New York and Philadelphia, Black children represented less than a third of the total dependent-child population. Nevertheless, both of these systems of service were sectarian, and Black children constituted a far smaller proportion of the total dependent-child population than they did the Protestant sector population of dependent children. In Cleveland, where the system was not as strongly sectarian, there was a split between public and private services, and Black children were overrepresented in the public sphere. Black children constituted less than a third of the dependent-child population in Cleveland, but almost half of the children under public agency care.

Thus, the reason why the Black child was becoming increasingly visible to the child welfare system—enough to warrant special study—was not only the "crisis" increase in Black population. Other factors involved were directly racist practices in the treatment of Black children and indirectly racist practices resulting from the fact that the system of services was not designed with the Black child in mind. Ironically, then, efforts to change the care of Black children came about in part because of the treatment of children imposed by these systems.

NEW YORK'S BLACK CHILDREN, 1937–1944

Child-care facilities at the beginning of World War II in New York were almost totally segregated in the sphere of residential institutions, and were partially integrated in the foster-care field. Adoption was virtually nonexistent. All services were sectarian. Table 5–2 shows the numbers of Black children and the agencies serving them in the Protestant sector. These data, published by the Exploratory Committee on Negro Welfare of the Welfare Council of New York City in 1939, were collected in 1937. Three factors are immediately clear from the figures presented: (1) three-fourths of the Black children being served were in foster homes; (2) almost half of all Black children being served were cared for through the Colored Orphan Asylum, and almost all of those in residential institutions were in this particular institution; and (3) several agencies which extended foster-care services to Black children excluded them from their institutional facilities. Black children constituted over 55 percent of the total

TABLE 5-2

Agencies Serving Black Children in Institutions and Foster Homes, New York City, 1937

	Institutional Care	Foster Homes
Colored Orphan Asylum	322	436
Edwin Gould Foundation[a]	—	500
Children's Aid Society		
Foster Home Department	—	41
Brace Memorial Farm	65	—
New York Child Foster Home		
Service[b]	—	200 (est.)
Brooklyn Children's Aid Society	—	83
Five Points House[b]	—	142
Brooklyn Nursery and Infants		
Hospital	?	?
Total	387 plus	1,402 plus

[a] Institutional facilities closed to Black children.
[b] No institutional facilities.

SOURCE: "Child Care Facilities in Three Cities," 1945, p. 39.

number served in the Protestant sector. The heavy concentration of these children in only four agencies indicates the relatively closed nature of the foster-care system.

Black children constituted a much smaller percentage of the Catholic children under care, approximately 10 percent, or about 700 children. (p. 39)* More of the Black children under Catholic care were in residential institutions than those under Protestant auspices, a reflection of the traditionally heavier emphasis upon institutional care among Catholic agencies. At that time, Black Catholic children were cared for in one of four institutions, two of which were only for Black children—St. Benedict's Home, and the Little Flower House of Providence in the Brooklyn Diocese. Foster-care facilities were administered primarily through the New York Foundling Hospital, which served both racial groups.

---

* All references in this chapter are to *Child Care Facilities for Dependent and Neglected Negro Children in Three Cities: New York City, Philadelphia, Cleveland.* Howard W. Hopkirk, ed. New York: Child Welfare League of America, Inc., 1945.

Virtually no Black children were being served by the Jewish agencies. The report noted that "the small group of Black Jews, the Falashas, did not use child care agencies." (p. 28)

The first and major problem in the care of Black children in New York City prior to World War II was that there were not enough facilities for their care. By the end of the war the situation was worse; there were more children, and the total array of facilities for them had not significantly increased. In fact, the end result of all of the activity on behalf of Black children during this period was actually a *decrease* in the total facilities available to them. The first major effort for Black children during these years was a reform of the Colored Orphan Asylum. Next came the formation of endless committees to study the situation of Black children and make recommendations, most of which resulted in a lot of activity and no action. The most beneficial action taken, which did actually increase services for Black children, was the formation of a new service especially for them, The Service Bureau for Negro Children of the New York Children's Aid Society, and the extension of adoption services to Black children by the State Charities Aid Association. Another specific effort at change was the passage of antidiscriminatory legislation regarding child-care facilities; the legislation had little effect, however, because it provided for sectarian priorities and because it was too vaguely worded to police the powerful autonomous private agencies. Let us now look at each of these efforts.

Reform of the Colored Orphan Asylum

Perhaps it is not surprising that the first effort of the child welfare community on behalf of Black children was a "reform" of the Colored Orphan Asylum. Reform of this one agency would, of course, constitute no major disruption of the rest of the system. In 1937 the Colored Orphan Asylum was severely criticized by the State Department of Social Welfare because the children were receiving poor care. The agency *was* giving inferior care—little else could be expected in an institution whose population had doubled, from 400 to 800, between 1930 and 1934. The reason for the expansion, of course, was that no other agency would take the children. The butt of the criticism, however, was the agency itself. The resolution of the problem was of ambiguous benefit to Black children—the Colored Orphan

Asylum reduced its population by moving 250 children from the residence to foster homes. In other words, this particular effort on behalf of Black children reduced by a significant number the available residential facilities for Black children, while Black children needed increased resources which would have improved *both* the quality of care *and* the extent of facilities.

In the entire history of this major facility for Black children in New York City, adoption has never been developed as a service. Institutions for white children with histories parallel to that of the Colored Orphan Asylum had by the 1930's extended their functions to include adoption.

Committee Work for Black Children

At least a dozen special committees were formed in New York City by various community welfare and child welfare bodies between 1937 and 1944, but none of them resulted in any significant action. Repeatedly the same facts were discovered; almost the only new finding with the passing years was that the situation of Black children was getting worse. Actually, one of the first committees, formed in 1938, not only clearly identified the major problems, but made most insightful recommendations calling for several radical changes in the child welfare system. Some of these recommendations eventually did come to pass in New York, but not for many years. Some still have not.

This early committee, the Standing Committee on Negro Welfare, was formed in 1938, the year after the Colored Orphan Asylum reduced its services, and was funded by the Welfare Council of New York City. Two subcommittees were devoted to the situation of Black children; both were chaired by Black leaders. Eugene Kinckle Jones chaired the Exploratory Committee of the Welfare Council, and Dr. Channing Tobias chaired the Joint Committee on Negro Child Care of the Welfare Council. The reports of both men were ignored.

The report of Eugene Kinckle Jones' committee spoke very directly:

> The Exploratory Committee's findings . . . show conclusively how necessary it is to increase both the amount and quality of welfare services to the Negro community. They show that a substantial part of social work's leadership has failed to maintain even that concern with the problems of the Negro popula-

tion which was evinced immediately after the World War. The Negro population's continued growth and the intensification of its social and economic problems placed a serious responsibility upon the social welfare leadership of New York City. Thoughtful observers recognize that the economic barriers and the social perplexities which handicap the Negro population have not been created and cannot be solved within that group alone. For instance, it would be completely impossible for the Negro community to assume the financial burden required for its own welfare needs. Those needs will be efficiently met only by interracial cooperation on such a scale as social work administration has not yet attempted.

Failure to satisfy the welfare needs of the Negro population as effectively as the needs of the white population have been satisfied can be ascribed to several causes: (1) Failure to examine and define the special needs of the Negro population which frequently vary from the general community welfare pattern. . . . (2) Lack of agency services to supply those needs which have been discovered. (3) Unwillingness of many agencies to include Negroes in their services even though the services are available and the needs are recognized. [pp. 47–48]

Dr. Tobias' report expanded these themes. He noted first the extent to which the combined practices of racial exclusion and sectarianism restricted the resources available for Black children, and also made the point that the lack of accumulated wealth in the Black community itself prevented the full support of Black agencies for Black children.

None of the sectarian agencies in New York was actually self-supporting; all received public monies for the subsidy of children under their care. In a system, however, where each group "takes care of its own," the absence of a Black-supported agency severely reduced the resources for Black children. Since most Black children were Protestant, their care was expected to come from the Protestant agencies; but most of these agencies had policies of racial exclusion. The Tobias report took note of this combination of noxious forces and practices:

> Here is the crux of the problem, for while the need for foster home care is especially great among Negro children, facilities for that care are especially inadequate. The private agencies

which place children in foster homes and supervise them there generally do not accept responsibility for Negro children, for fewer than one-fifth of the Protestant agencies will care for any Negro children.

No question has arisen regarding the adequacy of care by Catholic agencies of Catholic Negro children, but only 6 out of 34 Protestant agencies will care for any Negro children. Theoretically, the Negro group would be expected by many persons to care for its own children, but examination of its income level immediately reveals the futility of this suggestion. The 6 Protestant agencies mentioned now care for a total of approximately 1,500 Negro children, but the gross inadequacy of these provisions is shown by the fact that in a five-year period alone, between 1935 and 1939, the Children's Court adjudged 3,232 Negro children to be neglected and assigned them to the care of the Department of Welfare. [p. 48]

Dr. Tobias noted that the failure of the child welfare system to care for Black children had another extremely bad effect, one which we have mentioned in earlier chapters:

Nor does this number represent the actual total of Negro children who should be so adjudicated. Because of the notorious lack of facilities for foster home care, judges are said to be reluctant to declare these children neglected. . . . Thus the proportion of Negro children in correctional institutions rises, while the number of those committed to the Department of Welfare for preventative care is substantially decreased. [p 49]

Dr. Tobias' committee called for three fundamental changes in the child-care system: alteration in the existing private agencies to include Black children and to introduce Black participation in the management of services; the creation of a new agency specifically for Black children; and the introduction of public agency responsibility. These recommendations were ignored in 1938. In fact, it was not until a generation later that they began to be accepted.

In recommending that existing agencies hire Black personnel and extend Black participation in the management of services, Dr. Tobias pointed to one of the familiar myths offered by the white agencies to explain away their failure to serve Black children:

The inclusion of Negro workers in agency staffs is a vital factor in successful finding and supervision of foster homes. Several agencies now caring for Negro children are handicapped in their work by lack of effective contact with the Negro community. Staff members drawn from that community can enormously facilitate the agency program through establishing this community contact. Agencies which refuse to accept Negro cases sometimes do so through lack of understanding of the serious social factors involved, or through a feeling of inadequacy to solve some of the problems that would be met in this new work. For instance, several agencies have stated in the past that acceptable foster homes could not be located in most Negro neighborhoods because of income, housing, and neighborhood conditions which do not satisfy the minimum requirements. These agencies, however, took this position without having made the most skillful approach to homefinding. They had not canvassed many likely neighborhoods, nor had they used the services of Negro foster home finders, although these workers would naturally be most successful in finding homes in Negro neighborhoods. [p. 50]

Dr. Tobias' other recommendations were for the creation of new services through the new Service Bureau for Negro Children of the New York Children's Aid Society. The Bureau did not evolve into a separate agency, as we shall presently see, but the committee's recommendation—that this service should evolve, in time, into a public agency—is worth close examination.

Creation of New Agencies

1. In the case of continued refusal by private agencies to assume responsibility for existing child care needs, an obvious second choice is the creation of new agencies that will devote special attention to the needs of Negro children. One such effort is the new Service Bureau for Negro Children. . . . The Service Bureau for Negro Children is planned to carry a maximum caseload of 300 boys and girls and thus it can be seen that even its complete success will come a long way from meeting the emergency foster home needs of the Negro community. Care must be taken, also, that the creation of additional private agencies does not encourage agencies which now care for Negro children to relax their interest and reduce their services to this group.

Those responsible for the development of the Service Bureau's program hope that at the end of a three-year demonstration

> period the city will see its value as an extension to the Depart-
> ment of Welfare's service* to dependent children, as part of
> the whole development of a Department of Child Welfare.
> [p. 50]

Neither the Jones report nor the Tobias report was acted upon in any way.

The numerous other committees formed in the following years met with similar defeat. The most significant aspect of their reports is that they document the worsening of the situation. In fact, these reports seem to bracket the actual turning point when the Black child became the number-one child welfare problem in New York City. In the middle of World War II, at the peak of growing white affluence, the child welfare system, established to handle poor children, had a changed constituency—more than half the children were Black.

The Integration Ordinance: The Wrong Name and the Wrong Move for the Wrong Reasons

In 1942, municipal legislation was passed outlawing segregation in residential child-caring facilities which received public monies for the care of the children. The ordinance, which we shall presently quote, did not prohibit denial of service. It was only a vague directive to "integrate" facilities—"integration" being translated into a "reasonable proportion of inmates from any racial group." Such "integration" was an inappropriate goal, as "segregated" was an inaccurate description of the facilities.

The immediate impetus to the legislation was not in fact a concern for children. The bill resulted from the efforts of the City-Wide Citizens' Committee on Harlem, which had been organized through the New York City Office of Civilian Defense with some city leaders who were becoming increasingly concerned about "tensions" in Harlem. A Sub-Committee on Crime Prevention had made efforts to have more facilities available to dependent and neglected Black children, because of the age-old problem—known outside child welfare circles as well as within—that many "dependent" Black children were being treated as "delinquent" Black children because there were no services

---

* The Department of Welfare *subsidized* services, but the services were administered under the auspices of the voluntary agencies.

available to them under the former label. The enormous frustration this subcommittee faced in attempting to increase facilities for dependent Black children convinced them that persuasion was not the answer, and they asked for the Race Discrimination Ordinance, thinking that the law could do what moral appeals had failed to do. This legislation provided:

> No money shall be paid out of any appropriation made to any charitable institution for the care of dependent, neglected or delinquent children duly committed by the Commissioner of Welfare or a Court of appropriate jurisdiction if after due notice by the Commissioner of Welfare such charitable institution shall refuse to accept a reasonable proportion of inmates from any racial group because of race or color, provided that no institutions be required to accept persons from any race or group other than those who belong to its own religious faith. What constitutes a "reasonable proportion" shall be determined by the Commissioner of Welfare on consideration of the nature and activities of the institution and all its branches, the vacancies occurring in the institution, and the need of a racial group for the type of service rendered by the group. [p. 78]

This legislation is still in effect in New York City; it isn't working very well now either, but violations are somewhat more subtle and difficult to detect. It was hardly a model ordinance; the vagueness of "due notice" and "reasonable proportion" and, above all, the enormous limitation imposed by its subservience to sectarian demands are obvious drawbacks. But the legislation was effective in one sense: funds were in fact withheld from the nine Protestant corporations that refused to comply. Among them, the nine institutions had 626 institutional placements for children who were public charges (the only ones covered by the ordinance). These 626 placements were lost when the funds were withheld; so 626 children, all of them white, lost their shelter. The irony is even more apparent when the agencies that did agree to comply are examined. By the end of 1945, in the seven institutions that had not previously taken Black children but agreed to do so, only 100 Black children had been admitted. Three other agencies that had agreed to comply were yet to take their first Black child by 1945. As might be anticipated, the agency which showed the greatest willingness to comply was the Colored Orphan Asylum.

The Catholic agencies and institutions all agreed to comply, but their compliance did little to advance the cause of Black children. In the first place, the Catholic institutions had never excluded Black children, although they did have separate institutions for them, which the Archdiocese had already begun to integrate. Thus, compliance did not mean an increase in facilities, but simply a redistribution among the existing ones. Second, as long as services were distributed on a sectarian basis, no matter how much Catholic agencies expanded their facilities for Black children, the effect was minimal, for the vast majority of Blacks were Protestant and could not use Catholic agencies. The Jewish agencies all agreed to comply with the ordinance also, but again, because of the sectarian nature of the system, their contribution to Black children was nil.

Characteristically, the first agency to comply with the ordinance had been the Colored Orphan Asylum. In the spirit of integration, the name was changed to that which it bears today, the Riverdale Children's Association, and the policy was changed to include white as well as Black children. Although three years passed before application was made for a white child, the amendment had the potential effect of reducing the total provision that could be made by that agency for Black children—integration was not accompanied by an increase in facilities.

The Service Bureau for Negro Children: Action Collides with the System

The most far-reaching program developed between 1937 and 1944—far-reaching in the sense that it significantly increased the number of Black children served—was the Service Bureau for Negro Children, organized in 1939 as a unit of the New York Children's Aid Society. The Service Bureau's significance is demonstrated in the following agency statistics. In 1937 the agency had in foster care 41 Black children, and in one of its institutional facilities, Brace Farm, it had 65 Black boys. In 1943 there were 461 Black children in foster care, 34 Black boys at Brace Farm, and 15 Black girls at another institution, Walkill Cottage. In 1943 the Society had applications from 1,031 white children and 441 Black children; they accepted 111 of the Black applications or about 25 percent, and only 73 of the white applications.

The purposes for which the Service Bureau was established are well worth repeating here, because they go to the heart of some of the racist rationales which focus on Black people, rather than on the dysfunctional operation of the agencies and the system. These purposes were "to demonstrate to the skeptics of New York that it was not impossible, as they claimed, to find (1) an adequate number of Negro foster homes of the highest standing, (2) enough well-trained and competent Negro social workers to run the project, and (3) sufficient funds to maintain it." (p. 51) On the first point, the availability of Black foster homes, the Bureau reported that in 1943 it had applications from 1,131 families, of which 214 were taken into the program. On the second point, the availability of trained Black workers, the Bureau had been successful in securing a Black director, seven Black caseworkers, and three Black supervisors.

These successes should not only have dispelled some of the myths about the obstacles to service to Black children, they should have pointed the way for other agencies. They should in any case have insured the continuance of the Bureau. None of these things happened. They failed to happen largely because those in power chose not to make the changes necessary for future success.

The first decision necessary—to continue the Bureau's work—required the reallocation of funding to support it. Initially, John D. Rockefeller, Jr., Greater New York Fund, several other foundations, and several individuals provided funds for the three-year demonstration project. In addition, of course, as with all other voluntary agencies in New York, there was the usual subsidy through public monies for each child in care. As the three demonstration years drew to a close, the Advisory Committee to the Welfare Council Section on Dependent Children reported that if the work of the Bureau was to continue there were only three alternatives: (1) creation of a new agency to continue the work, (2) absorption by another existing voluntary agency, or (3) absorption into the Department of Welfare. The first to be considered was absorption into the Welfare Department, which, of course, would have been a major and most fundamental change in the child-care system, as the public agency gave no direct foster-care service, only the subsidy. This alternative was wrecked quickly on the rocks of sectarianism. The Welfare Commissioner had told the Committee that the three religious communities would have to agree before the City would take over the project. Such agreement was not forthcoming and the idea of transferring the project to municipal auspices was abandoned. The Children's Aid

Society then tried the next alternative: to obtain placements for the children presently under care through other voluntary agencies, with the plan that they would keep one-fourth of the children. The agencies refused them. The idea of creating a new agency was stillborn. In 1942 the work of the Bureau was absorbed into the Foster Home Department of the Children's Aid Society.

State Charities Aid Association

Another agency action of considerable significance was that taken by the State Charities Aid Association Child Placing and Adoption Committee. In February, 1939, this Committee assigned a special worker to develop an interest among Black citizens in adopting Black children. During the war years this special project was successful in placing for adoption between eighteen and twenty children each year. While this is hardly an astounding number, it was of great significance in the development of adoption services for Black children, because it was specific in extending this service to them.

PHILADELPHIA'S BLACK CHILDREN, 1937-1944

Philadelphia's child welfare system resembled that of New York in three respects: services were distributed on a sectarian basis; all services were under the auspices of private, voluntary groups; and all received public subsidy for the maintenance of children under care. As in New York, the sectarian nature of the system meant that almost all of the Black children were cared for in the Protestant sector. Unlike New York, however, none of Philadelphia's Protestant agencies caring for white children, whether in foster care or in institutions, served Black children. The care of Black children was principally distributed among three agencies, two sponsored by organizations in the Black community (the Women's Christian Alliance and the Bureau for Colored Children), and one under white auspices (the House of the Holy Child).

Efforts at improving the situation of Black children in Philadelphia during these years centered almost entirely on improving service in the agencies for Black children. There was no attempt to make any changes in the child care system, nor to stop policies of exclusion. The efforts to improve the Black agencies were very misguided, and met with only minimal success. They were consistently guided by a rigid professionalism and paternalism, not by a direct concern for the children. Resources were distributed among the Philadelphia agencies without regard for the poverty of the Black community (or for that poverty's racist roots). Agencies under Black sponsorship simply did not have access to the endowments, donations, and other private funding resources that white agencies did. The agencies further suffered in that the distribution of public monies was also discriminatory, as we shall see.

Black Agencies Under White Domination

The two agencies in Philadelphia caring for the vast majority of Black children were the Women's Christian Alliance and the Bureau for Colored Children. Both agencies were part of the tradition which dominated Afro-American efforts for their people in the first part of this century.

The Women's Christian Alliance grew out of a meeting of Black churchwomen in April, 1919, at the Allen A.M.E. Church in Philadelphia, called to discuss the development of a service for Negro working girls migrating from the South after World War I. The guiding personality behind this movement was Dr. Melissa E. Thompson Coppin, the tenth Black woman physician in the United States and the wife of Bishop Levi Coppin of the A.M.E. Church. The initial focus on work with young migrant women soon shifted to child care, and the Women's Christian Alliance was chartered as a child-placing agency in 1929. Dr. Coppin's sister, Mrs. Ada B. Carter, who was involved in the work since its early days, came to disagree with Dr. Coppin on the direction the work was to take, and in 1927 left to form the Bureau for Colored Children.

The Bureau grew more rapidly than did the parent agency, which maintained the name of the Women's Christian Alliance. Mostly because of its size, the Bureau for Colored Children received considerably more attention from official bodies than did the smaller agency. But the Women's Christian Alliance remained the second largest child-placing agency for Black children for many years; and the two agencies, founded, organized, and directed by members of the Black community, performed the major portion of the child-care work among Black children in Philadelphia.

After its inception in 1927, Mrs. Carter became the executive of the Bureau for Colored Children. In 1929 the agency had 329 children in foster homes and 20 in its shelter. By 1936, there were approximately 1,000 children in care, and in that same year the agency opened a residential institution for boys in Pomeroy (about 40 miles from Philadelphia).

From the beginning the agency was in acute financial distress, deriving almost its entire income from the board-and-care payments it received from the county commissioners and the Department of Public Welfare for individual children. Income from private donors was minimal. Furthermore, even some of the public monies to which it was entitled were not forthcoming. The Child Welfare League reported this discrimination: "The legislature has been appropriating funds to them for some time at the rate of $1500 per year. Because of certain technical requirements governing payment of state appropriations, they have not been able to secure payment of the appropriation for some years past." (p. 125) The agency was in a vicious circle: money was not to be forthcoming until the agency met "standards"; and it was impossible to meet the standards without an increase in financial support.

In 1939 the Bureau for Colored Children asked the Council of Social Agencies to make a survey of its work. The report that the Council issued made no less than fourteen recommendations for changes within the agency operation. All would cost money. The Council did not in any way suggest the possibility of their contributing to the agency funding, nor did they suggest any fund-raising operations, other than renewed pleas to the Legislature.

The recommendations revealed a misguided professionalism far removed from the reality of the situation. Even suggestions for decreasing the agency's institution population would cost more money, because a more highly trained and expensive staff would be needed to make the cut. For example, it was recommended that the population in the boys' institution at Pomeroy be reduced through "good case work." (p. 128) Obviously, reductions in population were not going to be made by transfering any of the children to other agencies, nor were the agency's facilities to be expanded through additional funding. In short, the white community was not inclined to assume any responsibility for the care of Black children in their own agencies; but at the same time they were maintaining tight control over the funds that belonged as rightly to Black children in Black agencies as they did to white children in white agencies. The Council of Social Agencies report contains a statement which—were it not that the lives of so many children were at stake—might simply be considered idiotic; in view of the reality, it can only be considered viciously paternal: "In summing up the findings, we have at no point lost sight of the financial difficulties which have beset the Bureau, *even when we seem to ignore them. If we appear to set up impossible standards—well, 'A man's reach should exceed his grasp.'* " (p. 126; emphasis ours) Just how far out of the agency's grasp the recommendations were is revealed in the figures on the agency's operation at that time, which were also included in the Council's report:

> Minimum costs for acceptable service at present price levels are more than one dollar a day per child, or about $400 per year. . . . *We must reject without hesitation any assumption that somehow colored children can thrive on less than those of other races.* Health and delinquency statistics alone refute this. We must, therefore, admit that an income derived chiefly from board at the rate of $4.25 per week *can by no possibility meet minimum costs of good care.* The very fact that the Bureau for Colored Children has been unable to avoid the accumulation of debts for operating expenses is proof of this. It is clear that eventually additional sources of income must be found if the Bureau for Colored Children is to meet even the minimum standards set up by the State Department of Welfare. [p. 127; emphasis ours]

In spite of this extraordinarily unhelpful report, the director of the Bureau again turned to the Council of Social Agencies in 1942. The Bureau's second approach was made when the Court increased the rate of board to $7.25 a week for its foster-home commitments to the agency. The executive of the Bureau then asked the Council of Social Agencies to help plan the use of the increased money. Since the increase in board rate was really of quite negligible benefit to the agency, it is apparent that the director was rather skillfully using this pretext to bring the agency's situation once again to the attention of the community powers. This time the results were more tangible. The Council appointed a Committee of executives from other agencies to meet with the Director and the President of the Board of the Bureau. This Committee pointed out to the Board the already painfully obvious fact that if the agency was to raise its standards it would have to raise its salaries, and that the increase in board rate would hardly be sufficient to do this. The Bureau representative then expressed the wish that the Bureau might get a grant from the Community Fund; the Bureau received encouragement to apply for membership in the Community Fund, which it did in late 1942. Again the Bureau was studied—this time in connection with the application. The report of this study indicates that the Community Fund was a little more realistic than the Council of Social Agencies had been:

Community Need for Bureau for Colored Children

There can be no question as to the need in Philadelphia for an agency to care for the mass of Negro children who must be given care away from their own homes. . . .

No community need is more pressing than that of adequate provision for the great number of dependent and delinquent Negro children being maintained with no other support than the board obtained from the County and City of Philadelphia. Since neither the City nor the State make adequate provision for the care of children away from their homes, the necessity for responsible private agencies able to offer such care is definite. . . .

Study in 1939 Revealed Great Financial Need

This study revealed grave defects in the work of the Bureau, many of which could not be rectified without more adequate financial support. The Council of Social Agencies backed the Bureau in a request to the General Assembly for an appropriation of $40,000 for the biennium to carry out an improved program of care. (The Legislature had been appropriating $3,000 biennially.) However, the appropriation was not increased. Moreover, the State appropriation has been held up since 1938 (because of certain technical requirements). Payments from City and County are made quarterly and foster parents cannot be paid until the cash is in hand. The Bureau for Colored Children has felt that it was caught in a vicious circle, being unable to improve its work without more funds, or to secure more funds without having raised its standards.

In July, 1942, when the rate of board for foster children received from City and County was increased, the Bureau turned to the Council of Social Agencies for advice as to how to use the additional income most effectively and worked out a new budget with the aid of a Council committee representing several foster care agencies. However, additional sources of income are needed if the Bureau is to obtain acceptable standards of care. Certain primary needs, such as a higher rate of board to foster homes and better health service can be partially met by the increased board rate, but it will not cover the increases in staff demanded by the volume of work handled, or the higher salaries necessary to attract duly qualified personnel. [p. 131]

The Bureau for Colored Children applied to the Community Fund for a grant of $73,900 and received $62,500. The $11,400 deducted had been earmarked for additional staff, which the Council disapproved: "The payroll has been increased to provide for a total of 5 supervisors and 22 social workers. Two supervisors and five visitors is the most that should be added in one year, leaving one supervisor and five visitors to be added the second year, thus deducting approximately $11,000. . . ." (p. 133) In short, the agency was to improve its standards—but at a pace deemed appropriate by the Community Fund. At the close of the war, the Bureau for Colored Children, now a Community Fund agency, was still handling by far the largest number of Black children in Philadelphia, with 809 children in foster care, 26 in its shelter, 56 boys in Pomeroy, and 150 children under supervision in their own homes.

The patience of the Bureau is attested to by the summary statement of the Child Welfare League in its review:

> The most important change in the situation of dependent and neglected Negro children in recent years in Philadelphia is the increasing obligation which the white-dominated community has assumed for their care. The part which the Bureau for Colored Children has had in bringing this about is worthy of note. Instead of using a negative approach and protesting against the white-dominated community for this lack of provision for colored children, the Bureau used a positive approach and asked the Council of Social Agencies and the Community Fund for help in caring for their children. [p. 161]

Although standards of the Bureau for Colored Children were raised through the addition of Community Fund monies, the sum was by no means sufficient to bring the agency up to the level of agencies for white children, a matter openly acknowledged by all concerned. It should also be noted that at no time were plans made for expansion of the agency. Thus, in spite of the fact that the Bureau's financial situation was somewhat eased, and the standards of care somewhat higher, little had been accomplished in terms of increasing the total community facility for Black children.

Just before the end of the War one addition was made to the Bureau's total array of services: it acquired the property formerly held by the Allerdice School, a residential institution for white girls. Benevolence was not exactly at the root of this gesture. The "school" had practically gone out of business because it was located in a neighborhood that had become increasingly Black over the years. Since the white girls in residence had become the only white girls attending the local public schools, the agency elected to close its door, transferring both its property and its endowment to the Bureau for Colored Children.

The House of the Holy Child: Progress and the Persistence of Paternalism

Another major development in the organization of child care for Black children during the war years was the merger of two agencies serving only Black children, but under white auspices. These two agencies—the House of St. Michael and All Angels for Colored Cripples, and the House of the Holy Child—began their merger in 1938.

The House of the Holy Child had been founded in 1899, by Miss Edith Wharton Dallas, as a remedy for the "most grievous condition in Philadelphia to be remedied." (p. 158) Initially the House of the Holy Child served only girls in a residential setting, but gradually it developed a foster-home program for both boys and girls. Though the agency was not a religious institution, the members of the corporation sponsoring the agency were all members of the Episcopal Church and the church gave financial support. The House of Saint Michael and All Angels for Colored Cripples, which originated under the auspices of the Episcopal Diocese in 1887, was the only one of its kind in the nation, devoted specifically to serving physically handicapped Black children. It closed its institutional facility in 1938, and the service was merged with, and continued by, the House of the

Holy Child. Eventually, in 1949, the work of both agencies was fully merged into one organization—Children's Services Incorporated. Both these institutions differed from the Women's Christian Alliance and the Bureau for Colored Children in agency auspices. The latter were originated by a Black women's organization and remained under the control of members of the Black community. The House of the Holy Child and the House of St. Michael and All Angels—like the New York City Colored Orphan Asylum—were originated and operated by members of the white community. This fact should be kept in mind as the relationship of this agency to the Council of Social Agencies is detailed.

The major changes which took place in the program of the House of the Holy Child during the war years were the dissolution of the institutional program and a trebling of the foster-home program, which did result in an overall increase in facilities for Black children in Philadelphia. In 1941 the agency had requested a study by the Council of Social Agencies, which recommended that the institutional program be dropped. At that time the institutional population had been reduced to only ten children, so the formal change to a total foster-home program was little more than recognition of an almost-accomplished fact.

Interestingly enough, the study of the Council of Social Agencies did underscore the need for institutional facilities for both Black boys and Black girls in Philadelphia, but a very realistic factor—expense—seems to have swayed the decision in favor of closing the residence:

> The Court looks with favor on expansion of the child placing program. The Court recognizes the value of institutional care for Negro children and feels strongly that the House of the Holy Child should be kept open, together with an extended program of foster home placement, and that additional funds should be sought to insure further extension. However, if both services cannot be perpetuated, the Court would be in favor of extending foster home placement. . . . [p. 140]

The report of the Council of Social Agencies continued: "The proposed budget covering the House of the Holy Child indicates that if the institution were closed and an office maintained in town, the House of the Holy Child could care for approximately double the number of children *with no increase in their request from the Community Fund. . . .*" (p. 142; emphasis ours) Apparently the corollary to this argument did not occur to anyone; with an increase from the Community Fund both programs could be maintained and expanded!

Another factor stimulated the closing of the residential facility for girls. In 1928 the original facility had been moved to Spring House, about fifteen miles from Philadelphia. This was a totally white community, and almost all community facilities—including medical care, recreational facilities, and religious institutions—were closed to the girls. Apart from the burden this exclusion put on the girls themselves, enormous amounts of staff time were devoted simply to transporting the girls to parts of Philadelphia where they could obtain the necessary services. An excerpt from the report dealing with this situation has implications today for the concept of "neighborhood-based" services, and especially for white agencies that wish to extend services to the Black community—from offices in white neighborhoods.

> A good institution must depend not only on an adequate building and grounds, but upon the staff which runs it and is responsible for the direct contact with the children. The Negro group has a limited field from which to draw experienced and well-qualified workers. Obtaining of a suitable staff is made doubly difficult by the distance of this institution from the city and the fact that workers must live in a community which has little or nothing to offer them. . . . Many of the children are placed in homes in the better Negro neighborhoods of the city. With offices and headquarters located . . . 15 miles from the city these workers spend a disproportionate amount of time in carrying out the supervision of these children. [p. 143]

The House of the Holy Child closed its residential institution.

By 1944, the House of the Holy Child had increased its foster-home program to 265 children. This is to be compared with the numbers of children under care by the two other agencies serving Black children: the Bureau for Colored Children had 960, and the Women's Christian Alliance had 394. The Child Welfare League report stated that in 1944 the standards of the House of the Holy Child "compare favorably with those in the agencies for white children with the best standards." (p. 161) We have already detailed the saga of the standards of the Bureau for Colored Children. As for the Women's Christian Alliance, the Child Welfare League only noted that at the close of 1944 the Board of Visitation had "just made an

adverse report on the Shelter of this agency and action was pending."
(p. 152) It should be noted here that the founder of the Women's
Christian Alliance agency and her followers steadfastly avoided membership in the Community Fund until 1968, out of fear of losing the
autonomy that they felt they had as an independent agency.

It seems clear that at the close of World War II the House of the
Holy Child, the agency under white auspices, had progressed and expanded much more rapidly than had either of the agencies under
Black auspices. There is only indirect evidence to suggest that there
was definite discrimination against the Black agencies because they
were Black. It must be remembered that at no time in Philadelphia
was integration of services ever an issue. All three agencies served
only Black children, and this was sustained as the accepted pattern
of care. What is certainly clear is the discrimination against Black
children. However much the white child welfare leaders decried the
low standards in the two Black agencies, however punitive the words
and actions toward them, the fact remained that these two agencies
were caring for the vast majority of Black dependent children in
Philadelphia, and no action was taken to provide new and "better"
sources of care. It seems obvious that not all of the concern about
standards in these two agencies was dictated by a concern for the
children being served.

Not only was little concern for the children apparent, but a most
paternalistic obliviousness to the Black community was also clearly
visible. In its final report on the House of the Holy Child, the Council
of Social Agencies saw a most important role for this agency in the
future of Black children in Philadelphia.

> In addition to the other aspects mentioned, there is still another
> demonstration which the House of the Holy Child is making,
> *that of assisting a racial group* to take responsibility for the
> solution of its own problems. The effectiveness of the Board
> could be strengthened by the addition of *progressive and inter-
> ested* Negro citizens. The Board should realize that "the most
> grievous condition" which Miss Dallas sought to remedy is an
> even greater problem today. *They are in a unique position*
> to provide the leadership to arouse the public and *the Negro
> community to work toward more and better care for Phila-
> delphia Negro children.* [p. 144; emphasis ours]

Why an agency founded by a white woman with a white board should have been in such a unique position to arouse the Negro community, rather than the agencies founded by Black women with Black boards, is a question that can be answered only in racist terms: a white agency is superior to a Black agency—even in serving Black children, even in arousing the Black community.

Summary

The efforts made in Philadelphia during the war years, though specifically directed toward improving the situation of Black children, accomplished little for them, because they were not directed toward the principal reason why the children were suffering. The situation of Black children at the end of the War was actually somewhat worse than at the beginning. As Mrs. Laura D. Nichols, then Director of the House of the Holy Child, was quoted in the Child Welfare League study report:

> In the past decade the quality of care for dependent white children in and around Philadelphia has been steadily improved, with professional training becoming more and more a requirement for workers. . . . Unfortunately the same has not been true to any large extent in the case of agencies serving Negro children exclusively, and other agencies in the meantime have, for various reasons, curtailed their intake of Negro children. Thus, while the ratio of dependent white children decreased and the provision for their care at the same time became more adequate, the reverse has been true in the case of colored children. [p. 148]

CLEVELAND'S BLACK CHILDREN, 1937-1944

As in New York and Philadelphia, the situation of Black children in Cleveland worsened during the war years. In Cleveland, however, only the feeblest and most ineffectual efforts were made to alter their situation. That Black children were discriminated against was flatly denied. Moreover, those in a position to make changes misguidedly believed that integration was the only solution—a solution not attained, but yet a goal which blocked other alternatives.

The Cleveland Child-Care System

The Cleveland pattern differed from that of New York and Philadelphia in two important ways. First, as is typical of the more western states, the public sector rendered a major amount of direct service. There was a strong private sector, not unlike that in the eastern states, but there was not the same plethora of voluntary agencies. In Cleveland the voluntary agencies were few and large. Sectarianism, however, was quite as strong in Cleveland within the voluntary sector as it was in the other two cities. Second, Cleveland differed from New York and Philadelphia in that there were no services exclusively for Black children. This did not mean that the Cleveland child welfare system was racially integrated. Black children in Cleveland were excluded from virtually every residential facility that existed.

On the face of it, the lack of segregated Black residential institutions and the development of the public sector might lead one to expect that the Cleveland system would be more progressive and that one would see great advances on behalf of Black children. The opposite was true. Not one advance was made during the war years. One does, however, see a curious kind of "progressiveness": the handling of urgent Black problems is enormously similar to that of the 1960's, particularly after the passage of the Civil Rights Act. Black needs and Black problems were never discussed as such; the exclusion of Black children was manifested indirectly. Exclusion of this nature is most difficult to demonstrate, especially in areas such as the child-care field—for there are no objective criteria by which to judge which children, and how many children, need substitute homes. But certainly in Cleveland the most pressing problem of Black children was not the rendering of segregated services as in New York, or separate Black services as in Philadelphia, but the rendering of *no* residential services at all. This exclusion in part accounts for the fact that the problems of Black children did not seem urgent in Cleveland during the war. It is far easier *not* to see the children who are *not* being served; children not being served at all exert much less pressure on the total child-care system than children being served, albeit in segregated and inadequate services, as in New York and Philadelphia.

In Cleveland, foster-home placement was predominantly in the hands of one public agency—the County Child Welfare Board—and one private agency—the Children's Service Bureau of the Cleveland Humane Society. In 1943 there were approximately 3,342 dependent children in foster homes and in institutions, about 950 of them Black. Of the Black children, about 90 percent were being served in foster homes under the supervision of the public agency. About 8 percent were in foster homes under the Humane Society, and the remaining few were in Catholic agencies and the few specialized institutions which did care for Black children. If the matter is looked at from a different standpoint, about 75 percent of the children in care of the County Child Welfare Board's foster homes were Black and about 25 percent of those in Humane Society homes were Black. There were five Protestant residential institutions; none of the five accepted Black children.

There is more than one reason why the number of Black children being served by the public agency was so disproportionate. The fact that none of the five Protestant residential institutions served them contributed to the situation. Another reason, however, was that, although the Humane Society always accepted children without regard to race, it disposed of cases in part on a financial basis. If the placement was expected to last less than a year, the Humane Society maintained the child; however, if it would last more than a year, the parents were required to pay 85 cents a day for the child. Children whose parents could not pay were transferred to the responsibility of the public agency. Since any kind of economic discrimination always falls more heavily on Black children, this factor helps to explain the concentration in the public service. There was, however, another reason why the proportion of Black children was smaller in the Humane Society caseload: a considerably higher proportion of Black children were screened out of the agency at the point of application. Thus, for example, in 1943 there were 1,560 applications to the agency. Of these, 227 families were Black. Sixty-two of the Black applications were accepted, or 27 percent. (p. 183)

There was little available to the children who were rejected, as the Child Welfare League's report makes plain.

The Denial of Racism: No Problem = No Action

In all of the reports studied by the Child Welfare League, Black children received scant mention. When they were mentioned, the points discussed were always the same—the lack of residential facilities and the suspicion of large numbers of unserved children.

The County Child Welfare Board noted that "there are about twenty-five Negro children for whom institutional care would represent the optimal solution, and there is an additional group for whom foster homes would be best, but cannot be found. *The fact that institutional placement for colored children is not available operates to shut off referrals of these children,* and a substantially large number might be discovered. . . ." (p. 242; emphasis ours) In a similar vein the judge of the Juvenile Court observed that "figures available as to colored children in need of care are wholly incomplete since these children *have never received the care they should have and facilities for such care do not exist, so that neither the social agencies nor the police call attention to large numbers of children who would profit by placement.*" (p. 242; emphasis ours) And the principal of the junior high school in the largest Black section of Cleveland said, "there have never been sufficient facilities for the care of colored children and many needs are therefore unmet . . . the people of the Central Area see this neglect of children, are conscious of it, and will be rightfully aroused if positive action is not taken." (p. 243) It seems clear that there were vast numbers of Black children not being served, and further, that the matter was no secret. Given such a situation, it is surprising that during the war years the Cleveland child welfare community did not overtly express mounting concern over the "mounting numbers of Black dependent children."

During the war one civic committee was devoted to an examination of Black children and their needs. It bore a name suggestive of our own climate of euphemisms: the Committee on Family and Children's Services in the Central Area. Its final report states the rationale behind the "color-blind" approach of the Cleveland child welfare system:

> As part of the Committee's orientation to the study, recognition was given to the fact that Cleveland historically has been *a city of liberal attitudes* and that this tradition applied to and included the Negroes in Cleveland's early history. Though not always obvious, it was accepted as fact that Cleveland's intellectual philosophy in respect to Negroes has been toward freedom *even when the Negroes came in masses.*

> Negroes in Cleveland have shared this philosophy. It was
> recognized also that historically there has been partial achieve-
> ment of this philosophy, but that the partial achievement to
> date is far short of the desirable, both in the interest of the
> Negro and the community at large. [p. 232; emphasis ours]

Given this philosophy, what did the committee and the rest of the
child welfare system do about the obvious and repeated "finding" that
there were no residential institutions for dependent Black children? It
was the only Black-related problem to catch sustained attention over
a ten-year span. Three possible solutions were attempted, but all three
came to naught. Nothing was done.

The first and most obvious solution was to extend existing residential institutions to Black children—*i.e.,* to "desegregate" the white
Protestant institutions. This was attempted; the Committee on Family
and Children's Services in the Central Area approached the Protestant
institutions and asked if they were planning to change their policy on
admission of Black children. The answer was "no," and that was that.
While these institutions did receive money from the Community Fund,
they did not receive public subsidy as did the ones in New York. Thus
any legislation like New York's Race Discrimination Amendment
would have little influence over these institutions, since there was no
public money to be withheld from them.

The second solution was for the public agency to open its own residential institution. This was rejected for two reasons. First, there was
a presumption that foster homes were a more efficacious form of care,
and since that was the service already being given by the public
agency, an extension into the institutional field was seen as a step
backwards. The second reason was a fear, in the Black community
and among both Black and white child welfare professionals, that any
such public institution would immediately become segregated, in that
white children would continue to be sent to the private institutions
and only Black children would enter the public institution.

The third solution considered was the establishment of residences
under the auspices of the Black community. In fact, at several different times groups of Black people had applied to the state for the in-
corporation of a voluntary agency to be operated exclusively for
Black children. Each time this had happened the application was
eventually withdrawn by the group in question because other members

of the Black community expressed strong opposition to a "segregated" agency.

What happened in Cleveland in relation to the children's residential institution comes close to the situation of the entire child welfare field in the post-World War years. Available solutions to the child-care problems of Black children repeatedly were found to be unacceptable for one reason or another by one group or another. While some reasons were (and are) nobler than others, the ultimate result, regardless of the reason, has been the same: the problems remain unsolved, and the children go unserved. In its closing comments on Cleveland, the Child Welfare League of America made a statement which could have applied to most communities for the next twenty years: "In Cleveland the approach of the Children's Council to the problem of foster care for colored children is consistently based on the idea that the needs of these children should be met through integrated programs. Practice in individuals agencies, however, has not yet caught up with this idea." (p. 253)

BLACK CHILDREN AND CHILD WELFARE AT THE END OF WORLD WAR II

World War II marked a turning point in child welfare race relations just as it did in national race relations. The events detailed in this study by the Child Welfare League of America were not idiosyncratic to the three cities involved. They were representative of virtually every large northern urban community. The details have been reviewed here not only because they contribute greatly to an understanding of this crucial period in the history of child welfare, but also because they demonstrate the forces operating to the disadvantage of Black children today. Of primarily historical significance are the external influences and pressures on the child welfare systems emanating from the broader social situation of the times. But the responses of the child welfare systems to these pressures, and the barriers to resolution of the conflicts they engendered, are thoroughly representative of the situation today. The same interplay of the forces of racism, sectarianism, professionalism, and bureaucracy is as evident today as it was in 1945. Let us summarize, then, the pressures and responses which the Child Welfare League report illuminated.

External Pressures

During World War II two major changes occurred which would for-ever alter the relationship of Black children to child welfare. One change was in the American population; the other was in Black–white race relations.

The massive southern–northern migration by Black people was not the only population factor affecting child welfare. The major change for child welfare—the change in the Black–white ratio of dependent children—was not brought about simply by an increase in Black chil-dren, but also by a decrease in the number of white Protestant depen-dent children. Affluence in the general white population had been un-evenly distributed among Protestants and Catholics, since the most recently immigrated populations, and thus the poorest, had come most often from Catholic countries. The increased affluence among white people during the war years simply accentuated this situation, for it was most dramatically seen among the white, Protestant groups. Thus, the pressure of the "enormous increase" in the Black population of many cities was in fact magnified by the sectarian nature of the ser-vices.

Black children constituted a relatively small percentage of the *total* dependent-child population even at the end of the war. However, the *total* dependent-child population was an irrelevant datum; because most Black children were Protestant, only the Protestant and non-sectarian services were potentially open to them. Thus, while Black migration and increased white affluence helped to change the Black–white ratio in the dependent-child population, the sectarian nature of the services greatly accentuated the practical impact of the accelera-tion of this long-established trend. These factors combined to change the Black–white ratio, even in cities such as Cleveland and Pittsburgh, which in fact had not experienced notably great wartime migrations of Black people.

The second factor which altered the relationship of Black children to child welfare was a change in Black–white relations, which stemmed largely from the blatant example of white racism in the armed forces. Perhaps at no previous time in history did Black Amer-ica so strongly pronounce its edict that the nation's racism was no longer to be tolerated. This growing impact of the Black presence on white Americans, and the guilt and fear and rage that it uncovered, was felt in the child welfare field as it was throughout the country. As we saw in the pages on New York, the antidiscrimination ordinance for child-caring institutions came about through committees established to prevent Harlem uprisings. The very fact that the Child Welfare League of America saw fit to do this study at the close of the war is testimony to the growing awareness among white Americans that Black Americans were determined to drag them and their society, including their child welfare system, into the twentieth century.

System Responses

Both these external factors, actually sharp accelerations of long-standing trends, contributed to the birth of a new era in child welfare. The responses of the New York, Philadelphia, and Cleveland child welfare systems to these external pressures were no more idiosyncratic to them than were the pressures themselves. Many facets of the Child Welfare League study in these cities were in fact prophetic of similar responses to similar pressures in many other communities.

Three generalizations about child welfare can be drawn from this study which are only slightly less true today. First, there was not one community in which the entire array of forms of services were equally accessible to Black children. The most inaccessible form of service was that of adoption, followed by institutional care. Insofar as these forms of services were closed to Black children, additional strains were put on the form of service that *was* open to them, that of foster-home care. The stresses on this form of service resulted in inadequacies in the care given—long delays in placement, inconceivable waiting by children in temporary, overcrowded shelters, and often the use of inadequate homes—and in closing the service to children for whom it would have been appropriate. The second generalization that can be made concerns the nature of the organization of child welfare systems. Each of the three systems studied was representative of a different type of organization, yet in none of the three instances was the basic organizational nature of the system changed during the period of study. The basic organization of each system revolved around three dimensions: (1) agency auspices, (2) racial patterning, and (3) the intersection of these two with each form of service given. Each of the three cities represented a different patterning of these organizational dimensions, although certain characteristics were common to all three. The third generalization is that each organizational pattern had aspects which were dysfunctional to Black children, in addition to the racism which was built into each basic structuring. Let us examine the three organizational patterns in detail.

New York

Services in all forms of care were under the auspices *entirely of voluntary agencies,* with public subsidy for each child in care. Within the voluntary sector, all services were organized along *sectarian* lines, as was true in the other communities. *Three types of racial patterning* were visible: agencies under white auspices which served Black children almost exclusively (one agency); agencies which served white children almost exclusively, though illegally (several agencies); and agencies which served both Black and white children (several agencies). This patterning extended over all forms of services, though very few Black children received adoptive services, and many institutions serving both Black and white children served only a small number of Black children.

Philadelphia

Services were *predominantly voluntary in nature with a public subsidy,* though there was a small foster-home service given directly by the public agency. Voluntary agencies were distributed along *sectarian lines.* Philadelphia differed from New York in that *only one racial pattern maintained:* all services were distributed along racial lines. Three agencies, two under Black auspices and one under white, cared for almost all Black children in Philadelphia. Since these agencies did not offer adoption, there were virtually no adoption services available to Black children.

Cleveland

Cleveland offered a contrast to the other two in both agency auspices and racial patterning. The system was both *public and private in nature, without a public subsidy* to the voluntary agencies. There was an extensive public foster-home service, but no public residential institution nor adoption service. Voluntary services were organized along *sectarian lines;* Protestant voluntary agencies operated on a *fee-for-service* basis. Both institutional and adoptive services were virtually nonexistent for Black children. *Racial patterning* also differed

from the other two cities—foster-home service was dispensed through
public and private agencies which served both Black and white children; institutional services existed for white children only. There was
no foster-home or institutional service operated only for Black children.

System Dysfunction for Black Children

These three different systems of services were representative of the
various patternings of services throughout the country. In spite of the
diversity represented here in both the public–private dimension and
the racial patterning, Black children suffered under all three. All three
systems tolerated overt racist practices, and all three had covert racist
aspects. The overt racism is seen in all three systems in the deliberate
exclusion of Black children by individual agencies, most particularly
in the institutional form of care. This exclusion was racist in the most
fundamental sense—white people did not want Black children eating
and sleeping alongside white children. Foster care has always been
relatively more open to Black children for just this reason—in foster
care Black children could be placed with Black children. Because
white people were in control of the institutional fabric of these communities, and, in the instance of residential care, acted on the basis
of racism and deprived Black children of this kind of service, Black
children were made to suffer.

The overt exclusion of children on the basis of race is, of course,
the most readily recognized form of racism. In each of these three
communities, however, covert racism can also be found in the *system
dysfunction for Black children,* which, while less obvious and less deliberate, was no less effective in depriving Black children of adequate
services. Each system had been established fundamentally to serve
white children, and little had been done to adapt any of them to
Black children's needs. In Philadelphia, the financial base of the system was an expectation that services would be provided through
heavily endowed voluntary agencies. Public subsidy for individual
children was expected to be supplemental to each agency's own resources; *i.e.;* it was an amount suitable to cover board and care of
each child; it was insufficient to cover other operating expenditures.
This system worked well for the white agencies and for the white
children served by them. But the Black agencies did not have the

financial backing that the white agencies did. The subsidy therefore was most insufficient to their needs, and the system failed to adapt to their situation. Black children in Philadelphia were deprived not because they were served through Black agencies apart from white children, but because the financial structure of the Philadelphia system did not recognize and adapt to the financial realities facing the Black agencies.

In New York, the highly decentralized child welfare system administered through fiercely independent and autonomous private agencies was dysfunctional not only for Black children but for white children as well. The plethora of highly specialized agencies, particularly residential centers for "special needs" children, left many children of both races unserved. But the burden fell most critically on Black children, barred as they were from so many of the specialized and nonspecialized institutions. The political and financial power of such agencies made it impossible to enforce legislation intended to protect Black children.

The Cleveland system was more open to Black children, at least those in need of foster homes, by virtue of the extensive public services. Yet even the Cleveland system was dysfunctional for Black children. The division of clients between public and private agencies along financial lines screened Black children away from the private services in disproportionate numbers. These basic factors in all three systems remained unchanged even when shown to be grossly discriminatory against Black children.

In both New York and Philadelphia there was strong evidence that rigid professionalism served to reinforce the structure of the system, and further to add to the burdens of Black children. In both cities it was a strong factor in inhibiting the growth of public-agency service. As we shall see, professionalism in itself was to serve as a major barrier to the extension of adoption services to Black children. And in both cities the well-intended adherence to professional standards ultimately served to discriminate against—rather than to help—Black children, as in the cases of both the Colored Orphan Asylum and the Bureau for Colored Children. Standards, which are properly a means to an end, were allowed to become an end in and of themselves. In neither instance was there evidence of a genuine concern for and understanding of the plight of Black children. When the professional standards were upheld, the professionals considered their job done—regardless of the effects on the children. Once the standards in the

Colored Orphan Asylum in New York were raised—through a *diminution* of service—the efforts for Black children ceased. The "analyses" of the Bureau for Colored Children—in the name of standards—failed to raise standards of care for the Black children being served by that agency. More importantly, the withholding of funds actually lowered standards, curtailing both quality and quantity of service. In both instances failure to understand the specific situation of Black children, including the specific situation of the agencies serving them, resulted not in better care for the children, but only in the reinforcement of the system of services which was itself solely to blame for the lowered standards.

Sectarianism was still another facet of all three of these systems which served to bar Black children from adequate services. Sectarianism of itself need not ultimately have racist elements. Only insofar as the various religious sects themselves ascribe to and perpetuate racist beliefs and practices need a sectarian-based system adversely affect Black children. But whatever the case, sectarianism as practiced in child welfare worked in two ways to the disadvantage of Black children. Neither feature was essential to a sectarian operation. First of all, sectarianism operated both to include and to exclude children. This is not necessary. The right of religious groups to take care of their own would not be violated by their also taking care of someone else's when they are not provided for. Thus the vast institutional resources of the Catholic child-care system might have been opened to Black children who were not Catholics, and Catholics could still have maintained their rights to care for Catholic children of both races. Mechanisms of exclusion inevitably operate to the disadvantage of Black children, even if not directed specifically toward them. The second dysfunctional factor about sectarian child welfare services was (paradoxically enough) that it was not *fully* sectarian. In effect it was a Catholic, Jewish, "all-other" system. The "Protestant" sector was in reality a nonsectarian system with agencies under a variety of auspices, most not directly church-related. Thus a Protestant was not guaranteed entry into the "Protestant" services. Sectarianism of this kind worked for white Protestant children. Sectarianism presupposes each group's "taking care of its own." White children were the "own" of white nonsectarian agencies; Black children were not. These two facets of sectarianism in these child welfare systems thus combined to the disadvantage of Black children—one served to exclude them from services, while the other offered no guarantee of their inclusion.

The furious struggle to maintain sectarian rights—so unproductive for Black children—was not one to be easily relinquished or modified. As in New York, even legislation to protect Black children was made subservient to the sectarian dimension.

Of the three systems studied in this chapter, New York in one sense had the most diversified racial patterning of services, with agencies exclusively for Black children as well as agencies serving both racial groups. Philadelphia had only segregated agencies for Black children, and Cleveland had no agencies for Black children. All three had agencies which served only white children. And in all three, Black children suffered.

There are many who would argue that the total segregation of the Philadelphia racial pattern was the most racist and the most harmful to Black children. But were the Black children of Philadelphia really worse off in a Black residential institution than the Black children of Cleveland who had no such institution? Were the Black children of New York better off when the Colored Orphan Asylum changed its name to the Riverdale Children's Association and, in the name of integration, took some of its services away from Black children in order to serve white children? Can the Philadelphia system be considered any more racist than the others, when it produced a child-caring system that had fifty or more Black people on agency boards, while Cleveland had none, and New York only a token few? Did the Philadelphia system result in any greater disenfranchisement of children through its rigid adherence to segregation than did the Cleveland system with its rigid adherence to the principle—if not the fact —of integration?

These were the questions in 1945; they are the questions today. Depending upon one's ideology, they can be answered in many ways. Unfortunately, they are always answered by adults, not by the children whose lives are most affected by the answers. And always, when adults answer in terms of their ideology, they answer for the world that they want, the world of tomorrow. But children do not live in the world of tomorrow. They live—or they perish—in the real world of today. As we shall see in the next chapter, the subjugation of children's needs to an ideological battle—a battle for a most humane ideology—was to thwart one of the major national postwar efforts made on their behalf.

6 Black efforts for black children, 1953-1959

At its annual conference of 1953, the National Association for the Advancement of Colored People, spurred on by its younger members and the generally disillusioned Black community, formulated a bold ten-year plan of civil rights action and leadership toward the end that Black people would be "free by '63." It was a slogan more than a program. But it was highly symbolic of the mood of the Black community. It signaled a determination among Black people, leaders, and organizations to lead the struggle for liberation rather than continue to rely on "well-meaning white people" to lead the attack on institutional racism in all its varieties. Before the 1950's, Black people had believed that reason, rhetoric, research, and religion would convince white people of the humanity of Black people and of the consequences of racism; the assumption was that once white people had been enlightened they would reform themselves, their prejudices, and their institutions sufficiently to provide an equitable place for Black people in the society. By the 1950's, however, the Black community had begun to feel that enlightenment might more effectively come from action for social change, than the other way around.

The 1950's were a decade of social action for social justice: NAACP efforts led to the Supreme Court decision of 1954: the Montgomery Improvement Association was born, to be followed by the bus boycott and the crusades led by Martin Luther King, Jr., starting in 1956; the Freedom Rides of 1957–58 took place; and the Student Non-Violent Coordinating Committee was born at a Black college in Greensboro, North Carolina, in 1960.

These were years of tremendous activity on behalf of freedom, not only in the larger society but also in that social institution we call child welfare. Here the major efforts at change in the interest of Black children were focused on the provision of permanent substitute homes for Black children in need of parents, and most specifically on the field of adoption. In this effort, as in the wider society, the key philosophy was "integration": Black and white together served and treated alike by white-dominated institutions.

In this chapter we shall discuss two major efforts spurred and led by Black people, to change the situation of Black children in the adoption field. These were major efforts in the general movement for reform in child welfare and indeed are indices of the overall efforts toward Black liberation during the turbulent decade of the 1950's. They left an indelible imprint on the course and nature of the struggle for equity in child welfare.

One of the two projects—the National Urban League Foster Care and Adoptions Project—was national in scope; the other—the Adopt-A-Child project—was limited to New York City.* The very focus on the extension of adoption services to Black children made these projects efforts toward fundamental system changes. They were not fully successful; but they were nonetheless landmark efforts. We shall review first the National Urban League project, describing its general background and origins, and then examining the Kansas City phase

* The data for this chapter are drawn solely from the records of the National Urban League, 1953–60, in the Manuscripts Division, Library of Congress. Three prominent Black social workers and educators who played important roles in these two projects have assisted us in preparing this chapter. Patricia Garland Morrisey first directed our attention to the two projects; Nelson Jackson helped us locate the data; and William Jackson helped us place them in social and historical perspective. None of them is responsible, of course, for our analysis or conclusions.

of the project in detail. We shall then look at the Adopt-A-Child
project in New York City, to analyze its goal and strategies, its success and failures.

THE NATIONAL URBAN LEAGUE FOSTER CARE AND ADOP-
TIONS PROJECT

The National Urban League, organized in New York City in April,
1910, began as an interracial organization focused on the social problems of urban Negroes. The founders were principally social workers
and philanthropists. Its first executive officer, George Edmond Hayes,
was a professional social worker, as were most of his successors, including the late Whitney Young, Jr. Nevertheless, the League did not
enter areas related to social work to any great extent until after World
War II.

After World War II, the League began increasingly to urge community institutions to abandon segregation and discrimination in a
wide array of services to Black people. It was in this spirit that the
Foster Care and Adoptions Project was launched at a national level.

Before the effort was made national in scope, several of the affiliated Leagues had begun to intervene on behalf of local Black children.
Often these activities had been prompted by complaints of discriminatory actions. In Los Angeles, for example, in 1946, the Urban
League became active in child welfare because it had been informed
that the largest local adoption agency had refused to take any more
Black children. When local affiliates did become involved, they invariably uncovered vast discrimination against Black children, as can
be seen in the reports of annual meetings of the National Urban
League. Child welfare thus emerged as a suitable concern for an
organization directed toward eliminating discrimination against Black
people. The National Urban League Conference of 1953 launched the
nationwide project on Foster Care and Adoptions for Negro Children;
it remained a project of the League until 1958.

The Overall Characteristics of the Project

The Foster Care and Adoptions Project varied considerably from city
to city. In about a dozen cities the League affiliate never instituted the

project. In many of these, the local councils of social agencies refused to deal with the Urban League or to permit its participation and intervention in child welfare matters. In some others, the League affiliate accepted the local agencies' view that there was no problem— *i.e.,* that there were no Black children waiting for adoption. Many of the affiliates that did participate had to overcome similar responses in their communities, but managed to do so by persistence.

In almost all participating communities, the first action was to determine the exact treatment being given Black children. In essence these were efforts to document discrimination in agency practices. Such discrimination was not limited to the children; in some communities the discriminatory incidents involved Black agency staff and Black couples who had wished to adopt. Many of these initial studies produced information which was potentially quite useful in making significant alterations on behalf of Black children. For example, they frequently pointed out many subtle ways in which Black children were being excluded by the operating procedures of the various systems.

The persistent documentation of discrimination against Black children met with denial in many communities but with some measure of agency cooperation in many others. When met with denial, many Urban League personnel were dogged in demonstrating the truth, and set out to dispel the rationales that agencies presented to show their own blamelessness. Two rationales were offered almost universally. The first was that Black women did not wish to surrender their babies for adoption, and thus the agencies had no call for such service. Repeatedly the Urban League affiliates demonstrated the many ways in which Black women were prevented from expressing any such wish, and repeatedly they demonstrated the existence of Black babies and children in foster homes and institutions who were without permanent parents. The other rationale was that Black couples were not interested in adopting children, so that the agency wouldn't be able to place them. Again, the Urban League was often able to demonstrate that Black couples were actually traveling to other communities to find babies. They were not only willing to adopt, but very eager to do so. The Urban League personnel were often able to show the agencies how their operations actually screened out and discouraged willing Black adoptive applicants.

Apart from their studies and surveys of Black adoptive parents, some League affiliates engaged in direct recruitment of Black applicants. Some of the longest-lasting results of the project came through these direct activities. The successful recruitment of adoptive parents gave hundreds of children permanent, loving homes. As part of their recruitment activities many of the affiliates also founded agency-related organizations—Black auxiliaries and volunteer groups—which have persisted to this day. This aspect of the work was perhaps the only one resulting in permanent, institutionalized agency practices.

When the League's methods of reasoned study, documentation, suggestion, and persuasion were met with cooperation, the projects were relatively successful—Black babies and children were given adoptive homes. But the success was relative, for once the Urban League withdrew its support and pressure, there was a lapse into old ways, old practices, and old beliefs. In many instances, however, the agencies were not at all cooperative, ignored Urban League advice, and eventually excluded the Urban League altogether, persisting in their old, ineffective activity. When this occurred the Urban League affiliates, committed as they were to reason and persuasion, good faith and good will, were simply powerless to bring about any changes. At no time did any of the projects fundamentally challenge white control over the services and the system. When that control was not willingly shared even to the extent of heeding suggestions, the efforts failed, the purposes and energies were deflected—and the children waited.

Kansas City

Of all of the National Urban League efforts, Kansas City best exemplifies the failure of reason, research, and moral suasion to bring about change when the establishment refuses to change. The Kansas City experience had two phases. The first was a three-year period of painstaking Urban League study and research to define the situation, identify the discrimination, and to suggest the pathways to change. At the end of this time the Urban League, thinking its case was made, was prepared to act directly for Black children. In a display of faith it joined forces with the white establishment; this sharing of control ultimately led to total dissipation of its goals and exclusion of its leadership.

Phase One: Dispelling the Myths with Reason and Research

The Kansas City Urban League began its activity on behalf of Black children in 1951. At the National Urban League Conference in 1953 (the same conference which launched the nationwide project), Thomas A. Webster, Director of the Kansas City Urban League, reported:

> Early in the Spring of 1951, at the conference with the Director of the Adoptions Department, the Board of Directors of the Urban League appointed a *study action committee* with the recommendation that the Adoptions Department furnish the same quality of casework and adoption service to Black unmarried mothers, to their children and to adoptive parents as that furnished white persons, and secondly, that the Adoptions Department employ professionally qualified Black caseworkers. [emphasis ours]

The Urban League study action committee conferred with the Director of the Kansas City Adoptions Department, met all of the judges of the family court in executive session, and later studied many aspects of the problem of placing Black children for adoption. The Adoptions Department responded with a classic rationale: its caseworkers found that illegitimacy among Blacks did not carry the same stigma as in white cases, and the Black family would always make room for one more child. The department further claimed that homes could not be found because of poor housing and low income in the Black group: if an adoptive couple had a good home and sufficient income, they were often above the age limit set by the department.

Under Mr. Webster, who served as staff director, the Urban League of Kansas City formed a Committee on Adoptions. Its careful three-year study was successful in exposing, if not dispelling, the common myths. The committee found that of all children adopted in Jackson County in 1952, only 3.9 percent were Black—although 12.3 percent of the city's population was Black. Although one out of every five children receiving care away from home in 1952 was a Black child, only one out of every twenty-five children adopted was Black. The committee concluded:

> The facts indicate that there are many Black children without family ties and therefore available for adoption [and] at the same time there may be many Black couples wishing to adopt children who are unaware of the steps to take to secure such children. Because of this, many Black children are doomed to remain in institutions or to be shunted around in foster homes. . . .

The committee pointed out that the Jackson County Welfare Office estimated that 25 percent of its financial assistance cases involved unmarried mothers, and carefully detailed the ways in which the adoption and child welfare system screened out Black mothers and their babies. Their findings are all too reminiscent of similar practices today. Most hospital-born Black babies in Kansas City were delivered at General Hospital No. 2. The hospital accepted maternity patients regardlesss of marital status, and the Medical Social Services Department saw most of the unmarried mothers delivered at the hospital. When it was acceptable to the woman, referral was made to Family Service for casework service. Medical Social Services reported that in a 9-month period beginning March, 1951, about fifteen Black mothers had expressed a desire to have their babies adopted. These Black mothers were referred to Family Service.

No caseworker from the Adoptions Department interviewed expectant mothers at General Hospital No. 2. At the Willows and Fairmont Hospitals, which were commerical maternity homes, Adoptions Department caseworkers (whose salaries were paid by the private hospitals) visited all mothers.

These commerical maternity homes were virtually closed to Black women. The "maternity home" for Black women was, in effect—as it is in most communities today—the obstetric ward of the county hospital, which was not supplied with adoption-oriented casework service.

In Kansas City the adoptions situation was complicated by the financial system of the Adoptions Department, a system which served to discriminate against Black women and babies. Although the Adoptions Department was a part of the Welfare Department, the county paid only office rent, lights, and local telephone service. All other monies had to come from fees paid by the adoptive parents. The fees were deposited with "the friend of the court," a local bank, which then paid out salaries and other operating expenses. This system made it essential for the Adoptions Department to place large numbers of children and to place them quickly. The largest number of available babies, and the most rapidly placed babies, were white. This dependence of the department upon the number of placements was fundamentally unsound. The Urban League committee recommended that the employees should be appointed and paid by the county. They pointed out that many states had given up the fee system.

The child welfare system also had sectarian elements. The Urban League found that the Catholic Welfare Bureau had in its custody illegitimate Black children who were adoptable. The Bureau had had difficulty in finding suitable adoptive homes for these children, and had contacted Catholic agencies in other dioceses trying to find suitable homes. In 1951, the Bureau had had three babies and three prospective Black adoptive couples. Two of the couples were rejected: one had their own child, and the agency required evidence of infertility; and one had become financially insecure when the father was injured during the application period. The third couple had withdrawn their application, saying they would not be satisfied with an adopted child.

The committee studied scores of local reports and surveys, reviewed the professional literature of national agencies, and consulted the U.S. Children's Bureau, the Child Welfare League of America, and the Family Services Association of the United States of America. At the end of the study, the committee attacked the general assumption that the Black tradition of mutual help, great fondness for children, and readiness to add another member to the family made it unnecessary to provide extensive services for Black children: "Our committee concluded that this assumption is merely a rationalization for not providing satisfactory services for Black clients." The committee believed that in Kansas City approximately 1,400 Black children in foster homes or institutions, or receiving public assistance while living with parents or relatives, might be available for adoption services.

The Urban League committee also investigated the common agency statement that Black adoptive parents could not be found. Their study revealed that many Black applicants failed to complete their applications after their initial contact with the Adoptions Department. The department supplied the names of recent applicants to the committee members, who then asked twenty or more of the families why they had not followed up their applications. The most common answers centered on the interaction with the agency. Many couples had become discouraged by the regulations. Many more had been ruled ineligible because they were expecting or had their own baby, or were too old or too poor. Finally, some felt it was just too much red tape. The committee felt that there was an additional factor at work—the attitudes and practices of the social caseworkers, which the committee concluded were of extreme importance in placing minority children. The use of interracial staff and policy-making boards, and in-service training on racial, social, and cultural problems were recommended as both desirable and necessary.

The committee's report on its three years of study and action, titled "Working Copy of the Report for the Study Committee on Adoptions of the Urban League of Kansas City," concluded with specific recommendations. The first was that qualified Black caseworkers be employed on the staff of the Adoptions Department to encourage a closer identity with and a more effective use of the agency's services by the Black community. The second was that the Adoption Study Committee of the Urban League should be revised to include a wider selection of Black lay leadership and should be continued to educate and stimulate more Black families to adopt children. The committee recommended that the Family and Child Welfare Division of the Council of Social Agencies, the Urban League, and the Adoptions Department explore the possibility of a special experiment in expanding adoption services to Black families. Finally, the committee recommended that as a basis for planning the demonstration project, a research agency be asked to conduct sample studies in the Black community to determine the desire, ability, and number of Black families interested in adopting children.

Up to this point, the Kansas City Urban League had relied on careful study of issues. It had presented data which were contrary to the beliefs expressed by the agencies at the outset. The Urban League had carefully shown that many, not few, Black children were suitable for adoptive services. It had quite dramatically demonstrated ways in which the child welfare system operated to discriminate against Black mothers and babies, and ways in which the procedures of the adoption agencies contributed to a paucity of adoptive homes. The recommendations of the Urban League were thus quite appropriately weighted toward action, and in particular toward changes within the adoption system and agencies. It seemed reasonable to expect that the next phase of the project would be one of action.

Phase Two: Rejection of Black Leadership.

The fate of the Kansas City project in the years 1954–55 is most dramatically revealed in the letters of Thomas Webster, the director, to the National Urban League office. This correspondence illustrates the frustration and disappointment experienced by many Black organizations and individuals attempting to join forces with white organizations. The steps in the process are all too typical of the 1950's. The first step was a sharing of leadership, which rapidly became a surrender of leadership. The next inevitable step was a diversion of the original goals, followed by complete submersion. In Kansas City, the recommended demonstration project—an action project—was deferred in favor of a survey—further study without action—and was eventually lost altogether. Even the survey that was conducted did not follow the direction of the original study, and the results were of questionable utility. The final step was the exclusion of the Black organization from future planning.

The first recommendation of the Urban League committee to be acted upon was the research for the demonstration project. On January 5, 1954, Thomas Webster wrote to Nelson Jackson of the National Office as follows:

> we have already gotten some commitment from Community Studies, the [private] research agency in Kansas City, and the Association of Trusts and Foundations for a sample survey to determine the interests and ability of prospective Black adoptive parents to accept the children. If the evidence shows that there are sufficient couples interested in adoptions, we will ask for a sizable grant for a two-year education and interpretive project. The Court wants us to get into the home-finding business and I have some serious questions about this.*

Three months later, Mr. Webster observed,

> Community Studies . . . have indicated that they are very much interested in the possibility of a demonstration project in the adoption field for Black children.
>
> They would like as quickly as we can to have an outline in some detail of what we feel it should involve, as well as a similar request to Wadsworth of the Association of Trusts and Foundations, as to what such a study would require in terms of finance. Sometime next week I shall send you my outline for your review so that we can be agreed on what we shall submit to them.

---

* Reluctance to take on a direct-service activity was common in the Urban League projects. In part it stemmed from the Urban League's traditional role of facilitator and coordinator, but not a direct-service agency; in part, however, it stemmed from the fact that an Urban League agency specifically for Black children was considered to be in direct opposition to the goal of integration, and integration was considered of prime importance. In only one city—Seattle—did the Urban League suggest a separate agency for Black children. It never became a reality.

A month later (on May 10, 1954), Mr. Webster wrote,

> The Kansas City Association of Trusts and Foundations is most interested in the proposal we discussed with them. They want as soon as possible a detailed outline of what we want to see done in Kansas City, through a one day conference and through the research and the testing of the findings, by placing Black children as a demonstration that it can be done. After the demonstration has been made we should have some recommendations for responsibility for various phases of the adoption program for the future. . . .
> Let me tell you that you made some fine impressions on your visit here and I think we can readily move ahead in the adoption field if we keep pressing the matter.

On June 3, 1954, Webster wrote:

> A little later, I will send you a rough outline of our Institute [the one-day conference Webster had mentioned in May] plans for October when you will be in this part of the country.

Two weeks later, on June 14, 1954, Webster sent Nelson a copy of the request for funds, remarking that it had already been submitted to the Association of Trusts and Foundations, and to one Judge Reiderer, whose suggestions had been included. The next day Webster wrote,

> At our June meeting of the Adoption Committee, we had the State Director, Dr. N. Carter, present. He agreed to include in his next fiscal budget funds for the employment of the home-finder on the Jackson County Welfare staff. Although this will be a temporary experiment, it will last long enough to permit some real concentrated effort to find Black foster and adoptive homes. This is one of the most encouraging steps in the three-year operation of our committee.

In October things had changed. Webster wrote:

> Here is the outline for the research and demonstration project for adoptive children that are hard to place. This is a request which Community Studies has submitted to the K. C. Association of Foundations and Trusts.
> *As you see, it is somewhat different from the approach that I had in mind.* [Emphasis ours]

Some controversy had arisen over the Institute which had been proposed. It was to be deferred: "The foundation would rather do the survey first and have the Institute later to discuss the findings."

The Community Studies outline, which was attached, proposed that a survey and demonstration project be set up to determine (1) the extent to which *hard-to-place* adoptable babies and children could be placed in adoptive homes, and (2) the most effective procedure for accomplishing this objective in Jackson County. Notice that the project was no longer specifically focused on Black children.

The project would test certain theoretical assumptions about cultural and economic factors as causing the inability to place more Black children in Kansas City and throughout the U.S. In the second place, the project would examine and assay certain accepted policies and practices in the general field of adoption. The project would seek to answer the following questions: (1) Is it difficult to place Black children for adoption because skin color and hair texture must be matched to prospective parents? (2) Are housing facilities, employment, and income factors in the placement of Black babies? (3) Are Black adoptive parents apprenhensive about the legal procedure and the formality of the adoption process? (4) Are the attitudes of the adoption workers factors in getting community understanding of and support for sound adoption practices? (5) Does the broad policy of adoption account for the general lack of Black adoptive homes? (6) What are the effects upon the whole program of different methods of rejecting applicants for adoption? (7) How successful are adoptions when requirements related to age, income, housing, and payment of fees are adjusted in certain instances?

The Community Studies outline proposed the following staffing pattern: (1) a home-finder or caseworker on the Adoptions Department staff to concentrate on the placement of older white children and Black babies and children for a two-year period, and (2) a community organization secretary to be assigned to the Urban League staff for a two-year period to work cooperatively with the Adoptions Department. The report noted that of the twenty-six Urban League affiliates working in this special adoptions project, the Kansas City Urban League was the only one that did not have a full-time community organization secretary.

In November, Mr. Webster wrote as follows:

Community Studies has just called me to say that they have

found a means to begin the adoption study we requested for the adoptable children *that are hard to place.*

This study proposes a survey and demonstration project. . . . The survey part comes first, that is, to learn what families are most likely to be in a position to adopt non-white babies and *older children of both colors.* Once these families are located, interviews will be made to discover what they know about adoption possibilities and the nature of their attitudes towards adopting children.

From these findings, a workable operating plan will be prepared for the demonstration phase. The demonstration phase of the project will be . . . designed to bring in families who will request adoption of Black babies *or older children* under the care of the Court. Actual method or methods used will be developed from the survey findings which also might determine a permanent program of operation for the country.

It is difficult to estimate the length of time required for the survey part of the project but a maximum period of one year should be arranged for. It the results are secured in less time, the demonstration phase could immediately be undertaken. It is believed that the demonstration or casefinding period should cover 12 months. A shorter period would be inadequate time to thoroughly test the operating procedures derived from the survey findings. . . . [Emphasis ours]

The inclusion of older white children in the project illustrates the extent to which the program had been distorted: it indicates a very fundamental change in the approach to the problem. Where the Urban League had previously demonstrated how the system itself was contributing to the children's plight, it had now bought the "hard-to-place" concept, a concept which basically places the problem *with the children,* not with the system or the agencies. The concept does disservice to both the Black and the white children. Since it leaves no room for consideration of *how* the services are operating to their disadvantage, it allows no potential for change which would obviate the problems. In Kansas City, as elsewhere, there was no basis for a belief that the same dysfunctional aspects of the system were responsible for the plight of the Black children and the "older white children." The lumping together of both precluded examination of just how the white children had gotten older without being served adequately—a difficulty that could hardly be entirely resident in them. The projected survey no longer focused on the agencies and the system; it had become only a study of the people, the potential applicants. Webster went on to describe this aspect: "Community Studies . . . will conduct the two-year study . . . in two phases; one will be an attitude study of potential adoptive parents; the second phase of the demonstration project, to actually place children for adoption and to develop methods for a permanent plan for adoption for Jackson County."

On August 18, 1955, Webster sent the National Office a copy of the completed survey. The survey exhibited the ethnocentrism demonstrated by all too many white researchers in attempting to develop answers about Black people. The question they asked was, "What is the potential pool of adoptive applicants for Black children?" The way they answered it was to compare Black households in the city with white households on a number of characteristics. The underlying assumption was that the number of Black adoptive applicants could be determined from the number of Black households that did not deviate from the general patterning of white households—*i.e.,* that would meet white standards. They found differences. But they did not recommend many agency changes to adapt to these differences. For example, a larger proportion of Black women worked; they recommended that when a Black working mother and her husband applied for a baby, the income standard should be $4,000 instead of $5,000 annual income—to allow for the $1,000 loss of income that would occur when the mother stopped working. Community Studies did not consider changing the standards so that the mother could continue to work—a change which would have screened in many couples. The study did recommend, however, that the age limitations be raised for Black couples.

Of course, in view of its own findings two years before, the Urban League was disappointed by the results of the survey. It now wished to shift rapidly to the demonstration project—the action that would actually place Black children in homes.

On July 16, 1955, a local newspaper announced that the Juvenile Court Judge had appointed a Citizens' Committee to direct a campaign for more widespread adoption of children in Jackson County institutions and foster homes: "The Committee is aiming at finding real homes and legal parents for children who have been made wards of the Juvenile Court and are being maintained at County expense. They range in age from a few months to 17 years." The Committee included a number of prominent people; *it did not include the Executive Director of the Urban League.* The Urban League Committee decided to work closely with this Citizen's Committee. The rest of the story is perhaps best told by Webster. At the close of the national project, the National Urban League sent out a questionnaire to its affiliates. One question was, "What problems have you met in this venture?" Webster's reply was: "Community Studies took over the Adoption project, and published three reports and was to advise us how we could work with the Citizens' Committee appointees. *Frequent inquiries have produced no response.*" The final step in the process was complete—the Urban League was excluded from the project it had initiated. No changes had been made in the adoption or child welfare systems, and no improvements had been made in the placement of Black children.

Lessons Learned from the National Urban League Project

The Kansas City experience in the National Urban League Foster Care and Adoptions Project is representative of events in many of the participating communities. Nevertheless, it is important not to underrate the ultimate impact of this extensive project. The benefits to Black children cannot be measured solely in terms of tangible results, such as numbers of children placed, but must also include the social-psychological forces which such an endeavor can engender. It was the first—and the last—national effort on behalf of homeless Black children. As such the national results deserve scrutiny. When the seeds of social change are planted, they may dry up, like Langston Hughes' "Raisin in the Sun." Or they may germinate and sprout at a later time in history.

Benefits of a Black-Specific Effort.

The immediate tangible results of the various affiliate projects were the numbers of children placed in permanent adoptive homes. The absolute numbers were less than overwhelming; however, in most of the participating cities the number of Black children given permanent adoptive homes increased by one-fourth to one-half in the years 1953 and 1954, the most active years of the project. If we consider that between 1959 and 1967 the percentage of nonwhite children adopted throughout the nation *remained constant* (9 percent of all nonrelative adoptions), such increases in a two-year period are indeed amazing.

What may have been of greater importance than the immediate placements were the effects of the project on many, many more children, for many years to come. These benefits stemmed from the social-psychological impact of the project activity. The Urban League had firmly implanted in these communities the *expectation that Black children could and should be adopted*. Up to this time there had been no widespread expectation on the part of white or Black communities, or white or Black agencies, that adoption was a reasonable solution for homeless Black children. Though the expectation is still unfulfilled, there has been no retreat from it since the time of the Urban League activity. This expectation is directly related to the overriding philosophy of the National Urban League and its affiliates: that Black children should be served in the same manner as white children—and should receive the same *forms of service,* including adoption. As we saw in Chapter 5, adoption was hardly ever mentioned during the 1940's as a solution to the problems of Black children, even babies. These benefits, both short- and long-range, accrue largely to the fact that the effort was focused specifically on Black children.

Failure to Dispel the Rationales of Racism.

Two racist myths should have been shattered by the Urban League experience. However, a quick perusal of the child welfare literature in the last twenty years testifies that myths die hard. The first is the ever-present myth that illegitimacy bears no stigma in the Black community, and the second is that the Black community takes care of all of its children. The Urban League affiliates, in community after community, repeatedly discovered Black children without permanent homes, a finding that should have dispelled this convenient mythology. There were thousands of Black babies and children under care of child welfare agencies and in need of permanent homes. These children were not being cared for by their mothers, whether married or unmarried, stigmatized or not stigmatized; and they were not being cared for by loving grandmothers, aunts, or neighbors. Whether there is a grain or more of truth in these myths—something nobody knows; whether Black people do or do not ascribe a high degree of stigma to the status of illegitimacy; whether Black people do or do not provide extraordinary mechanisms for the care of unrelated children; there are, and there will continue to be, Black children in need of parents.

The second benefit that should have accrued from the Urban League experiences was dispossession of the myth that Black families will not adopt. The Urban League demonstrated that adoptive homes could be found for Black children among Black families. If the number of children placed could double in one year, then why not in the next and the next? The impact of the increased exertion in recruiting Black homes was quickly erased. The most successful recruiting drives yielded many applicants, but relatively few homes, in part because of the agencies' rigid eligibility requirements, which yielded a high rejection rate, and in part because agency procedures encouraged Black applicants to withdraw their applications. Although the various Urban League affiliates repeatedly pinpointed factors in agency orientations and practice which created these situations and perpetuated them, only rarely did the agencies attempt to remedy their negative impact on Black applicants. The National Urban League projects almost universally failed to bring about these kinds of changes.

The Kansas City experience exemplifies a dominant theme in the child welfare field in relation to Black adoptions. The initial period of Black adoptions just after World War II was one of simply opening services to Black children who previously had been excluded. When these agencies were unable to place Black children as fast as white children, the agencies began to define the children and the families as "problems." The fact that the agencies had long excluded Black children and families, and thus were totally inexperienced in serving them, was quickly forgotten. The children were "hard to place"; the families were "hard to reach." In other words the "problems" became: (1) "What's wrong with Black children? They don't get themselves adopted"; and (2) "What's wrong with Black families? They don't adopt children." From that point on, all the energies, and especially the research energies, were directed toward these questions. That the questions themselves might have been the wrong questions was rarely considered.

Goals and Strategies Employed.

INVOLVEMENT OF THE BLACK COMMUNITY. There is one characteristic of the National Urban Leage approach that perhaps contributed to the failure to dispel these myths. As was typical of the Urban League, the affiliates served as advocates for and representatives of the Black community. True, one of the more lasting results of the project was the founding of many Black auxiliaries and volunteer groups. But involvement of this kind is not very different from the kind of Black involvement that is still being offered by white agencies and that is still failing to produce very tangible results. It is involvement as recipient, as client. The Urban League affiliates did not involve their

Black communities in control, direction, and planning. They were not involved in the life of Black people and the Black experience. Unfortunately, neither the many studies by the Urban Leagues nor their actions to place Black children enlightened us very much about the real attitudes, values, and standards in various parts of the Black community toward the phenomena of relinquishment and adoption of babies. In fact, very little light was shed on the intricate subcultural milieu of the participants in this very basic human drama. In part this was because the Urban League projects were not conceived, designed, or staffed with this in mind. But it was also partly because the Black community was meaningfully involved in these projects *as a community.*

INTEGRATION. In all candor, it cannot be said that the primary goal of the Urban League was more adequate care for Black children. To be sure, more adequate care seemed an inevitable outcome of the attainment of integration, but the primary goal was that white institutions should cease discrimination, that they should treat Black children the same way that white children were treated. Unfortunately, the Urban League's strong insistence that the *same system* serving white children, *operating in the same way,* should serve Black children, had the ironic effect of actually strengthening the system and forestalling changes that would have made it more specific to the situation of Black children.

We do not wish to imply for a moment that those involved in this effort were not deeply concerned with the fate of Black dependent children. We maintain, however, that their concern was misguided, because it was not specific to Black children: it was a concern with all Black problems. And the Urban League, like many Black, and white, liberal organizations at the time, believed that racial integration was the solution to all of the problems—employment, education, dependent children, and all the others. More important, the League believed that integration was a readily attainable goal—a belief more deeply rooted in hope than in fact. With great faith, the Urban League thought it possible to change child welfare agencies into institutions that would and could serve the needs of all the children of its communities without regard to race, creed, or color, or previous condition of servitude. This philosophy limited the possible array of solutions that could be developed for Black children, for it precluded the development of direct services by the Urban League and by other Black groups and organizations.

The strategies traditionally employed by the Urban League also played a part in cutting off alternative solutions. The Urban League was an advocate, planner, and coordinator, and its strategies were predicated on the belief that reason and morality, understanding and persuasion would eventually triumph.

During the life of the project none of the affiliates engaged in activist strategies for social change. Although other organizations were using them increasingly, the Urban League engaged in no petitions, protests, or court cases. Nor was the NAACP's expertise in legal remedies called upon. At that time the Urban League seemed to be using impeccable means to a given end, but from our historical perspective they seem more limited. As the 1960's came to a close, many advocates of social reform had come to believe that more power must be mustered on the side of justice, and that exclusive reliance on reason and persuasion might be inappropriate. This lesson had been learned in large part from experiences like the Urban League project.

THE MAINTENANCE OF WHITE CONTROL. Both the successes and the failures of the National Urban League project are in part attributable to the underlying philosophy and goal: that Black children should be served in the same way and by the same system as white children. The League's enormous dedication to this goal produced the patient and persistent efforts which led to the placement of many hundreds of children. But the same single-mindedness also closed the door to alternative solutions and strategies which might have had more lasting and far-reaching results. Ultimately, however, the National Urban League was not responsible for its failures. Nowhere did the white child welfare agencies, public or private, enter into the effort to place Black children in permanent homes with enthusiasm and wholehearted commitment. They were reluctant partners at best. The same may be said of the local welfare councils. Even in communities where they actively participated, none was willing to surrender or even share control. This very fundamental aspect of racism, white control, remained intact.

ADOPT-A-CHILD

In 1953, the same year the National Urban League launched its project, several Black social workers in New York City had already started a series of discussions which led eventually to the first city-wide coordinated effort to place Black and Puerto Rican children in adoptive homes.

The origins of this special project were described in November, 1954 by Edward S. Lewis, of the New York Urban League. In a memorandum, he wrote:

> Almost two years ago . . . Mrs. Camille Jeffers [a nationally prominent Black social worker, then on the New York League staff] set up an appointment for me with several representatives of the adoption agencies in New York City.
>
> I thought it would be relatively easy to discourage this group from attempting to tackle the problem of adoption placements for Black kids, by pointing out the magnitude of the problem and indicating that it would cost a lot of money in New York City. They were not, however, discouraged. They then asked for my suggestions for other projects and indicated that money would be forthcoming.
>
> Very much to my surprise, the representatives of the agencies became enthusiastic about this idea and began to discuss it with similar organizations. This enthusiasm was apparently transmitted to them and led to a series of meetings in which various aspects of the project were discussed. In due course, committees were formed and two foundations, The Field Foundation and the New York Fund for Children, gave a total of $48,000 for this special effort.
>
> One of the unique features of this project is that every major adoption agency, cutting across religious and sectarian lines, is represented. According to the observation of one committee member, and a member of the New York Fund, this is the first time in her experience that she has seen all of the top agencies in the adoption field uniting around a single purpose such as this one. I had earlier pointed out the difficulties in connection with this sectarian approach to social work in New York and indicated that if it were possible for Catholic and Jewish children to be adopted in decent homes, these two groups should get together and eliminate the final block where Black and Puerto Rican children stay in hospitals for months and even years without ever being given an opportunity for a normal family life and development.

Once the grants had been received, Adopt-A-Child was founded, in January, 1955. It was established as a three-year pilot project to increase the number of homes for children of minority backgrounds.

Adopt-A-Child was interracial and interfaith and represented thirteen public and private adoption agencies in New York City and Nassau and Westchester Counties, and the Urban Leagues of Greater New York and Westchester County. In 1958 a fourteenth adoption agency, in Suffolk County, joined Adopt-A-Child. (Member agencies are listed in Table 6–1.)

The purpose of Adopt-A-Child was to develop and implement methods of recruiting adoptive families for children of Black, Puerto Rican, and mixed racial ancestry in New York City and the surrounding areas, and to coordinate interagency cooperation. It was to experiment with various techniques in home finding and share its findings with member agencies.

Before the end of the three-year demonstration period, Adopt-A-Child asked The Field Foundation and the New York Fund for Children to continue their contribution for another three-year period. This request was granted only in part, and lack of funds terminated the agency on December 31, 1959, after five years of operation.

Participants and Programs

The governing body of Adopt-A-Child was the Board of Directors, consisting of lay and agency representatives, which acted in an advisory capacity. An executive committee composed of adoption agency executives and the officers of the Board of Directors directed operations. For the first three years of its operation, the Adopt-A-Child staff consisted of an Executive Director, a part-time public relations consultant, and an office secretary. At the beginning of the fourth year (1958) a full-time referral and clearance worker was added to the staff, but this part of the project was not underwritten for the year 1959.

The responsibilities of the Executive Director were to develop and implement techniques for disseminating information about adoption to the community, and to work with the member agencies for a better understanding of the community. The referral and clearance worker's responsibilities were to give information to families, refer families to the adoption agencies, operate a clearance service, and work with the Executive Director in the community education program. In September, 1959, when William Jackson, the Executive Director, left to become Dean of the Graduate School of Social Work at Atlanta

TABLE 6-1

Member Agencies of Adopt-A-Child

Adoption Service of Westchester
17 Longview Avenue
White Plains, New York 10605

Angel Guardian Home for Little
 Children
6301 Twelfth Avenue
Brooklyn, New York 11219

Catholic Home Bureau
132 East 22nd Street
New York, New York 10010

Louise Wise Services
10-12 East 94th Street
New York, New York 10028

Lutheran Child Welfare Association
422 West 44th Street
New York, New York 10018

Nassau County Department of
 Welfare
Old County Court House
Mineola, New York 11501

New York City Department of
 Welfare
2 Lafayette Street
New York, New York 10007

New York Foundling Hospital
1175 Third Avenue
New York, New York 10021

Sheltering Arms Children's Service
122 East 29th Street
New York, New York 10016

Spence-Chapin Adoption Service
6 East 94th Street
New York, New York 10028

State Charities Aid Association
105 East 22nd Street
New York, New York 10010

Suffolk County Department of
 Public Welfare
75 Fourth Avenue
Bay Shore, New York 11706

Talbot-Perkins Adoption Service
108 Willow Street
Brooklyn, New York 11201

Westchester County Department
 of Welfare
424 County Court Building
White Plains, New York

Urban League of Greater New York
204 West 136th Street
New York, New York 10035

Urban League of Westchester County
60 Union Avenue
New Rochelle, New York 10801

SOURCE: National Urban League Collection, Documents Room,
Library of Congress.

University, the referral and clearance worker, Ernestene Sells Roye, became the Executive Director.

A major mechanism for change was the Clearance Committee, on which all member agencies were represented. Its function was to promote interagency placements through committee discussions and sharing of information, so that a wider selection of children and families was made available for interagency placements.

Originally the Clearance Committee also conducted the clearance service. When Ernestene Sells Roye joined the staff, she took over the service, with the Clearance Committee acting in an advisory capacity. The goal of the clearance service was to arrange placements as quickly as possible. Regular monthly meetings of the Clearance Committee, and close contact with the clearance worker, helped agencies to work more closely together in finding families for children. At these "matching sessions" the agencies pooled information about families and children awaiting placement. Beginning in March, 1958, the clearance worker issued a monthly listing of children and families to encourage interagency exchanges. The number of children placed by the member agencies as a result of clearance service efforts between January, 1958, and December, 1959, was thirty-two. Over the three-year period prior to January, 1958, the total number placed through Clearance Committee efforts was thirty-six.

Community activities were a central feature of the Adopt-A-Child program. Hundreds of radio and television spot announcements, news stories, feature stories, and the like, were broadcast or published in newspapers and magazines. Three attractive and easily read brochures were prepared and widely distributed. Special displays and posters were placed in churches, banks, stores, beauty parlors, social agency offices, etc. A professional artist donated his work in developing the brochures and posters.

Special emphasis was given to reaching the Black and Puerto Rican communities, and Adopt-A-Child held many community meetings. Two were particularly large. The first of these, "The Community Conference" in November, 1955, was sponsored by several community groups and resulted in a decision to review agency policies. The second was the "Volunteers Workshop" held in March, 1958, which produced several community volunteers for Adopt-A-Child's program. Smaller meetings with Black religious, social, fraternal, and professional groups were held continually. Panels of adoptive parents and adoption workers appeared; movies, recordings, and slides were used, and discussion periods followed. Informal social gatherings ("At Homes") were held in the homes of interested community members who invited friends who were interested in adoption. "Open House" was held one evening a month at the Adopt-A-Child office. Families who requested information from Adopt-A-Child were invited to come and discuss their questions about adoption. Each Open House resulted in at least one referral.

Adopt-A-Child had an active volunteer program. Volunteers gave time to office work, distribution of literature, manning of displays, sponsoring "At Homes," and generally discussing adoption with friends. The agency also got adoptive parents to appear at panel discussions and on radio shows and to allow pictures to be used for publicity.

Most of the inquiries to Adopt-A-Child were made by telephone and letter by families residing in New York and neighboring states. Inquiries were also received from nearly all the other states, Puerto Rico, and the Virgin Islands. (See Table 6–2.) Regular follow-up contacts were made with families in the area and invitations extended to an Open House or individual appointments arranged.

Between May and August, 1959, Adopt-A-Child conducted two special follow-up programs. The first concerned thirty-six selected families who had previously made inquiries to Adopt-A-Child. Twenty-nine of the families were reached; their questions were answered, and adoption procedures and practices were interpreted for them. Three of these families were referred to agencies, and one placement was made. The second follow-up program concerned eighty-four selected families referred to agencies by Adopt-A-Child in 1956 and 1957 who had withdrawn from the agencies. Twenty-nine of the families were reached. Thirteen explained that they were not ready because of financial or housing problems or the indecision of one spouse; five said they were still interested; five said they did not understand the procedures after explanation by Adopt-A-Child and an agency; three were no longer interested because of pregnancy or having taken a child privately; three did not respond. Of the five still interested, one family consulted an adoption agency but no child was placed.

For a year before the Adopt-A-Child office closed, preparations were under way to continue the overall efforts it had originated. The Board recommended (as had Channing Tobias in 1939!) that the

TABLE 6–2

Inquiries to and Referrals by Adopt-A-Child, 1955–1959

Inquiries Received	Adoption	Other[a]	Total
Geographic distribution of inquiries			
Metropolitan Area	2249	300	2549
Upstate New York	456	5	461
Other states[b]	1470	5	1475
Total	4175	310	4485
Disposition of inquiries			
Referred to member adoption agencies	1134		1134
Referred to other local agencies[c]		270	270
Referred to out-of-state agencies	865	18	883
Total inquiries referred	1999	288	2287
Total inquiries not referred[d]	2176	22	2198
Total	4175	310	4485

[a] Foster care, services to unmarried mothers, and other social services.
[b] Includes out of country.
[c] Includes foster-care, maternity, family-service, and other social agencies.
[d] Includes inquiries which had insufficient information for referral; inquiries for information with requests that referral be made at that time; and requests for information only.

SOURCE: National Urban League Collection, Documents Room, Library of Congress.

public agencies of the state and city be asked to assume more responsibility in this area, since the majority of the children were public charges. The agencies did in fact take on additional responsibility for placing children of minority backgrounds, for family recruitment, and for a clearance service. The clearance service functioned actively for several years. The Board of Directors and Executive Committee continued as a body to encourage all the agencies to extend their services in behalf of minority-group children.

Recommendations for Institutional Reform

One of the major contributions of the Adopt-A-Child project was a set of recommendations drawn up in May of 1956. Many of these recommendations are still not generally accepted in the adoptions field, some fifteen years later. Still others are considered revolutionary or professionally unsound. But a few have been adopted by almost all agencies that have a special interest in the placement of Black children. Many seem to make so much sense, it is a wonder they caused so much controversy in the mid-1950's. These recommendations attest directly to the kind of institutional reform which was desperately required of the established adoptions agencies. They were addressed not only to the member agencies of Adopt-A-Child, but to the adoption field in general.

1. Group Meetings

   That the agencies experiment with the use of group meetings with Negro and Puerto Rican families to determine their need and effectiveness.

2. Use of the Same Worker to Complete the Home Study

   That the same worker be assigned to the family throughout the study, wherever possible.

3. Evening, Saturday, and Sunday Interviews

   That the adoption agencies provide evening, Saturday, and Sunday interviews in an effort to accommodate families who are unable to keep appointments during the agencies' regular office hours.

4. Minimum Income Requirement

   That it be publicized in the Black and Puerto Rican communities that the adoption agencies, in general, do not have minimum income and savings requirements. However, families must be self-supporting.

5. Age Requirements

   That the age requirement for Black and Puerto Rican families be more flexible and that this be publicized in the community and be made clear to applicants by the caseworker in the first interview.

6. Medical Examination

   That the adoption agencies, in recognizing a lag or bottleneck in many cases around the returning of medical reports, might assist families by helping to provide access to low-cost, community medical services.

7. Sterility

That the medical certificate of sterility should not be required.

8. Fees

That the adoption agencies use a flexible and realistic approach to application of a fee system. They should bear in mind the socioeconomic factors operating in most Black and Puerto Rican communities, not only in relation to wage and income scales, but actual living costs.

9. Verification of Marriage and Birth

That it be publicized and interpreted to the community that certification of marriage and birth are legal requirements of the courts which must be fulfilled by the agency before adoption is approved by the court.

10. Working Wives

That the employment of the wife is not a barrier to adoptive placement.

11. Placement of Children in Congested Areas

That the approval of a home for placement should be based on the adequacy of the living conditions and relationships in the home. No family should be refused solely on the basis of neighborhood.

Some of the member agencies adopted some of these recommendations; some of them adopted none. No agency adopted all of them.

Progress and Problems

In the fourth year of Adopt-A-Child operation, the total number of placements of children of minority background in New York was 204, an increase of almost 100 percent. In the fifth year the total number of placements was 237, more than 100 percent over 1954, the year before Adopt-A-Child was established. These data are shown in Table 6–3.

This success was wrought in spite of the massively irrelevant professional standards and bureaucratic rigidities which the adoptive agencies applied to Black families who were seeking to adopt Black children. For example, most agencies set an age limit for adoptive

TABLE 6–3

Number of Placements of Minority Children by the Fourteen Adoption Agencies Affiliated with Adopt-A-Child, 1954–1959

| | Before Adopt-A-Child | | Joint Effort Through Adopt-A-Child | | | | |
	1954	1955	1956	1957	1958	1959	Total
Black	76	84	109	156	142	166	657
Puerto Rican	26	29	30	12	24	37	132
Asian (Including mixed racial)	6	13	13	8	9	26	69
Other	7	9	13	10	29	8	69
Total	115	135	165	186	204	237	927

SOURCE: National Urban League Collection, Documents Room, Library of Congress.

applicants; the agencies generally required a separate room for the child and an adequately maintained neighborhood; and some agencies required financial reserves or a minimum income. As a final example of the agencies' unproductive practices, the family study period was long, often covering several months and sometimes more than a year. In view of these and similar rigidities, Adopt-A-Child's success is indeed impressive.

Change came very painfully and very slowly even in the face of innovative ideas advanced by the staff and Board of Adopt-A-Child. For example, by 1958, some agencies had accepted the idea of working mothers. However, the adoptive working mother was expected to be at home for the months between the time the child was placed and the time he was legally adopted.

Relations Between Adopt-A-Child and the Agencies

Despite the elaborate communications system connecting Adopt-A-Child and the regular adoption agencies, and the efforts of all concerned to present a unified interracial, interreligious, and interagency front, theirs was an often suspicious, sometimes hostile, and very precarious alliance. There was a built-in, consistent conflict of interest. The staff and Board of Adopt-A-Child often acted from its identification with the Black community and on the basis of the cultural and socioeconomic realities of that community. These realities were by and large foreign to the experience and contrary to the expectations of the policy-makers and administrators of the white adoption agencies. Many, including some Black professionals, did not recognize the legitimacy of an effort specific to Black children and the Black community. For them there were some children out there, who just happened to be Black, who needed the best homes they could find. And "best" was defined in terms of white, middle-class standards, preferences, and conditions. For example, the agencies did not permit the advertising of Adopt-A-Child to say that Black families were desired for Black children; it could say only that families were desired for Black children. A more serious result of the adoption agencies' color-blindness was their reluctance to place Black babies in Black families and Black communities that did not meet white, middle-class standards. A staff report from Adopt-A-Child stressed this aspect of the problems between itself and the established agencies:

> The working wife, families living in concentrated and congested areas, and advanced age of couples applying for adoption are some of the realities which the adoption agencies must accept when considering Black and Puerto Rican families for adoption. This does not refer to the lowering of necessary standards which relate to the health and emotional tone of the people. It refers to the acceptance of the socioeconomic realities in which people must live.

The agencies maintained their autonomy, and in particular their authority to deal with the families recruited by Adopt-A-Child in any way they wished. They turned them down wholesale. During the first ten months of intensive and enthusiastic action by Adopt-A-Child, 240 Black and Puerto Rican families applied to Adopt-A-Child. Of this number only six were "awarded" children by member agencies. Only half of those referred were processed by the agencies. These sorry facts once again demonstrate the way progress is barred by failure to yield control.

Still another manifestation of the strained relation between Adopt-A-Child and its affiliated agencies was their difference over the size of the problem. Adopt-A-Child, through careful if informal research, estimated that there were 2,000 Black and Puerto Rican children available for adoption in October, 1955. This estimate was supported by Justice Justine Wise Polier. At the Action on Adoption Conference, November 19, 1955, she stated:

> If we examined the records of our Negro and Puerto Rican children in long-term care in our institutions and foster homes, we would find that this estimate (2,000) . . . was low and did not include many older children, children with physical or emotional problems whom we therefore, are satisfied to designate as "too hard to place". [Adopt-A-Child report, in National Urban League records]

The established agencies, however, mounted a "quiet, but overt and concerted effort to challenge these figures whenever and wherever the occasion presented itself." The Department of Public Welfare joined in this effort. It issued a report saying, for example, that there were only 408 Black and Puerto Rican children available "on referral" during that period. The battle of numbers was intense.

The established agencies resisted in other ways the aggressive and committed advocacy of Adopt-A-Child on behalf of adoptable Black children. An Adopt-A-Child staff report observed:

> Originally, Adopt-A-Child was conceived as a community centered approach to homefinding, using community organization methods. However, it was discovered later that some of the agencies considered community organization methods mainly that of promotion. The presentation of facts either by mass media or speaking before small groups was highly acceptable.
>
> It was, and still is, difficult for some of the agencies to accept and participate in an interactive experience with representative community persons and groups. Moreover, the agencies found it even more difficult to accept as part of the

community organization process, the testing of their theories and methods that they now take for granted.

It should be noted that this was the kind of community organization effort so often missing in the National Urban League projects.

The adoption agencies' traditional secrecy about their criteria for adequate adoptive parents was still another source of strain; selection criteria were not even shared with Adopt-A-Child, which was recruiting families for them. There was also conflict over the goals of recruitment. Many of the adoption agencies considered the referrals from Adopt-A-Child as a "windfall"; that is, they used the referrals from Adopt-A-Child to select a family for an individual Black child more carefully, rather than to place additional children.

Interpersonal strains were frequent in the relations between the Adopt-A-Child staff and volunteers on the one hand, and the casework staffs of the adoption agencies on the other. With staffs of some agencies the Adopt-A-Child staff had a "mutual exchange of ideas and experiences" which resulted in "strong, warm, and confiding relationships." With most of the agencies, however, there was little of this sharing and exchange. Consequently, the relations, though "professionally correct," were formal, distant, and often reflected mutual distrust. The lofty "commitment" and "cooperation" in statements of executive directors and of official agency policy were revealed as hypocritical by the actions of established agency caseworkers. Such contradictions were a striking feature and a continual problem in the project.

Many of these conflicts reached a peak when some of the agency representatives tried to withdraw the autonomy exercised by Adopt-A-Child, which allowed it to speak out on matters of adoption in ways which conflicted with individual agency preferences. This move took place despite the fact that Adopt-A-Child had agency representatives on its Board and generally acted and spoke on the basis of a majority opinion of its Board members. A staff report remarked with a certain amount of passion,

> Some of the agencies expressed concern over the fact that Adopt-A-Child is autonomous. They would have preferred to see the project subordinated to one of the adoption agencies. Then it would be possible to control the program and activities of the project. As it stands now, these agencies resent the fact that Adopt-A-Child now acts and speaks for all the

agencies in areas which were the domain of the individual agencies. As an action-research project, Adopt-A-Child tries to find within the community and in the cooperating adoption agencies, the strengths on which to build and the weaknesses that can be modified to bring about a maximum response from the community. An attempt to pursue the problem objectively has been interpreted by some of the agencies as deliberate attempts by Adopt-A-Child to embarrass and attack the affiliated adoption agencies. This defensiveness is one of the ways the agencies protect what they feel is their prerogative to resist change, not recognizing that it distorts their perception and judgment.

Alignment in such conflicts did not always follow racial lines. The activities of Adopt-A-Child often proved embarrassing to some of the very few Black caseworkers scattered among the fourteen adoption agencies. Some, though not all, and perhaps not even a majority, expressed the view that Adopt-A-Child was "lowering standards" for Black children. These Black professionals insisted that Black families "measure up" to the standards of adoption which had been set by white agencies and which they had accepted as valid. Some Black workers were more rigid than some white workers in this regard. One said vehemently that she did not believe in "coddling" families "just because they are Negroes." A number of Black workers strongly opposed the establishment, continuance, and operation of Adopt-A-Child on the grounds that its specific focus on Black and Puerto Rican children made it a "Jim Crow" agency. Such misunderstanding on the part of otherwise very enlightened people is a frequent concomitant to any specialized effort on behalf of Black children. However, as the project proceeded, was accepted in the general community, and showed enormous success, the resistance of the Black workers diminished. It must be said in this connection that there was strong Black support in the profession at large and in the community for Adopt-A-Child.

ADOPT-A-CHILD AND THE NATIONAL URBAN LEAGUE PROJECT—SUCCESSES OR FAILURES?

We have already recorded the principal successes of the National Urban League project—the numbers of children placed, and the less tangible, but more far-reaching social and psychological gains in the creation of the expectation that Black children could and would be adopted. We have noted also its failures: it did not change the systems of care which blocked service to Black children and it did not remove or diminish white control over these systems. Adopt-A-Child also placed hundreds of Black children in permanent adoptive homes and had even greater efficacy in changing expectations in New York City regarding adoptions. Both endeavors were more successful than the efforts recorded in Chapter 5, particularly those led by the agents of white child welfare. They were more successful partly because they were attempts to change the existing system—to open a new form of service for Black children.

Adopt-A-Child was more successful than any of the individual Urban League projects. It also came closer to challenging the basic racism in the child welfare system, and was the more radical project. It was more radical in that it rendered a direct service specifically for Black children, as the Urban League projects had not. While many of the Urban League efforts had participated directly in the recruitment of adoptive applicants, Adopt-A-Child went a giant step further. Where work through existing agencies had been the overriding idea of the Urban League, Adopt-A-Child was an agency in its own right. It went beyond simply recruiting applicants, to dealing directly with them, screening them and referring them. Thus Adopt-A-Child was also more radical than the Urban League in the relatively autonomous character of the agency. Adopt-A-Child challenged the usual way of doing business at that time in New York City. It brought together into one coordinated effort the disparate interests of the powerful sectarian and voluntary agencies. As we have just seen, Adopt-A-Child's very autonomy was both the key to its successes and a contributor to its demise. The agency's autonomy led to clashes with the member agencies that resented it. Perhaps these very clashes indicate the greater success of Adopt-A-Child than of the Urban League affiliates. Too often the admirable spirit of cooperation evidenced by the Urban League led to cooptation, obliteration of goals, and inaction; but it seldom led to open conflict.

Oddly enough, neither of these pioneering efforts by Black workers and professionals for Black children is often mentioned today. The Urban League project, unique in its national scope, is all but forgotten. Adopt-A-Child is sometimes mentioned in textbooks and by child welfare experts. But it is mentioned as a failure. Even some of the participating agencies, which spurned the specific advice of Adopt-A-Child to change their modes of operation, recall the project as a

failure. Adopt-A-Child is considered a failure because it did not produce very many Black applicants who met agency standards and who
ultimately adopted children. Some have even used Adopt-A-Child as
"evidence" that there are not sufficient adoptive parents for Black
children and that further efforts on their behalf should be abandoned.
We challenge this interpretation. That the program did not result in
"very many" adoptive homes is true. But the failure was not that of
Adopt-A-Child. The failure was the agencies', and their failure lay in
their unwillingness to yield control.

Consider the number of applicants referred by the Adopt-A-Child
workers, and the number accepted by the agencies. Consider the fact
that more than half of the referrals were not even processed by the
participating agencies. Adopt-A-Child itself was channeling and sort-
ing the potential applicants—and was obviously acting with a high
degree of discretion and judgment. Why, then, we must ask, was
there such extensive weeding out, which evidently resulted in the loss
of hundreds of homes for Black children? The failure to yield control
over the final selection of applicants, or even to modify the process,
was in many ways a direct rejection of the judgment of the Adopt-A-
Child staff. We do not think that the relatively small numbers of adoptions completed are evidence of failure by Adopt-A-Child or of a
dearth of interest in adoption on the part of the Black community.
The failure reflects, rather, the basic racism inherent in the system,
the persistent maintenance of total control by white-dominated
agencies.

We must ask still another question. What might have happened had
Adopt-A-Child been a fully autonomous effort, a complete agency
unto itself? What might have happened if, when the white agencies
refused to share control, Adopt-A-Child had taken control and established an autonomous Black agency? Perhaps then many of the applicants found unacceptable by the agencies making the ultimate decisions would have received children, and many many more children
would have found their way into permanent, loving homes.

SUMMARY

In this chapter we have described two major reform measures initiated
from the Black community with a major leadership role being played
by Black professionals. These two efforts were somewhat more suc-

cessful than earlier efforts had been, in part because the major reformers were more aware of and realistic about the nature of childhood and family life in the Black community, and because they were
abler and more willing to point up some of the essential dysfunctions
in the general system of child welfare services. These reform measures
led by Black professionals were able to shatter the foundations of
many of the myths about the Black community and their patterns of
child care. At the same time, they demonstrated that the major obstacles preventing the child welfare agencies from serving Black children were an inadequate philosophy and structure of services supported and perpetuated by the established economic and political
interests, rather than the alleged lack of interest, motivation, suit-
ability, or need on the part of Black children and families. The success
of these reforms was severely limited, however. Part of the reason was
the integrationist ideology which informed and permeated these efforts.
Even the Black reformers were victimized by the Anglo-conformist
doctrine that white modes, culture, and institutions are the best for all
children without regard to race, creed, or color. But their success
was much more severely limited by the intransigence of the established
agencies, which resisted change at every hand. Thus, in the face of the
most convincing research showing exclusion of and discrimination
against Black children, and in the face of airtight reasoning, eloquent
rhetoric, and impassioned religious fervor, the established agencies
and their agents refused to expand their services to meet the needs of
Black children on any basis which even remotely approached equity
with their efforts on behalf of white children. One of the most important lessons which emerges during the 1950's was that additional
weapons of change must be used to supplement—if not replace altogether—research, rhetoric, reason, and religion in bringing about
the social changes which will enable Black children to benefit equally
from the rewards, protections, and services offered by the major institutions of their society. It was clear from the National Urban League
project and Adopt-A-Child experiences that new and different weapons were necessary for substantial social change—the weapons of
political power, economic power, and social power of a variety of
types.

7

Extending adoptive services to black children, 1960-1970

In the later 1950's, a few adoption agencies began to respond to the "crisis" of Black children in need of parents. Increasing numbers of Black mothers, freed from the social constraints which had previously bound them, began leaving their newborn babies behind in hospital wards for adoption. These "boarder babies," so called because they were in hospitals only for their room and board and not for medical treatment, caught the imagination of some child welfare workers and of the general community. A number of white agencies began to cut through the knot of racism, bureaucracy, sectarianism, and professionalism which had for so long closed off adoption to Black babies. In 1968 we set out to study the most successful of these agencies—to analyze their innovations and to measure their success.*

* Our study was conducted under the joint auspices of the Metropolitan Applied Research Center in New York and the National Urban League. This chapter is a highly condensed version of a small portion of our original monograph, "Black Children in Need of Parents" (Manuscript, 1968.) At MARCH we benefited greatly from the searching and critical questions and suggestions

Our purpose was to examine in detail efforts at change which had been specifically undertaken to improve and expand services to Black children. In selecting the agencies for study we were, therefore, guided by the criteria of innovation and some demonstrable measure of success. By a "successful" agency we meant one which had made dramatic increases in the numbers of Black children placed in permanent homes (giving evidence of change within its own operation) or one which, relative to its peers, was placing high numbers of Black children. We sought, in effect, to study agencies which were assuming a leadership role in the placement of Black children. Those we chose to study were undoubtedly among the leaders in this field, but they were not the only ones. There were other agencies, across the nation, which even at that time had approached the number of placements of those we selected.

The agencies we studied are located in four large northern and western urban centers with substantial Black populations, a circumstance which influenced their assumption of leadership, and which in turn renders their experiences particularly relevant to other agencies similarly located. They were: in New York City, the Louise Wise Services, the New York Foundling Hospital, the Division of Adoption of the New York City Department of Public Social Services, and the Spence-Chapin Adoption Service; in Chicago, the Child Care Society and the Children's Division of the Cook County Department of Public Aid; in Los Angeles, the Los Angeles County Department of Adoptions; and finally, in Philadelphia, the Women's Christian Alliance.

THE STRUCTURES OF CHANGE: THE AGENCIES

These eight agencies were all making outstanding contributions to the adoption of Black children in their communities. Yet they were a very diverse group of organizations, both in auspices and in the relative proportion of Black children among those served by the agency.

of Kenneth B. Clark. At the same time we benefited immensely from the advice and assistance of Hylan Lewis. At the Urban League our work was facilitated by Whitney Young, Jr., Betti Whaley, Jeweldean Londa, Leonore Tate, and Morris Grant, who enabled us to find our way around New York and the National Urban League, and into the hearts of a dedicated band of social workers. We were aided in our selection of agencies by the United States Children's Bureau and the Child Welfare League. None of these associates are responsible, however, for our analysis or interpretations of our data.

Auspices of the Agencies

Three of the agencies were public. The Los Angeles County Department of Adoptions, inaugurated in 1947 as the first public adoption service in California, was unique in that it was a separate department, rather than a unit within a public welfare department. The Division of Adoptions of the New York City Department of Public Social Services originated in 1957, with a specific mandate to serve "hard-to-place" children—especially Black children. The third public adoption service, the Children's Division of the Cook County Department of Public Aid, was launched in 1958, specifically to render adoption services to children who were already in foster homes.

Two sectarian agencies were included. The Louise Wise Services, founded in 1916, was a Jewish agency focused on the field of adoptions. This agency's extension of services to Black children was a landmark venture in breaking through the rigid bonds of sectarianism which long characterized the New York City child welfare system. The New York Foundling Hospital was a Roman Catholic institution dating back to 1869, which began placing significant numbers of Black Catholic children in adoptive homes in 1966.

The two nonsectarian private agencies, the Spence-Chapin Adoption Service in New York City and the Chicago Child Care Society, had very different origins. The Spence-Chapin agency was born in the merger of two private adoption agencies in the early 1920's. Being a nonsectarian agency in New York, its responsibility to Protestant children had always included a responsibility to Black children. But it was not until the late 1950's that the agency began to fulfill that responsibility in any significant way. The Chicago Child Care Society originated as the Chicago Orphan Asylum in 1849. This agency's efforts to extend adoption to Black children began in 1955, when it launched its "Negro Adoption Project."

The Women's Christian Alliance differed from all of the others in that it was created and sustained by the Black community in Philadelphia. Chartered as a child-placing agency in 1926, it was incorporated in 1941 and a Board of Directors established. The Board had always had a Black president; in 1968 twenty-six of its members were Black, while five were white. There was no stated policy on acceptance of children who were not Black. However, the agency had never been asked to take a white child. The agency was a creation of the Black community, expressly for Black children, directed and staffed predominantly by Black people.

The Women's Christian Alliance

Because the Women's Christian Alliance was and always had been a Black agency, its entry into the Black adoptions field presented somewhat different problems, and was accomplished by somewhat different techniques, from the problems and techniques encountered in the other agencies studied. For example, "entry" into the Black community presented no difficulties. For this reason we shall discuss the Alliance briefly here before examining the problems and techniques that were common to the other agencies.

The Women's Christian Alliance began its adoption program in 1959. At that time in Philadelphia, all adoptions of Protestant children were channelled through a single agency. Although there was no direct policy excluding Black children from the service, that agency had never served them in substantial numbers. The Women's Christian Alliance had referred a few Black babies to the agency, but none had been accepted, and in some instances the Alliance had received no reply at all. Black children were not considered "hard-to-place," but rather unadoptable. Then in 1959 the Alliance surveyed the children under care in foster homes, and found that 359 children were legally free for adoption. Many were, of course, older children, and some were physically handicapped. Many others, however, were infants or very young children free of any special needs. The first year after the survey the Alliance placed six of these children in adoptive homes. A foundation grant was secured to extend the project for three years, and in 1964 the agency was approved by the Department of Welfare of the Commonwealth of Pennsylvania as an adoption agency, meeting local and state standards.

By 1968 the adoption program was placing about twenty-five children a year. This was not an astounding number, but other agencies in Philadelphia rarely placed more than five or ten Black children a year at most.

Proportion of Black Children Served

The agencies differed not only in auspices but in the relative proportion of Black children among those placed for adoption. As Table 7–1 shows, the agencies fell into three major patterns. The first pattern was a high volume of total placements with a low proportion of Black children placed. The second was a relatively low volume of total placements and a high proportion of Black children. Finally there was the third pattern—a relatively low volume of placements, one hundred percent Black.

With the exception of Los Angeles County, which had an extraordinarily high volume of placements, the absolute numbers of Black children placed were not dramatically different from one type of agency to another. The relative figures did differ dramatically, however: in Type I agencies, the proportion of Black children placed ranged from 8.9 percent to 11.8 percent; in Type II agencies, from 49.5 percent to 56.5 percent; and in the Type III agency, 100 percent.

The range of agency types is indeed broad, and suggests that success in placing Black children is not limited to any single category of participation. If anything, these figures indicate that the extension and improvement of adoptive services to Black children can come about only through a variety of approaches, with different types of agencies playing different roles in relation to the total effort. These agencies ran the gamut of existing adoption services: they were public and private, sectarian and nonsectarian, and large and small; and a range of racial proportions were represented. If there was such variation among these leaders, it appears that all existing adoption agencies can extend their services to Black children successfully.

All of these agencies had made a deliberate commitment to the extension of adoption services to Black children. In this sense, they surpassed many institutions and organizations in the child welfare field. But at the time of our study all were grappling with the problems of fulfilling that commitment, and of sustaining it. In essence, all of these agencies' experiences testified to the need for such deliberate commitment, and at the same time to the insufficiency of that commitment. Commitment must be accompanied by relentless, vigorous, and sometimes painful changes, both fundamental and superficial, at every level of the organization's structure and operation. These agencies were all engaged at this level; they were far ahead of their field, but they were far behind their expressed goals. No agency expressed satisfaction with its present achievement. Nor should they have been satisfied: the gains had been small.

TABLE 7–1

Adoptive Placements by Type of Agency and Proportion of
Black Children Placed Relative to Total Placements, 1967

TYPE I: High Volume, Low Proportion

	Total Placements[a]	Number Black	Percent Black
Los Angeles	2483	222	8.9
Louise Wise	278	31	11.2
Spence-Chapin	465	54	11.6
New York Foundling Hospital	366	35	11.8

TYPE II: Low Volume, High Proportion

	Total Placements	Number Black	Percent Black
Chicago Child Care	107	53	49.5
New York D.S.S.	130	67	51.5
Cook County	92	52	56.5

TYPE III: Low Volume, All Black

	Total Placements	Number Black	Percent Black
Women's Christian Alliance	25	25	100

[a] The total number of placements includes, in addition to white for
each of the agencies, the following numbers of other minority group
children:

Los Angeles: 354　　　　　　　　　Cook County:　2
Louise Wise:　15　　　　　　　　　N.Y.　D.S.S.: 24
Spence-Chapin:　10

SOURCE: Billingsley and Giovannoni, 1968, p. 12.

CHANGING AGENCIES AND CHANGING PRACTICES FOR BLACK CHILDREN

Black children in need of parents are involved in an intricate network
of relationships. They are part of the Black community. They are part
of a family, even if estranged or orphaned. Their lives depend on the

love and nurturance of other parents who can rear them. They are also a part of a broader society that rejects and is hostile to them. And their fate is in the hands of an agency of that society. These elements, intricately involved as they are in the lives of the children, of necessity concern the agencies controlling their lives. Indeed the agencies cannot serve only the children, they must serve all of the publics involved. These are the Black community, the potential adoptive parents, the children's own natural parents—and the children themselves. We have elected to discuss first the agency relationships with the Black community. Not only did the agencies themselves most frequently view this relationship as their most problematic one, but we believe it to be the most crucial relationship of all. It is in the relationship to the Black community that the most fundamental aspect of racism in child welfare is projected—white control.*

The Black Community

Among any people the welfare of their children is a primary concern, and in any community the protection of that welfare is a primary function. While the institutions of the total society are concerned with all children in that society, the various subsocieties within it are particularly concerned with their own members. The right of many ethnic and religious subsocieties to carry out these functions—to rule over various aspects of the socialization and protection of their children— has been clearly recognized. In the case of the Black subsociety there has been no such recognition. Nor do sufficient institutions exist within the Black community to carry out these functions. Thus most children born into the Black community for whom adoption is the elected form of parental care must be surrendered to agents of the white society, and then members of the Black community must petition these agents to return the child to the Black community. He will be returned, if at all, on conditions laid down by the white establishment. The Black community and its members do not stand in a position of control. They are subjects. This is quite in contrast to the position of many other major ethnic subsocieties.

Innovations intended to better *serve* the Black community as clientele are quite different from those intended to bring the Black com-

* The Women's Christian Alliance, being already an agency of the Black community, is, of course, excepted from in this discussion.

munity into *partnership and control.* Child welfare agencies, including those in this study, have made little innovative effort toward partnership. In fact this has been perhaps the most crucial failure of the agencies studied. They seemed to be at least partly aware of their predicament in this regard, insofar as their major self-criticism was their inability to "reach" the Black community. However, to these agencies "reach" meant to reach *clients,* specifically adoptive parents. There seemed to be less appreciation of the failure to engage the Black community in a partnership. While in the largest sense the agencies had not succeeded in this regard, there were some efforts to bring members of the Black community into positions of control as board and staff members, and as directors of new satellite agencies.

Black people were included on boards primarily by the private agencies, as public agencies do not customarily have controlling boards. The Los Angeles Department of Adoptions was an exception since it had always had a five-member advisory board, each one appointed by a member of the County Board of Supervisors. All five members had always been white, and no change appeared imminent. In New York, the thirty-member Mayor's Advisory Committee on Adoptions, which advised the mayor on policies regarding adoption in the public sphere, was about half Black. The Chicago Child Care Society had an interracial Board of Directors consisting predominantly of upper-class men and women and a few middle-class professionals. In New York, both the Louise Wise Services and the Spence-Chapin agency made deliberate efforts to bring Black members onto their boards as they expanded their services for Black children. About five members of the thirty-member board for Louise Wise were Black, and about three of the forty members on the board of Spence-Chapin. As in the Chicago Child Care Society, the Spence-Chapin Black board members had usually been very famous people. Members of the Louise Wise board, on the other hand, had been Black professionals from fields related to child welfare. This was a departure from the usual practice of limiting Black representation to one or two very famous or prominent people.

Black representation on boards of directors does make some slight inroads into the control of these agencies, although such representation of the Black community is not overwhelming. Further, board members are not selected by the Black community, but by the boards themselves, which have been all, or almost all, white. A curious fact arises here. The boards of social agencies have traditionally been composed of wealthy white citizens, citizens who are hardly representative of a wide spectrum of the white community or of the white clientele. This rather skewed representation of white people is seldom challenged. When it comes to choosing Black board members, however, social agencies bog down, trying to decide "who represents the Black community?" Such a question has delayed and stymied many an attempt to increase Black representation on social agency boards. Concern about representativeness would certainly be alleviated by doubling or tripling Black membership, providing for input from a broad spectrum of the interests in the Black community.

The number of Black people in positions of control should be increased in order to improve services to Black children and clientele, but there is a more compelling reason as well. Black people also pay taxes and contribute to United Funds, often through payroll deductions. Lack of participation in the control over the expense of that money is deeply unjust, for private as well as public agencies. In the case of tax-supported agencies, Black people are rendered virtually powerless by their gross underrepresentation in government at all levels.

Satellite Agencies.

Two of the agencies in this study had made some direct structural changes in their operation in order to increase Black community participation—the Los Angeles County Department of Adoptions and the Spence-Chapin agency. The Los Angeles County Department of Adoptions in 1967 opened a sub-office in the district of Compton, a predominantly Black area of Los Angeles. The Department had several district offices across the enormous geographic spread of Los Angeles, so that the Compton office was not a major change in the operation of the agency. Yet it was a deliberate effort to locate services in a Black community, with a predominantly Black staff, most living in the community. Both of these aspects of the Compton office, the location and the staffing, were highly innovative.

The social workers in the Compton office had been strongly identified with the Black community. In less than a year of operation, they had, for example, established an auxiliary, WINGS, composed of Black residents of Compton, many of them men, which was actively recruiting homes. This auxiliary differed from others of its type, including BABY, a Black auxiliary to the Los Angeles Department as a whole, in that it had a local, community orientation and had relative autonomy from the agency, since it was an independent community development.

Two problems were recognized by the workers trying to build the Compton service. Their work was primarily direct service, but their self-elected secondary role as community organizers took time and energy that they wanted and needed to devote to their primary task. Furthermore, the caseworkers felt untrained and somewhat inadequate as community organizers. Their second problem was conflict with overall agency policy on public relations with the Black community. Increasing awareness of inadequacies in the public-relations appeals to Black parents was accompanied by frustration in not having sufficient power to alter these approaches. Both these problems may arise from the basic problem of attempting to operate a Black office in a white agency. Thus, while the establishment of the Compton office— a unit in a Black community with a Black staff—was an innovative step in itself, considerable further innovation—more autonomy and more help in involving the Black community—was needed if it was to fulfill its promise.

The Spence-Chapin Adoption Service was the other agency which established a satellite office.* This satellite, the Harlem-Dowling Agency, differed from the Compton office in that it was planned from the beginning to become an independent agency of the Black community.

Harlem-Dowling opened in the Fall of 1969, Black-sponsored, Black-staffed, and devoted to Black children and families. The stimulus for this endeavor came from Spence-Chapin's Black administra-

---

* In reviewing the first draft of the study referred to here, in a letter dated May 7, 1969, Mrs. Jane D. Edwards, Executive Director of the Spence-Chapin Adoption Service said, in part:

"I was so greatly impressed with the entire study, its purpose, its philosophy and recommendations, that I asked our Board of Directors to approve of Spence-Chapin helping to set up an agency in the black community that will become an independent agency. We have already employed a Director of the Project who has visited the Women's Christian Alliance in Philadelphia. We are now organizing a community advisory council which will develop into the new agency's Board of Directors. We are in the process of leasing space in Harlem which should be available in mid-summer. Although it was just about time for Spence-Chapin to expand its services again or to develop a new project which would be even more relevant to the times, it was your report which inspired me to suggest the creation of an agency that would exist within and primarily serve the Harlem community."

tive staff, who had become increasingly aware of the many ways in which Black children were being inadequately served. Ready support for the agency came from Mrs. Alice Hall Dowling, then President of the Board of Directors, and the agency in Harlem now bears her name.

Black Administration and Staff.

In addition to Black board participation and satellite operations, a third way to increase Black participation in control and administration is through staffing. All of the agencies in this study seemed aware of the importance of Black staff at all levels of operation, but varied both in the number of Black personnel and in the way they were deployed.

In the child-care field and in professional social work, discrimination against Black social workers is not a thing of the distant past. Many agencies refused employment to Black professional social workers on grounds of race, quite openly, right up to the passage of the Civil Rights Act. Further, in many child-care agencies deployment of personnel was openly racist. A typical pattern was for Black social workers to work only with Black children and clients, while white workers maintained integrated caseloads. Black social workers, should they rise to supervisory positions, were allowed to supervise only Black workers, while white supervisors had both Black and white supervisees. Such unevenness in assignment was not based upon recognition of special qualities that Black workers had to offer, but was obviously based on a rigid hierarchy of white over Black. It is not surprising that today many Black social workers are highly sensitive to this pattern, and many are ambivalent about taking on Black-specific assignments. Some Black social workers in Los Angeles, for example, refused to take assignments in the Compton office, referring to it as the "Plantation."

In general, public agencies have traditionally been more open to employment of Black staff. The Los Angeles agency, for instance, has always had a relatively high proportion of Black social workers, but top administrative positions have mostly been held by white people. In other agencies studied, the proportion of Black personnel varied, although a similar pattern occurred in all. All of these agencies had Black personnel in higher administrative and supervisory positions but relatively few Black social workers at the operating level. The executive director and director of casework at Spence-Chapin were both

Black, but the rest of the staff was almost entirely white. Two of the directors of the New York public agency have been Black; in 1968 the administrator and three-fifths of the supervisory personnel were Black, but the social workers, again, were predominantly white. In Cook County, while seventy-five percent of the workers were white, the director, associate director, six of the eight administrative supervisors, and nineteen of the twenty-seven field supervisors were Black. Finally, the Chicago Child Care Society had a white director, but the one supervisor was Black and three of the seven social workers were Black.

It is difficult to determine how this pattern emerged. Since supervisory and higher-level personnel must be quite experienced, it may have arisen simply because the adoption field at one time attracted a higher number of Black social workers than it does now. Consequently the less-experienced people at the worker level are not as readily available. Some of the agency personnel expressed the belief that this was why they were failing to recruit more Black caseworkers. They thought that fewer social work students were electing casework at all, let alone adoptions, and that even fewer of the Black students were choosing these fields, preferring the more activist roles they perceived as available in community organization. There is no information on employment patterns among Black social workers to verify these notions. Thus it is difficult to sort out how much of the pattern reflects career patterns of Black social workers and how much is due to agency hiring practices.

There is a second, and perhaps equally important, question. What effect has this pattern had on the service rendered to Black people? The fact that these agencies had Black personnel in high positions surely cannot be unrelated to the greater success they have had in serving Black children.

Increasing the numbers of available Black professionals is not solely the responsibility of these agencies. It rests heavily on the social work profession and its educational institutions. However, since all of the agencies expressed a pressing need for more Black personnel, they might take other, more immediate steps. Many tasks in child welfare, and in adoptions specifically, can be more than adequately handled by people without a Master's degree and without a college degree. The majority of adoption agencies, including many of those we studied, have a rather peculiar hierarchy of assignments:

the most experienced professional workers are assigned to adoptive parents, those less qualified to natural parents, and those least qualified to the children. This is a carryover from the classic adoption model—when the children were white infants requiring little but holding and transportation. Natural parents received little attention, and most of it was focused on the relinquishment decision. This traditional pattern accentuates the shortage of Black workers. It does not make good sense to have a Black worker with a Bachelor's degree spending much of her time with infants, while a white holder of a Master's degree works with Black adoptive parents, who might be very much influenced by the race of the social worker. Essentially it would seem that the deployment of scarce Black personnel must be carefully and deliberately planned with a Black clientele in mind, rather than being based on any routine traditional patterns.

In most of these agencies the appallingly low number of Black social workers at the operative level persists, and personnel continues to be predominantly white. There is a continuing need for staff development and education at all levels of agency operation. All of these agencies were mindful that something more than ordinary supervision would be necessary in reorienting agency staff at all levels to the adoptive placement of Black children. Special staff-development seminars were employed by several of the agencies, not only when they began placing Black children, but as a continuing process.

While all of these agencies recognized the need for continuing staff education, and while the mechanisms for such education were established, the continuing problem was, of course, what to teach. Where in a white agency, embedded in a white system, was the information which would make the agency personnel more appropriately responsive to the needs of a Black clientele? The issue of Black community control is relevant here. The matter is not simply one of staff development; it is one of reeducation. White staff, administrators, and board members must enter into the situation as pupils—pupils of Black teachers selected by Black people and teaching what they think should be taught, not what the audience may want to hear. An excellent example of such reeducation is being carried on by the National Urban League in contract with the Family Service Association of America. Black staff members of the League, and other members of the Black community whom they select, meet with groups of board members, administrators, and staff members of the affiliated agencies

of the Family Service Association in various parts of the country to
teach them about racism, at both an intellectual and an emotional
level. Unfortunately, the Child Welfare League of America rejected
a similar offer by the National Urban League after two exploratory
meetings.

Black Adoptive Parents

The second public to which the agencies must relate is that of the
Black adoptive parents.

All of the agencies had difficulty in finding sufficient numbers of
Black homes for the Black children they had available for placement.
While many in the field of child welfare look to the Black family as
the explanation for the dearth of Black adoptive homes, the agencies
we studied on the whole did not consider such factors, but rather their
own operation, as being at fault. This is a major reason why they
have been more successful than other agencies in placing Black children. All were aware that their own practices, based as they were on
the situation of white children, had to be changed.

During the period when most of these agencies were initiating their
efforts for Black children, there were an estimated 182 white adoptive
applicants for every 100 white infants. (Hylton, 1965, p. 379) This
oversupply of white applicants and undersupply of white babies had
persisted for several decades. In this situation the fundamental task
of adoption agencies was choosing which applicants to reward with
a child. Such a task is essentially a screening-out process: the mechanism of selection had to effectively disqualify a high proportion of
adoptive applicants. Professional adoption practice developed within
this context. The situation of Black children was and is quite reverse.
There are many more Black children awaiting adoptive placement
than there are Black couples applying and being approved to adopt
them. Black children's situation, therefore, dictates an opposite selection mechanism from that developed for white children—a screening
in rather than a screening *out*.

There are three major steps in the screening process. The first is the
initial decision to make inquiry of an adoption agency, the next to
make the inquiry, and the third to follow through to completed adoption. The problems in each area, and these agencies' innovations to
correct them, are worth examination.

Recruitment.

The agencies' first task was to stimulate interest in adoption among members of the Black community, in order to increase the initial pool of applicants. It was in this area that the agencies had perhaps met their worst failures, and where they appeared least successful in manipulating their own behavior.

Kenneth Watson of the Chicago Child Care Society has noted the importance of community perceptions in influencing and perpetuating agencies' modes of operation: "That agency which accepts for placement only white infants of college students will strive to find such children in order to attempt to meet the demands of families . . . the community will perceive it, and I am afraid it will perceive itself, as that agency to which couples go who want a 'very good' baby." (Watson, 1968, p. 3) If this thinking can be extended to the case of Women's Christian Alliance, then its sufficiency of unsolicited applications arises in part from the Black community's perception of it as the agency where one goes for a Black baby. Thus, the agency's special recruitment efforts could be focused very efficiently on stimulating interest among those who had not considered adoption, since it did not have the added burden of channelling those already interested to the agency.

All of the other agencies seemed to have undertaken certain standard procedures in order to increase interest among Black families. These were the mass media—press, radio, and television; establishment of Black recruitment auxiliaries; personal contact with Black institutions and organizations, particularly churches, by agency personnel; and finally, recruitment by the agencies' own adoptive parents. Those agencies with foster-home programs found Black foster parents to be useful recruiters.

The mass-media approaches were planned by the various (often white) public relations personnel to reduce whatever resistances they thought existed among Black people against coming to the agencies. Thus, there were various pamphlets, posters, etc., aimed at dispelling misconceptions about adoption. For example, one agency had a booklet in which twelve questions about adoption procedures were asked and answered, such as, "Do you have to have your own home?" "May the new mother be employed?" and "Do you have to be under thirty-five?" Another approach was to use pictures of Black children and parents in television spots and public advertising. Almost all agency reports and pamphlets used a picture of a Black child in need of a home, and a picture of a Black adoptive family. The public-relations efforts employed varying degrees of directness in asking for Black families and in asking for homes for Black children, but they seemed to be more direct when it came to the need for homes for Black children. There is a difference, however, between asking for homes for Black children and asking for Black homes for Black children.

The public-relations efforts elicited at least two negative impressions among the staff members we interviewed in these agencies. The first was that the emotionalism of the appeals for homes—photographs of a small, tearful, Black, homeless child—often elicited more hysterical than genuine interest. Moreover, even when the approach was specific to Black families, the agencies received a high influx of inquiries from white families, but only a small increase in the number of Black inquiries. Although they continued to utilize the mass media, none of the agencies seemed particularly impressed with the results. The appeals were based not on any validated information about Black families, but rather on what were *supposed by the agencies* to be misconceptions about adoption among Black people. It could well be that none of these suppositions was valid. More important, it could well be that large areas of concern were being overlooked—the simplest one being the potential apprehension a Black couple might feel in approaching a white agency. Perhaps pictures of Black agency personnel would have been more effective than those of tearful Black children ever could be.

Apart from the mass-media contact with the Black community, agencies employed *direct personal contact* through Black organizations. Usually this meant that agency personnel appeared at meetings to explain their programs and to recruit applicants from the immediate audience and their acquaintances. One agency routinely sent an interracial team, while another sent only their white public-relations staff. One agency, which had routinely used white public-relations staff, sent a Black casework supervisor during a period when there were public-relations staff vacancies. In spite of the fact that she received a much warmer welcome in all contacts—and was more successful in recruiting—she was relieved of this assignment when the pressure of her other work became too great. Several of the agencies noted that white personnel appearing before Black audiences were receiving an increased amount of hostility toward the agency and the child welfare system in general. Nonetheless, only a few agencies had any immediate plans to employ Black personnel specifically for this task, or to deploy what Black personnel they did have to this kind of activity.

The effectiveness of such personal appearances had not been systematically evaluated, but it was possible that they were wrongly directed. The agencies seemed to have access to limited numbers and kinds of organizations in the Black community. A considerable amount of effort, for example, had gone into work with churches, and there was increasing doubt that these efforts were paying off at all. Some innovative efforts were, however, being made to expand agency visibility in the Black community. Satellite offices are an example. One New York agency had held an annual men's smoker at a motor hotel in Harlem, using whatever contacts they had in the Black community to attract an audience. Each of these affairs had yielded four or five adoptive homes. This approach left the usual channels, such as churches and lodges, and offered the agency an opportunity to develop contacts with organizations they might not ordinarily have reached. Equally interesting was the focus on men, rather than women or couples, which had been the usual approach of adoptive recruiting.

All of these efforts at recruiting applicants by extending the agency to the Black community had a major limitation: they approached Black people essentially as *clients,* not as *partners.* It may well be that the failure to create a partnership was the factor hobbling all the efforts to extend the client relationship. At one agency, a Black staff member observed that the agencies were always asking the Black community to help *them* with *their* problem, rather than to see the problem as a responsibility of the Black community itself. The latter approach might mean extending the agency beyond Black social organizations to politically oriented groups as well. All of the white agencies saw their relationship to the Black community as their biggest problem, and this was the problem where they were least imaginative and innovative. Until the gap is bridged somehow, the situation of Black children in need of homes is not likely to improve very dramatically. This becomes particularly apparent when the problems in the next phase of the adoption process are brought into focus—the period of inquiry and follow-through.

Screening In Those Who Came In.

Although there is not very much information on the matter, the data that exist indicate that there is an enormous drop-out rate, after the

initial inquiry, among adoptive couples of both races. The loss of
Black applicants at this early stage is much more serious than the loss
of white couples because of the differences in the supply-and-demand
situation for Black and white children.

Impressions about the drop-out rate among Black prospective
adoptive applicants is based on data from single-agency studies and
data from special community-wide recruitment drives. Fanshel
(1957) provided data on drop-outs in his special study of a single
agency in Pittsburgh. He reported that the proportion of Black applicants completing the process was 19 percent, while among the white
applicants it was 40 percent. He further divided those who failed to
complete into those who withdrew and those rejected. Sixty percent of
the original Black applicants withdrew, whereas only 41 percent of
the white withdrew. The rejection rates between the two were similar
—21 percent of the Black applicants and 18 percent of the white. The
second source of data on Black applicant losses is from special community-wide recruitment projects, notably the Adopt-A-Child project
in New York and the MARCH project in San Francisco, which was concerned with Mexican-American children as well as Black and white.
These data simply record the total number of inquiries and the number of children placed during the life of the project. The Adopt-A-
Child experience yielded a success rate of about 34 percent. MARCH
was far less successful, having recorded 866 inquiries and only 64
actual placements, a success rate of about 7 percent. (MARCH,
1959) All three of these reports were made in the late 1950's, but
unfortunately they still serve today to document the "enormously
high Negro drop-out rate."

Precise data were not available from all of the agencies we studied
on the Black applicant loss, either in absolute terms or relative to the
white applicant loss. Our general impression, substantiated by the data
that were available, was that the loss was not as severe as Fanshel,
Adopt-A-Child, and MARCH reported, but was still an unhappy one.
Generally speaking, the loss rate among Black applicants was con-
ceded to be somewhat higher than among white applicants, but not
much higher—about half of all white applicants dropped out and
about 60 percent of all Black applicants. The losses seemed greatest
after the point of initial inquiry and decreased sharply among those
who kept a first appointment.

The Los Angeles agency had the most complete data. During 1967,
the loss rate among Black applicants was 48 percent, among white

applicants 41 percent, and among Mexican-American applicants 53 percent. The New York public agency presented an interesting pattern. Between July, 1962, and April, 1968, the agency received 2,286 inquiries from Black applicants (34 percent of the total), 3,129 inquiries from white applicants (46 percent of the total), and 1,339 from Puerto Rican and other ethnic applicants. During this same period, the agency placed 230 Black children, or 64 percent of their total placements. Judging from the number of inquiries recorded and the total number of placements made, the drop-out rate appears to be enormously high, and—oddly enough—considerably higher among white than Black applicants. But the very high drop-out rate indicated here may reflect nothing more than the size of the operation. To accommodate even a fraction of the Black applicants with children (bringing the drop-out level up to that in the Los Angeles agency) would have required a much larger operation. Such a feat could not be accomplished without a vast increase in the agency's resources of staff and money.

The Women's Christian Alliance, the Black agency, had something of a drop-out problem, but it was probably less severe than in any of the other agencies we studied. Of approximately 80 inquiries from Black couples in 1967, about 55 went on to pursue the adoptive process. The agency personnel attributed the withdrawal of applications largely to misconceptions by those applying. However, the agency had only a small adoption program, and the lack of resources was probably playing a part in the withdrawal rate there.

While these agencies reported a less severe drop-out problem, it was still a problem. Sufficient homes are not to be had unless it is corrected. If the present drop-out rate is maintained, only a hundred-fold increase in the number of inquiries can produce a satisfactory number of completed adoptions.

The term "drop-out" is in some ways misleading: How valid is the distinction between "withdrawal" and "rejection"? Even in Fanshel's careful analysis, one reason, "infertility requirements," appears as a reason both for "rejection" and for "withdrawal." The infertility requirement was, of course, imposed by the agency, not the applicants. When a group of Black social workers initiated a follow-up study of "drop-outs" at the Los Angeles agency in 1970, they found that many of these families classified as "drop-outs" were in fact encouraged to withdraw by the worker; in some cases the worker had known that they would have been rejected had they pursued their applications, for such reasons as previous arrests and outstanding child-support payments. Thus, the extent to which agency operations, requirements, and procedures contribute to the voluntary withdrawal of applicants demands serious attention.

The agencies we studied, mindful of their failure to reduce the loss rate of Black adoptive parents, had made a number of changes aimed specifically toward screening in, rather than screening out, parents. These innovations in practice were made not only at the point of inquiry but throughout adoptive study and final placement as well. All of the agencies had a policy of reaching out to prospective Black applicants in ways which they did not use with white applicants. The major tacks taken were (1) to give an immediate individual appointment at as convenient a time and place as possible; (2) to follow up by telephoning those who did not keep appointments, and (3) to keep an open-door policy toward those who dropped out, with encouragement to return. By contrast, white couples at these agencies were not usually given an individual appointment. Rather, their first face-to-face contact with the agency occurred in a group meeting, and they often had to wait to be assigned to one. Such differential treatment to Black applicants seemed to be well accepted at all of these agencies. They were all of the opinion that it had helped reduce the number of early drop-outs, but none had put the idea to systematic examination.

Following Through to Adoptions.

Beyond the special handling of initial inquiries, the agencies had made great strides in altering practices so as to increase the number of possible homes. More innovative steps had been taken in this area than in any other. Most of them had to do with eliminating rigid eligibility standards for Black applicants. (In many instances, these restrictions were subsequently dropped for white applicants as well.) Among the standards changed were (1) fees, (2) infertility, (3) first marriage, (4) married couples only, (5) employment of mother, and (6) income and home ownership. Not all of the agencies had all of these restrictions and not all of them had abolished them. Neither of the Chicago agencies had any fee; nor had the New York public agency. Spence-Chapin and the Los Angeles agency had a sliding scale of fees, with different bases for Black and white applicants. While abolishing the fee did not automatically increase the number of homes, the fee did appear to be a drawback when it was present. In a recent study, middle-class Black families in Los Angeles often quoted the fee and the whole cost of adoption as a barrier to adoption. Some Black social workers believe that some Black applicants find the idea of "buying a child" reminiscent of slavery and particularly repugnant. While the Los Angeles agency did have a fee, 43 percent of their Black adoptive couples were not charged a fee in 1968; among other California agencies, only 18 percent of the adoptive couples paid no fee. Among these agencies, 54 percent of the Black couples paid $200 or more, but only 22 percent of the Los Angeles families were charged this much. This seems to be one reason for the agency's success.

Black families, even though they may have current income equivalent to whites', much less often have inherited wealth, or even small help from their own families in setting up their households. Thus, an outlay of even $400 or $500 for agency and legal fees can preclude adoption when the family simply is not able to save that amount. There really seems to be little logic to the fee. The amounts of money collected, especially from the small numbers of Black families who now adopt, are not large. As a test of motivation, the fee is hardly valid. Willingness to pay $150 to $200 to adopt a baby cannot be taken as an indication of serious intent to support the baby for the next eighteen or twenty years.

The infertility requirement no longer existed in any of these agencies for Black couples, and in fact a large proportion of adopting parents had children of their own. Many of the agencies thought that the fertility tests previously imposed had driven many Black men from the agency. Thus, whether couples were childless or not, such tests were no longer required. The infertility requirement itself seems to have been nothing more than a carryover from the practices established to weed out the oversupply of white couples. Certainly there is no reason why a childless couple invariably should make better parents than a couple with children.

The agencies no longer excluded working mothers from adoption. However, they did exercise a prerogative of approving the substitute care provided during mothers' absences. Again, the working-mother restriction was also a carryover from the white situation, as certainly many natural mothers continue to work without any particular societal condemnation for doing so.

Agency policy was somewhat more nebulous on couples where one or both partners had been previously married. None of the agencies had a specific ruling against such couples, but the stability of the present marriage was generally examined more closely. Similarly, age was no longer a total barrier. However, the agencies were still reluctant to place a very young child with parents past fifty. Previous difficulty with the law by an applicant did not automatically exclude him, but his chances of receiving a child were probably reduced.

Income and home ownership have always been rather vague requirement of agencies. In these agencies the general requirement for Black applicants was sufficient income to maintain the child and sufficient room to house him. No fixed or written standards were applied. No doubt, a different yardstick was used for "sufficient" income for Black and white couples. "Sufficiency" is a rather intangible concept. Middle-class workers would quite naturally be led to consider the home with material advantages the better home. Similarly, the agencies had no educational restrictions, but the more educated couple, Black or white, was no doubt prized more highly. While we do not wish to imply that the agencies were excluding couples with lower socioeconomic status, we do think that there may well be some differences in the kinds of children they get. The "good baby"-"good parents" frame of mind described by Bradley (1966) probably operates for Black applicants and children just as it does for whites.

While the agencies have relaxed restrictions on Black adoptive couples, all of these agencies were most frequently placing children with Black, middle-class couples where the mother was of child-bearing age. Other factors of couse enter into adoptive parenthood.

The most detailed data on the characteristics of Black families who have completed legal adoptions come from California. In 1968, the Los Angeles agency placed children with 146 Black couples. Among these couples, 34 percent of the Black adopting fathers had at least a high-school education, and 35 percent had been to college. Almost a third of them, 31 percent, had not finished high school. The educational distribution among the Black adopting mothers was approximately the same. This was quite at variance with the education of all adoptive couples in California (seven-eighths of whom were white): only 11 percent of the fathers and 13 percent of the mothers had not completed high school; 61 percent of the men had attended college and over half of the women. The ages of the Black adoptive couples at the Los Angeles agency were also at variance with the age distribution among adoptive couples statewide. While about half of both groups were in their thirties, there was considerable difference in the other age ranges. About a third of the Black couples were over forty, but only about 15 percent of the couples statewide. Thus, the Los Angeles agency did appear to be defining "acceptable adoptive parents" among Black couples quite differently from the going definition for white families, in particular screening in more older couples and more couples with less education. Fertility restrictions had been generally relaxed throughout the state. Still, 60 percent of the Los Angeles Black adopting couples had children, while this was so for only 40 percent of the couples statewide.

While the adoptive parents for Black children in all of these agencies were overwhelmingly Black married couples, all the agencies had extended into transracial adoptions and most into single-parent adoptions. The agencies did not rely heavily on either type of adoption, but they had made considerably more transracial placements than single-parent placements. These two innovations received somewhat less enthusiastic support than those in relation to Black couples. The agencies were attempting these changes with misgiving and reluctance.

SINGLE PARENTS: The agencies that had done a few single-parent adoptions felt able to justify them only on the basis that the alternatives open to the child were less desirable than not having a father in the home. Whether the single-parent home will ever become a common adoptive resource for Black children remains to be seen. The present level of agency reservation, however, indicates that it will not come about in the near future.

The most complete information on single-parent adoptions came from the Los Angeles agency, where Mrs. Ethel Branham had studied 36 single-parent placements made by that agency between December, 1965, and December, 1967. Mrs. Branham noted that the average single parent was a forty-one-year-old Black woman, possessed of a college degree, probably married at some time in the past, and with nothing in her present situation or her inclinations to preclude remarriage. All were able to provide male companionship for the children, including usually both relatives and men whom they regularly dated. Mrs. Branham summed up her profile of these women by saying: "For the most part, these women had full lives, enjoyable occupations, and yet had something else to give." (1970, p. 5) In general, Mrs. Branham's report would indicate that agencies might well reexamine their reservations about such Black men and women as a future resource for waiting Black children.

TRANSRACIAL ADOPTION. Placement of Black or mixed Black children with white families is much more common than the single-parent adoption. By 1968, the Los Angeles agency had placed one hundred children with parents of a different racial background. The Louise Wise Services had placed about fifteen children in such homes, and the other agencies had placed a few. The success of these adoptions was still to be evaluated, and the problems posed for child and parent had not yet been investigated. As with single-parent adoptions, there were reservations on the part of the agencies; transracial adoptions were seen as second best to placements with Black parents, but preferable to other alternatives for these children.

Transracial placements have been more numerous and more acceptable to the agencies than the single-parent ones. Apparently the agencies place more value on having two parents, even if they are white, than on having one Black parent. From the point of view of the Black child, this is quite conceivably erroneous.

Increasingly, Black social workers are voicing strenuous objections to transracial adoptions as being based on ignorance and denial of the Black child's situation. This controversy can be expected to heighten. There are, in fact, several reasons why agencies should be discouraged from pursuing transracial adoption on any large scale. To date, transracial adoptions have not made nearly as sizable a contribution to the placement of Black children as have placements with Black parents. In the agencies which have led in the adoption of Black children, the vast majority have been placed with Black couples. Those agencies that make the *highest* proportion of transracial adoptions are also the agencies that place *fewest* Black children. In California, for example, in 1968, transracial placements at the Los Angeles County Department of Adoptions accounted for only 13 percent of the total number of Black children placed. Among the other agencies in California, agencies which placed far fewer Black children, transracial placements accounted for 21 percent of placements. In a few agencies which placed fewer than ten Black children, transracial placements accounted for over half the placements.

Second, the failure to recruit enough Black adoptive parents for all the Black children in need of homes may well relate to the agencies' failure to involve the Black community. Persistent reliance on white couples may only deflect energy away from this more basic problem.

Still a third reason arises from the past and present undersupply of adoptable white infants. Adoption, as we have noted, originated as a means of serving white couples who wanted children. White infants for adoption are becoming increasingly scarce, and some believe that in the not too distant future there will be very few at all. However, the pressure on the agencies by white couples has not decreased. There is the distinct possibility in such a situation that the white couples' desires will be given priority over the needs and welfare of the Black children.

These are the reasons why many Black social workers advise against programs of transracial adoption. Many people of course point out that transracial adoption, while problematic, may be the best alternative available for a Black child. Conceivably it is, for some individual children. But that decision must be made from the standpoint of the child. Sound policy would dictate that transracial adoptions be supervised and directed by a Black social worker or Black consultant.

Subsidized Adoption.

Perhaps the most promising development in the late 1960's, and one intended primarily to benefit Black and other minority children, was subsidized adoption. Subsidized adoption is identical to other adoption in all ways except that the adoptive parents receive financial assistance toward the maintenance of the child. It differs from long-term foster care or quasi-adoption in that the child is legally adopted. At the time of our study, the Chicago Child Care Society had experimented with subsidized adoptions for several years. The other agencies had not undertaken such programs; however, legislation in California and in New York had made it possible for these states to subsidize adoptive parents.

By 1970, enabling legislation had been passed in Michigan and Maryland as well as in California and New York, and legislation was pending in several other states. The amount of payment varied from state to state. The 1969 Michigan legislation set a maximum of $600 a year. In the other states, payment was geared to coincide with the amounts paid for foster care. The California legislation, introduced by Senator Dymally in 1968, allowed only for a pilot program; payments to any adoptive parent were to be made only for three years from the time of the first payment. Because the program proved successful in increasing the number of homes and was financially feasible as well, a permanent program was adopted in 1971. New York's law became effective in 1968.

All of the laws have characteristics in common. First, the intended recipients are "hard-to-place" or "special needs" children. While the

Michigan, Maryland, and New York laws are relatively vague on this point, the California bill is explicit, stating the purpose to be "the placement in adoptive homes of children who because of their ethnic background, race, color, language, physical or mental or emotional or medical handicaps or age have become difficult to place in adoptive homes."

The emphasis on children who are demonstrably "hard-to-place" because they have not been placed has great political expediency. The underlying appeal is that subsidized adoption will be cheaper for the state than continued foster care, which is an expense already encumbering the states. Should the laws be strictly implemented only for such children, however, the programs may become self-defeating: securing a home for a child through subsidy only *after* other means have demonstrably failed may contribute unnecessarily to the population of "hard-to-place" children. It would be more beneficial to children to view the subsidy as a preventive measure against "hard-to-placeness," as well as a curative one. Such an approach obviously cannot at present gain wide support among legislators and the many taxpayers whom they represent. For them the benefit to children is secondary to the financial benefits to the state.

All of the legislation is notably vague as to the economic means of adoptive parents who may receive subsidy. This is fortunate, for to link the program to a means test for adoptive parents would surely reduce its effectiveness in recruiting parents. All of the legislation is too new for us to evaluate its effectiveness in multiplying homes for Black children, or for that matter to determine how all of the policy implications, such as means of parents, will be worked out. The Los Angeles agency has made a few placements, but so far the program has been used most extensively by that agency to waive the fee for parents who had already applied. Mrs. Jane Edwards of the Spence-Chapin agency has estimated that approximately half of the children in the agency's long-term foster program might be adopted by their present foster parents if the New York legislation is fully implemented.

Whether subsidized adoption programs will significantly increase the number of adoptive homes for Black children will not be known for some time and will depend on how they are implemented. While all of the New York agencies studied seemed to be looking forward eagerly to the possibilities which the new legislation might open for Black children, at least one agency administrator anticipated many problems in administering such a program. One of these is the selection of homes. While the idea of a means test is abhorrent to the agency, there is a strong possibility of just such a development, unless there should come about some change in the basic policies toward paying parents. Another problem is the type of publicity to be given the program. If not all parents are to be paid, then the publicity must keep some from expecting the subsidy while encouraging others to expect it. The publicity will be very pertinent to the usefulness of the program in increasing the numbers of adoptive parents applying. With all its problems, however, subsidized adoption offers a most concrete solution for Black homeless children, whose potential parents must be drawn in large part from among those who are economically unable to care for them. Subsidized adoption offers the promise of a redefinition of "potential adoptive parents" for Black children which can significantly increase the total pool of homes.

That adoptive parents should receive some kind of compensation for their child-rearing efforts would be a commonplace idea in practically any other country than the United States. Most other industrial nations have some form of family allowance for parents, whether adoptive or natural. However, the concept of income maintenance has not yet won acceptance in this country. Unless they are destitute, American parents are still expected to rear their children without financial assistance. Despite its "un-American" flavor, however, subsidized adoption will probably be widely accepted, though not for humanitarian reasons. Subsidized adoption is cheaper than foster care. Reduced administrative costs, elimination of casework supervision, and partial assumption of financial responsibility by many parents all reduce the cost of care. The most extensive figures available to support this contention derive from the experiences with the program in Chicago. Shireman (1969) reports:

> Subsidized adoption offers considerable financial saving to the community. The median long-term subsidy by the Chicago agencies is $720 per year, the median cost of foster care is $1,900 in Chicago. . . . In addition, cost of service to each child in a subsidized adoptive home is at most one-twelfth of the cost of service to a child in foster family care.
>
> Could subsidized adoption be effected for the 51 children in CD [Cook County Children's Division] homes whose foster parents would like to adopt them, but need help in meeting costs of care, a saving of $24,480 per year could be estimated. [p. 1]

The Natural Parents

The third public to which the agencies had to relate was that of the natural parents. For any group of children, the services rendered by an adoption agency depend heavily upon the services to natural parents. The agencies can do more than take relinquishments. They can pro-vide counseling, arrange financial assistance, and help in finding housing, employment, and hospital and medical care. Many mothers who approach an adoption agency ultimately do not relinquish their babies, but often receive these other services. The Los Angeles agency, for example, estimates that almost half of all the parents who come in ultimately keep their children. Thus, the services given by an agency cannot be measured solely by the number of children placed or relinquishments taken.

Figures on services to the parents of Black children are diffcult to come by. As we have noted, only about 5 percent of the Black babies born out of wedlock in this country are served through adoption agencies, while the figure for whites is 75 percent, and the potential pool of Black parents in need of services cannot be estimated, short of special study. It is safe to say, however, that the agencies studied were not going out of their way to recruit the natural parents of Black children, since such children are at present in oversupply. The effort of the Louise Wise Services in recruiting Black mothers for their maternity homes was a notable exception.

Perhaps the best that could be said about most agencies' operation in this area was that they no longer deliberately excluded Black children, either by refusal of service to all parents of Black children, or by quota systems on the number of relinquishments which could be taken for Black children, with periodic closing of intake to parents—which is always a closing to children, too. Exclusion has been as characteristic of public agencies as it has been of private ones. It is not only the responsibility of the adoption agency, but of all who come into contact with the parents of Black children. Medical and welfare personnel, for example, are frequently the first professionals that a mother may come to for service. While they may well refer the parents of a white child to an adoption agency, they routinely fail to give parents of Black children such referrals.

While none of the agencies studied had deliberate exclusion policies or practices, their laissez-faire approach to the problem was in itself a means of exclusion. In the present child welfare system, channels of entry are much more likely to be blocked for Black parents than for white parents.

The present system works an additional psychological hardship on the parents of the Black child. The agencies' difficulty in placing Black children is common knowledge. Thus, the parent considering relinquishment of a Black child is not in the same decision-making situation as a white parent. The white parent can assume that the child will be placed rapidly, without lingering in a foster home or institution. The Black parent has no such assurance. Thus, she bears a heavy psychological burden in planning to relinquish a child. The situation was different in the Louise Wise maternity homes, which had about 25 percent Black mothers and 75 percent Jewish. The agency made a pointed effort not to discriminate on the basis of race in serving these women, and informed all women in the homes that it would accept their babies for adoption. The great majority did relinquish their babies, and the "culture" of the homes might be said to be "relinquishment oriented." Under such circumstances, where relinquishment was quite an acceptable form of maternal behavior, the Black mothers chose to relinquish their babies almost as frequently as did the Jewish mothers.

Given the systematic deterrents to mothers of Black children, it is safe to say that the adoptive services being rendered to them are not randomly distributed among potential users. Initiative among the mothers themselves is a prime determinant of their even encountering an adoption agency. Data from California support this view. Among the mothers of Black children placed for adoption by the Los Angeles County Adoptions Department in 1968, only 28 percent were under seventeen years of age and 19 percent between eighteen and twenty, whereas 53 percent were over twenty-one. Forty-five percent had not completed high school, 29 percent had a high school diploma, and 22 percent had attended college. These data suggest that the young teenager, and less well educated women of all ages, may have been underrepresented. However, the Los Angeles agency appeared to be serving more of the very young and the less well educated than other agencies in California. Statewide, the mothers served were both older and better educated. Sixty-one percent of them were over twenty-one, fully 36 percent of them had attended college, and another 29 percent had graduated from high school.

The extension of adoption services to Black children must ultimately mean an extension of services to natural parents. It must mean particularly an active search for poorer girls and younger girls, and deliberate efforts to unblock the usual channels of referrals, particularly schools and public hospitals. Agencies are reluctant to do this because they fear that there will not be enough homes for the children who will enter care. Such a fear may be based on too narrow a conception of the problem. Many such children eventually enter the child welfare system as abandoned dependent children. And when they do enter, as older children, possibly with emotional damage, the prospects for adoption are lessened.

The array of services available to natural parents must also be extended. Adoption agencies should have more to offer parents than adoption. A fundamental issue arises here. If the primary function of adoption is to provide babies for couples wishing to adopt, then natural parents and their children will remain of secondary concern. If, on the other hand, the primary function is to provide homes and services to children, then the natural parents are a valuable resource, and a multifunction approach becomes vital. The commitment to such a function is one of the most fundamental changes that agencies must make if they are to adapt to the needs of Black children.

As they increased their contact with Black mothers, all of the agencies we studied found that their modes of service were not sufficiently responsive to the needs of these women. Not only were changes in casework techniques and services indicated, but programmatic changes as well.* The problems of the Black mother and child are not the same as those of the white mother and child, first of all because they are Black.

* The whole field of adoption and its various agencies is, of course, in a continual state of change and development, as indicated by a letter dated December 28, 1971, from Mrs. Doris McKelvey, Assistant Director of Louise Wise Services: "Very few young pregnant girls are coming to the agency with the thought of surrendering their children for adoption. Many more are coming to us in the postnatal period when their child is past the infancy stage. This has meant that the agency has had to refocus and redirect its services to meet the needs of young parents who are attempting to keep their children rather than relinquish them for adoption. This means that currently we offer many services to young mothers postnatally. These services include not only the traditional casework but also help with concrete needs such as housing, employment, education, day care, etc. . . . Contemporary adoptive agencies that are attuned to this changing picture need to, therefore, readjust their services and find many ways of being creative with regard to Black families and children."

In considering the potential pool of natural parents who might be served by adoption agencies, let us reexamine the implications of the fact that the number of white infants being relinquished is diminishing. The Los Angeles County Department of Adoptions had significantly fewer white children relinquished during 1969, and the Louise Wise agency had noted a decline in the number of Jewish women coming to that agency as early as 1965. This decrease is variously attributed to the liberalization of abortion laws, the increased use of oral contraceptives, and a diminished stigma of illegitimacy among white middle-class girls. The implications of these changes for Black children are uncertain. On the one hand, the decreased demand for services for white children might mean a redistribution of resources for Black children. On the other hand, the resources may simply be cut back. Such was the case in Los Angeles, at least, where the budget for the Adoptions Department was cut in 1969–70 on the basis that fewer babies were being relinquished. But where is the evidence that the decrease in white applications is any indicator of need among Black children? Surely the ratio of Black children in the dependent-child population would be a more justifiable indicator of their needs than the supply of white infants can be.

The Children

The final public served by the agencies is that of the children themselves. In looking at the ways in which these agencies serve children, it is necessary to expand our view beyond the immediate situation of adoptive placement. As has been stressed earlier, adoption is but one part of the total child welfare system in any community. Thus, adoption agencies, as part of such a system, bear a relationship to children in the total system, not only to those under their immediate care. Moreover, the agencies frequently must perform tasks for the children awaiting adoption which are common to those performed by agencies in other parts of the child welfare system. Once children are relinquished to an agency, the agency becomes the substitute parent until they are placed in an adoptive home.

As has become the custom in recent years, the agencies we studied were placing children in pre-adoptive foster homes, rather than in institutional care. Thus any given agency had a large program of short-term foster care at any given time, as an integral part of adoptive practice. This was, and is, especially true of Black children; white infants are so quickly placed that they are frequently taken home from the hospital by the adopting parents, thus precluding any type of pre-adoptive placement. Pre-adoptive foster parents understand that the children placed with them will eventually be removed by the agency. They are ordinarily paid at a higher rate than ordinary foster parents and may receive a retainer fee even when no child is currently in the home, so that the agency will have the home available at all times, especially for infants.

The pre-adoptive foster-care programs varied according to whether the agency was single-purpose or multipurpose. Thus, the Chicago Child Care Society, the Children's Division of the Cook County Department, the Women's Christian Alliance, and the Spence-Chapin agency all had long-term foster-care programs which exceeded in magnitude the adoption programs. On the other hand, the Los Angeles agency, Louise Wise Services, and the public agency in New York had adoption as their single purpose. The New York public agency was a division of the welfare department, but as a separate division it was removed from the general foster-care programs.

Multipurpose and single-purpose agencies have different relationships to the children. If an agency is responsible only for adoption, and a child is not placed in an adoptive home, the agency has the prerogative of transferring that child to another agency or division for disposition, usually foster or institutional care. This was perhaps most dramatically illustrated by the Los Angeles Adoptions Department in 1955, when it transferred children out of the department to the Bureau of Child Welfare because adoptive placement for them was not achieved.

The single-purpose agency also has the prerogative of extending its functions to include long-term foster care. The potential in increasing services to children through development of new programs, rather than legitimating exclusion, was well illustrated by Spence-Chapin's long-term foster-care program, which began while the agency had been primarily focused on adoptive placements. There was already a cadre of pre-adoptive foster-home parents. These parents were the first resource; the agency expanded through recruiting additional foster homes specifically for babies. Now, however, they were not recruiting pre-adoptive homes, but homes for foster care of an indefinite and long-lasting nature. Of course, some long-lasting foster care had always evolved out of that which was supposed to be temporary, but this practice of planning for long-term foster care was considered quite innovative in the profession.

Spence-Chapin's long-term foster-care program had had effects upon the agency's adoption services for Black children. Table 7–2 shows what happened to the infants admitted to long-term foster care each year from the program's inception through 1967. One can readily observe the persistent increase in the proportion placed in adoption, and the very dramatic increase in the number of babies

TABLE 7–2

Children Received into Spence-Chapin Adoption Service Long-term Foster-care Program, 1962–1967: Numbers and Proportion Returned to Mother, Adopted, and Remaining in Program

Year	Children received	Returned to Mother		Adopted		Remaining	
		Number	Percent	Number	Percent	Number	Percent
Carried over from 1961	129	—	—	—	—	—	—
1962	104	11	11	5	5	88	84
1963	224	41	18	29	13	154	69
1964	209	47	22	52	25	110	53
1965	254	71	28	48	19	135	53
1966	286	72	25	46	16	168	59
1967	277	93	34	54	19	130	47

SOURCE: Billingsley and Giovannoni, 1968, p. 89.

adopted. The proportion of children returned to their own mothers also increased; consequently, the proportion of children remaining in "long-term foster care" had reduced steadily. Essentially, what happened was that the agency had, through the initiation of a new function, long-term foster care, extended *all* types of its services to increasingly large numbers of Black children. The increase in adoptive placements should not be considered an accidental by-product of the long-term foster-home project. It was a planned-for result for a deliberate effort to take Black children under care. Once this deliberate step was taken, the resources of the agency, including adoption, became available to Black children who otherwise might never have been brought into the agency. The enormous increase in the number of Black children placed for adoption in a single year, 1962–63, from 5 to 29 children, is illustrative of the resources that can be mustered once children are admitted into the system.

From the standpoint of Black children, the multipurpose agency may well be preferable. If agencies cannot get rid of children, they must do something for them; when the pressure of the children's presence is actually felt, there is more likelihood that innovative services will be developed. This is particularly important for the Black child. As long as child welfare systems are so structured that agencies can pass children along, one to another, from one function to another, it is the Black child who is most likely to receive the least desirable form of care. There are several indications that this happens in the larger child welfare systems to which the agencies studied belong. In New York, for example, Black children accounted for less than 10 percent of all children adopted in 1967. However, Black and Puerto Rican children comprised over 80 percent of the children in institutional-shelter care. Similarly, in Los Angeles in 1967, 8 percent of the adoptive placements were Black children, and a similar proportion were Mexican children; however, these two groups comprised half of all children in foster homes.

Clearly individual agencies cannot expand indefinitely. The entire child welfare system must be geared to provide both the amount and the kinds of services that Black children need, if they are not to remain unserved or badly served. At present the number of agencies in the systems and the volume of services given are geared to the needs of white children, and the systems are too constricted even to begin serving Black children adequately. Thus, the expansion of service by the agencies studied will not alone solve the problem, but the solution may well lie in the expansion of present agencies combined with the creation of new agencies specific to the needs of Black children.

When agencies extend themselves to Black children, particularly through those programs which are adoption substitutes, they become in a real sense substitute parents. These programs are of demonstrated value, and certainly warrant extension by other agencies. However, in such programs the agencies retain ultimate control over the children's lives, and the agencies themselves are staffed and controlled by white people. The implications for Black children should be considered. Increasing awareness of the sense of Black peoplehood has pointed up a particular and specific developmental task with respect to Black children. Children's Services Incorporated, in Philadelphia, an agency serving only Black children in foster care, has assumed a leadership role in incorporating into its foster-home program elements specifically designed to serve the children's needs in relation to their identity. This program has included African history and culture seminars, the provision of libraries on Black history in several foster homes, Black selfhood sessions conducted by recent college graduates, and visits to Black arts festivals and cultural events. The deliberate efforts by this agency stem from a basic conviction and understanding of the position of Black children in society, and especially of Black children in foster care. As an agency publication put it: "Quality services to 'neglected' and 'dependent' Black children are unique in child welfare. Services perceived, designed, and delivered with the understanding that their 'neglect' and 'dependency' stem largely from conditions of conflict between their Blackness and larger society are true innovations." Not only are they true innovations, they are innovations which all agencies, Black and white, that serve Black children must incorporate into practice.

PART THREE

8 Patterns of organizational reform in child welfare

In Chapter 2–7 we have traced the treatment of Black children in the child welfare system from colonial times to the 1960's, documenting both past and present manifestations of racism in the treatment of Black children. This history is a prime example of the operation of overt and covert institutional racism. For over two hundred years—until, in fact, the last decade—the dominant child welfare institutions of the country openly excluded Black children. This overt racist discrimination has been replaced by a covert but nonetheless effective racism in the maldistribution of services to Black children. The policies of exclusion have largely ceased, but the services still are not reaching the children. We have detailed the gradual shifts away from the exclusion of Black children and have presented the current national picture in the distribution of services to Black children. We have also examined some of the special efforts made to stop overt discrimination against Black children, especially in relation to the service of adoption. There we saw Black children in the day-to-day functioning of child-placement agencies and systems, and the practices which underlie the past and present maldistribution of services.

The behavioral racism reflected in all of the inequities inflicted on Black children by white child welfare agencies and systems is accompanied by several manifestations of ideational racism which in fact serve to perpetuate and protect the behavioral manifestations. As we have seen, efforts for change specifically for Black children have almost always been met with a rationale which absolves those perpetuating the discrimination. These rationales all rest on a pervasive negative conception of Black people—of the children, of their families, of their communities, and of their institutions. Each facet of these rationales reflects the negation of Black people and the Black experience. And this same negation of Blackness pervades the language of child welfare practice. Black children have come to be known in agencies not as Black but as "hard to place." This negative conception is reflected in the almost total absence of Black children from the child welfare literature until the last decade. That literature totally eclipses the enormous efforts of Black people—of Black organizations and Black institutions—after the Civil War and into the present century to provide a network of child welfare services.

If there is one message that should emerge from the earlier chapters of this book, it is that of the pressing need for change and the tragically slow pace at which meager changes have come about. At the national level, the distribution of services to Black children has barely changed in the last fifty years. Many of the problems and dysfunctions of the 1940's are all too present in the child welfare systems of the 1960's and the 1970's. Why? Why have not new and more relevant services been developed, why have the inequities in the existing ones persisted, and why, in the face of the most earnest efforts to overcome discrimination against Black children, has so little effective, manifest change come about?

We argue that these efforts failed because they were not sufficiently radical. More specifically, they were not conceived or pursued from a Black perspective. They did not grow out of the Black experience. In addition, they were not based on recognition that some of the dysfunctions were inherent in the existing system of child welfare services.

Historically, efforts at changing the major systems and institutions of child welfare have been thwarted principally by the continuation of white control. White control has been at once the most pervasive manifestation of racism in the system, the source of its greatest dysfunctions, and the most effective barrier to change. To imagine that solutions to Black children's problems are to be found within the existing child welfare system, as it is currently structured, is, we believe, sheer folly. Thus, we call for a restructuring of the present system based on a new conceptualization both of child welfare and of Black children.

Fundamental to the restructuring of services and the system of delivering them, as well as to our entire analysis of Black children and child welfare, is a new and broader conception of Black children in the context of their family and community. Indeed, as long as the problem is conceived of as a matter between Black children and the established, white-dominated child welfare system, neither can the past and present failures be understood, nor the solutions and directions of change charted.

In effect, the most commonly held assumption concerning Black children and child welfare is that the Black child's problems stem from his negatively valued family and disorganized community, and that his solutions lie in the institutions of the larger white society. We propose that the reverse interpretation is the more valid one, and we are borne out by the history of American child welfare. The incorrectness of the assumption that the resources for Black children lie in the white society is at once the tragedy of the history and the most fundamental barrier to ·change. The entire child welfare system seems presently predicated on this erroneous assumption. The major sources of power and control over the distribution of child welfare services are white; but the resources themselves—the love, the nurturance, and the sustenance—are in Black families and Black people. It is time, we think, that control over the children's resources be turned over to their people.

THE DIRECTIONS OF REFORM

What, then, are the directions of reform in child welfare? In *Black Families in White America* (Billingsley, 1968) it was argued that two broad categories of social change were indicated in situations affecting Black family and community life. The first were "external" changes—changes in the character, structure, and operation of the major institutions of the larger society which are responsible for meeting the needs of "all the people," to make room for a significant, substantial, and equitable Black presence. At the same time, "internal" changes are necessary—local, community-based institutions must be specifically conceived, designed, controlled, and managed by members of the Black community. (pp. 151–52) This two-pronged approach to social change seems highly consistent with the compartmentalized existence of Black people in America and the "double consciousness" so eloquently described by Du Bois (1903).

Others are also thinking along these lines. At the Congress of African Peoples in Atlanta, Georgia, in September, 1970, the special workshop on social organization in the Black community adopted unanimously the following statement of objectives: "We will by any means necessary move to infiltrate and co-opt *all* the existing social institutions for the purpose of gaining, maintaining, and using our power correctly. We will at the same time move to create alternative social institutions which are based on a Black ideology." (Congress of African Peoples, 1970, p. 3) This resolution also called for specific efforts to apply this objective to "adoption agencies, welfare and health centers, and day care centers." (p. 4) A similar theme was expressed by Black child-development professionals meeting in Washington, D.C., June 10–13, 1970, under the sponsorship of the Black Women's Community Development Foundation. This conference— billed as the first national conference of Black child-development experts—brought together parents, legislators, and practitioners in a wide variety of fields with a special interest in children. Their general purposes were to:

> Develop a set of Black standards and guidelines for child development programming in our communities; (2) develop ways of disseminating the findings and results of the conference to the general Black community; (3) discuss ways of identifying, locating, funding and using sources of technical assistance for child development centers; (4) discuss ways of helping communities establish and control their centers and use them for total community economic development; (5) discuss an overall position and strategy regarding child development, welfare trends and issues, e.g., adoptions, institutional infant care, white institutional and government research and surveys; (6) organize the conference into a permanent body to be inclusive of other concerned individuals, organizations, and institutions. [Conference of Black Child Development, 1970, p. 10]

The proceedings of this conference are a serious beginning on all these stated purposes, and a permanent organization has been established.

Still another call for Black leadership in the definition, design, and control of child welfare programs has come from the Institute of the Black World, formerly a part of the Martin Luther King Center in Atlanta. The Institute staff and associates are currently working on a set of "agenda papers" designed to be definitive statements and analyses of the Black agenda for the 1970's in the major aspects of life. In the area of health and welfare, the task force at the Institute has taken the position that Black people must exert their energies to "humanize" the larger society by developing strong Black alternatives to existing policies and institutions that will serve the needs of Black children and families. Black solidarity is the hallmark of the Institute's work. Lerone Bennett, Jr., a member of the Institute, has expressed this credo as follows: "We believe in the community of the Black dead and the Black living and the Black unborn. We believe that that community has a prior claim on our time and our resources, and that we must respond when it calls." (Manuscript, 1971, p. 1)

Finally, the National Association of Black Social Workers, in its second annual convention held at Howard University in Washington in February, 1970, has taken a similar stance. The organization is devoted to the creation and operation of "viable Black institutions," and individual members are asked to pledge: "I will consciously use my skills, and my whole being, as an instrument for social change, with particular attention directed to the establishment of Black social institutions such as schools, hospitals and voluntary agencies." (*Black Caucus,* 1970, p. 5) At the same time, members are urged to transform the existing white agencies in which they currently work. (p. 64)

How, then, can we humanize the white institutions which affect children and at the same time develop viable Black institutions to serve their needs more effectively? The first requirement is to recognize that existing institutions were not conceived or structured to be relevant to Black children, Black families, or Black communities. Consequently they are grossly dysfunctional for this task. Their dysfunction arises from a complex interplay of the forces of racism, professionalism, sectarianism, and bureaucracy.

Before proceeding with our discussion of these problem areas, we wish to point out that we do not negate the efforts made by the agencies which we studied in Chapter 7. By 1968, these agencies had made substantial inroads on the basic racism in child welfare. The steps that they had taken should encourage and serve as examples for other agencies. Nonetheless, even they had not gone nearly far enough. More radical changes must be made if Black children are ever to be adequately served. The problem of racism does not lie with any individual agency; rather, it goes beyond the single agency to the racist system of child welfare in which it is embedded.

Racism

Those who would conceive, design, administer, and support child welfare programs that are relevant to the needs of Black children and who would strive to eliminate the negative view of Black people must undergo a process of remedial education. The purpose of such education is to put Black people into a more realistic and positive perspective. Such education must be intellectual and emotional. It must be sustained, and it must be conceived and executed by Black people. No one-shot lecture or speech will do the job. It will be painful and expensive, yet this kind of remedial education, which we have all missed in our formal and informal education, must be a part of the program of child welfare.

For such reeducation to take place there must be a deep commitment to the effort from top to bottom, from boards to administrators to staff. Furthermore, the Black teachers must be selected by the Black community. The idea that the white community can designate some "responsible" Black representative is totally incompatible with any sincere desire to learn.

We must learn a new concept of the Black community. We must learn that it is a historical and contemporary ethnic subsociety, sharing important conditions, experiences, values, and sentiments. The rising moves toward ethnic solidarity in the Black community must be understood in this context and aided and abetted by the child welfare system. A fundamental requirement is the abandonment of two important misconceptions of the Black community still current. One is the view that there is no Black community, but only individuals and families who happen to be Black and who are sometimes forced to live together in the same neighborhood because of prejudice and poverty. This view precludes recognition that the community has a meaningful institutional and cultural life of its own. The second view holds that there is a Black community, but that it is a depressed, poverty-ridden ghetto which should be destroyed or overcome. In the second view, the community values are negative and dysfunctional for child care. The children should be "rescued" and placed in better surroundings by the white child welfare system. This view underlies the paternalism which characterizes the child welfare system today.

Finally, a remedial education program must help us develop a more realistic and positive conception of the Black family itself, as it functions within the Black community and within the wider white society. The view is still very common in child welfare that Black family life is disorganized and unstable, and that consequently not enough qualified Black families can be found to rear the large numbers of dependent and neglected Black children who need parents.

Those of us who would analyze, conceive, design, and execute child welfare programs must begin to think Black when we think of Black children. We must consider them in a context of Black family and community life instead of adhering to the white perspective which is as perverted as it is pervasive. That perspective grows out of an over-concern with the structure rather than the function of Black family life. It ignores the historical and contemporary child-care patterns in the Black community. Most damaging of all, it ignores the need for the child welfare system to change itself in order to meet the needs of the families, and instead implies that families should change in order to conform to the child welfare system. Black families now must convince white child welfare experts that they are "qualified" to rear their own children or to decide what substitute care their children should receive. As we have observed, other important social groups exercise these rights. And their children get better service.

The basic change that must come about if racism is to be eliminated in child welfare is a sharing and at some points an abdication of power and control in favor of the Black community. We do not make specific recommendations here. Rather, we recommend that decision-making functions be shared with and transferred to the Black community, so that the specifics of alteration can be decided upon by Black people. The Black community in Philadelphia may decide on an optimal situation for its children that is quite different from the optimal solution for the Black community in Los Angeles. What is incumbent upon the present child welfare system is honest relinquishment of control through deliberate change in the mechanisms of control to open them up to Black people. If there is a sincere sharing of power, the specifics of change can then come from the Black communities.

Other Sources of Dsyfunction

If racism, pure and complex, is the chief barrier to be overcome for the child welfare system to meet the needs of Black children, still other barriers are represented by bureaucracy, professionalism, and sectarianism. Each of these forces, which are endemic to our present system, has an honorable tradition in child welfare. They have helped provide services to countless thousands of children who might otherwise have been neglected. In the contemporary scene, however, these forces are often perverted to serve as handmaidens to racism, to the detriment of Black children.

Bureaucracy—multilevel authority, extreme specialization, elaborate rules governing eligibility, and rigid functional and jurisdictional divisions—prevents Black children from coming into care to the same extent that white children do. When they are in care, bureaucracy prevents their placement in permanent homes. One reason for this is that the bureaucracy was designed expressly to serve the needs of white children. The assumption has been that these rules and procedures are humane and universal. If they did not serve Black people as well as they did white people, that was the fault of the Black people, or the fault of the general society which made them poor or culturally deprived, or the fault of the government; in any case, it was somebody else's fault, not the fault of the child welfare system.

The bureaucratic nature of the agencies is fortified by *professionalism,* which also all too often prevents established child welfare systems from serving the needs of Black children. Even in the agencies we studied in Chapter 7, where official policies were undergoing great change, there were still very firmly held professional values which were completely outside the experience of Black families and children in the urban ghettos. Consider, for example, the professional view that adoptive homes should have two parents who are married to each other, have never been married before, and have been married for a certain amount of time; that the wife should not work; that there should be no other children, and there should be sufficient room for the child; and that the adoptive parents should pay a fee ranging from a few hundred dollars to a few thousand. Surely these values did not evolve in reference to Black children or Black families. Yet it is hard indeed to convince white adoption workers that these values prevent them from serving Black children who need homes and from finding Black families who would take them in. We need not only a realistic set of standards for Black children and families, but a different and distinct one which grows out of their experience and life styles. Only when such standards are adopted can these children be said to be treated equally with white children. To impose white standards on Black children is not equality, but a subtle form of professional insensitivity at best, and racism at worst.

Sectarianism also works to the detriment of Black children. Religious belief or ascription, or the lack thereof, plays a role in child welfare that is as insidious and dysfunctional for Black children as it is widespread, respected, and protected by both the private and public sectors of the child welfare system. The notions that a newborn child has a religion, that his natural mother has the right to decide what religious preparation he should receive in the home which cares for him, and that the state or agency has the right to impose the mother's religion on the child and his new parents, are all foreign to the experience of Black people. Thus sectarianism, which may serve very well the needs of Jewish families, or white Catholic families, or white Protestant families, is a major obstacle to meeting the needs of Black children and families.

THREE SYSTEMS OF CHILD WELFARE AGENCIES

We need, then, to abandon the notion that a single white-conceived, white-dominated, and white-administered system of child welfare, hampered as it is by racism, bureaucracy, professionalism, and sectarianism, can possibly meet the needs of all children of all races and subcultures. We need to adopt a pluralistic, multiethnic conception of child welfare services, and to develop, deliberately and systematically, different child welfare services that will explicitly consider these ethnic realities. We need to reform, revise, and build on the present framework of child welfare services to develop a tripartite system: (1) a white system of child welfare services, much like the best of the white ethnic and sectarian systems now in existence; (2) a system of public agencies developed specifically with Black children in mind, while operating to serve all needy children; and (3) a Black system of child welfare services to serve Black children in a specific way.

White System

The Jewish Child Care Association of New York City, the Lutheran Children's Services, and the Catholic Association of Children's Agencies are excellent examples of white child-care systems designed expressly to meet the needs of groups of white children. By and large, these systems were conceived and designed by members of the groups to be served, and are administered by those groups. They receive substantial financing from those groups; however, public monies are a major source of support for all. These systems need to be expanded in some instances, and in all instances they need better financing, including a larger share of local, state, and Federal monies.

These white agencies for white children must help meet the needs of the large numbers of Black children who are in need of care. Some Jewish, Catholic, and Lutheran agencies have already demonstrated an awareness of such a responsibility, among them the Louise Wise Services in New York, the New York Foundling Hospital, the Children's Aid Society of Philadelphia, and the Chicago Child Care Society.

There are two major reasons why these voluntary, white agencies have a responsibility to Black children. First, the need is tremendous, and these agencies have a humanitarian and professional commitment. All were founded and operate ostensibly to meet crying human needs. In order to be true to this calling, they must devote some, and in many instances, substantial, portions of their resources to one of the great human tragedies of modern times.

Second, the agencies are financed in large and increasing measure by public funds from government sources. The money they receive from community-wide campaigns for voluntary contributions must also be considered public funding, at least in part, because of the tax-exempt status and other privileges accorded these voluntary agencies. These white agencies are obligated to serve public needs by their public support.

But if white agencies are going to make any meaningful and positive contribution to the welfare of Black children, they must change. They must transform themselves from white agencies to multiethnic and multiracial agencies. They must attack the racism in their conception of Black people, in their conception of their own function, in their board and policy-making bodies, in their staff, and in their relationship to the Black community.

Essentially the Black perspective must become meaningful to the white agencies, and the Black community must become a partner. Agencies which now devote ten percent of their resources to Black children and families must move that up to thirty percent. At the same time, as a means and an end of this activity, they must involve the Black community as a partner in every phase of the agency. The programs must be designed by Black people who know the Black community, the wider community, and the profession of caring for children.

These programs must be developed and set in motion by boards of directors which are not simply white upper class, but include a substantial proportion of Black people of all social classes. A substantial proportion for some agencies will be a third of the board. For others it will be two-thirds. This must include a sufficiently wide cross section of the Black community so that the range and complexity of that community will be reflected in board deliberations, and so that leadership from this ethnic group can emerge and be sustained. Additionally, agencies and their boards must educate themselves about the conditions in and resources of the Black community. Futhermore, they must go out of their way to develop and recruit Black staff in substantial numbers, at least in proportion to the agency resources devoted to Black children, the proportion of Black board members, and the proportion of Black children served. Finally, agency boards must give up some of the autonomy they now have in deciding on programs for the placement of Black children. Such decisions must somehow be shifted to the Black community, through board members, staff, or community advisory committees, or parents of the children served. In short, if these white agencies wish to serve the needs of Black children to some substantial degree while maintaining their major commitment to white children, they must be transformed from white agencies to multiracial ones. In the process they must develop structured attacks on the racism, professionalism, and bureaucracy so rampant today. Even the exemplary agencies in our study have not moved far enough in this direction to make a major impact on the problems of Black children and the functions of their agencies. The need is urgent.

There is some slight hope that existing institutions will undertake the type of transformation we are urging, although this hope is like the shore dimly seen. One white institution that has undertaken such a transformation is the Family Service Association of America. The national staff and Board of Directors have taken seriously the challenge of making their organization relevant to the needs of Black people. It is difficult to know exactly when the process began. Some time after the assassination of Martin Luther King, Jr., and the issuance of the Kerner Commission Report in the spring of 1968, the Family Service Association, along with a number of other organizations aspiring to serve the Black community, began an intensive examination of its own structure and functioning, in order to improve its service to Black families. One landmark in this effort was a conference in November, 1968, attended by the national staff and Board of Directors together with regional representatives from around the country. At this conference, known as The Princeton Institute because it was held at Princeton, New Jersey, these officials subjected themselves to a most thoroughgoing analysis of their organization and their own involvement in and support of institutional white racism. And they did this under the leadership of two of their own Black board members plus a team of Black professionals called together by the National Urban League. This institute led to a number of structural changes in the national organization. Changed procedures resulted in a substantial increase in Black board and national staff members. In addition, a new division of the agency was established under a dynamic Black social worker, Mrs. Frances Brisbane, to focus on the needs of Black people. A special issue of the *Journal of Social Casework* was devoted to Black families. Several other measures were taken which indicated real efforts by the national association to obtain the kind of remedial education necessary for it to relate more effectively to the Black community.

A second landmark in this organization's efforts to attack racism in its own house occurred a year later, at the Association's Biennial Conference in Philadelphia, in November, 1969. On this occasion a Black Caucus was formed within F.S.A.A. on the initiative of Benjamin Finley of Chicago. The Caucus succeeded in organizing itself sufficiently to negotiate with the planners of F.S.A.A. for the purpose of "turning this conference around and making it relevant." On Monday, November 17, which subsequently became known as the Day of Black Challenge, the Caucus conducted the entire program. It later presented a well-organized series of demands to F.S.A.A. The organization has taken the demands seriously and has made valiant efforts to meet them, with modest and spotty success. The Caucus became a permanent organization and meets regularly at the expense of the Association to conduct its business.

An outgrowth of the Caucus work was the formation of a Task Force on Institutional Racism within F.S.A.A. It was formed as an organ of the Board of Directors and reports directly to the Board. The Task Force has a two-to-one ratio of Black Caucus members to F.S.A.A. staff and Board. Its specific and only task is to focus on racism within F.S.A.A., point it up, analyze it, and propose ways of dealing with it. While the Task Force reports directly to the Board, it considers itself mainly responsive and reponsible to the Black Caucus. It takes the responsibility of overseeing the implementation of the demands of the Black Caucus. At a meeting sponsored by the Association in Albuquerque in August, 1970, a Chicano Caucus was formed. It works in conjunction with the Black Caucus.

In November, 1970, one year after it was formed, the Black Caucus assayed the progress which had been made. It observed the following efforts: (1) The national staff and board had made commendable efforts to change their organization from a white racist one one to a multiracial, multiethnic one designed to serve the Black and Brown communities. (2) Some, perhaps most, members of the national staff and Board seemed to have become more sensitive to their organization and to the needs of Black people. (3) A long-range educational program to recognize and combat the forces of racism had been launched. (4) Some specific personnel changes had been made. Ten new Black Board members had been added. Seven of the eight staff vacancies which had occurred had been filled by Black professionals, and one local agency had hired a Black executive, the first in the history of the national association. (5) Each of the major regions of the country had conducted a modified "Princeton Institute," and a special issue of *Social Casework* had been devoted to Mexican-Americans. (6) The Association officials had exposed themselves to continual dialogue with members of the Black Caucus. (7) They had engaged in continual explanations to other white associates that change and internal self-examination were needed to root out racism. (8) They had tried valiantly to raise money to increase their efforts at transformation.

These efforts are more than can be claimed by most other social welfare agencies. Yet members of the Black Caucus meeting in November, 1970, did not feel much optimism that even this organization could sufficiently transform itself to be an effective instrument of service to the Black community. There were many obstacles: (1) lack of support and open resistance by member agencies of the association, (2) lack of extra financial support for the bold new ideas for family service to Black and Brown communities, (3) unwillingness on the part of the national staff and board to let the F.S.A.A. go the whole way and die as an organization, if necessary, for the new cause. Thus, the kind of transformation urged by the Black Caucus meets a certain hard resistance by the white rulers when efforts reach a certain critical level. There always comes a time when a staff member threatens to resign in a huff if his domain is altered; when a member agency threatens to resign from the association; when a large contributor threatens to discontinue his support. It seemed to Caucus members that as long as the organization remained substantially controlled by white members, no matter how enlightened and committed, their pressures, publics, associates, prior commitments, and prior loyalties would not allow the organization to go all out in responding to the needs and demands of Black people.

In 1972 the Family Service Association of America is still a white racist organization in all essential features, despite the best efforts and good will of many of its staff and officers, and the most urgent demands of its Black Caucus. And while it has come a long way in four years, it seems a long way still from the kind of transformation which is required if it is to serve its Black and Brown constituencies as well as it does its white constituency.

Public System

A second type of system, which has greater promise for Black children, is the public system developed specifically with them in mind, while open to all needy children not being adequately served by the private child welfare system. In our study we have analyzed the emergence of Black-oriented public adoption agencies in Los Angeles, Chicago, and New York. Other large cities have established, or are establishing, similar agencies. In our view, these agencies have greater promise in meeting the needs of Black children than do the private organizations. Their wider scope more nearly matches the scope of the problem. The Los Angeles County public agency places considerably more Black children than any private agency in the country. In

New York City, it is the public agency which places the largest volume of Black children, despite the fact that it is underdeveloped compared with the voluntary agencies. The public agencies may also outstrip the voluntary ones in Chicago and Philadelphia. This is the case largely because the volume of placements by the voluntary agencies is so pitifully small.

If the public agencies have tremendous potential for meeting the needs of Black children it is also true that they have not lived up to that potential anywhere in the country, even allowing for the current financial and political limitations. Perhaps the most crippling handicap of these agencies is the conception of the agency and its function held by those who create and administer it. They do not have a positive conception of their function or of Black people. They see themselves in business to serve "disadvantaged," "hard-to-place," "problem," "unfortunate" children who are left out of the more favored placement systems. Consequently, they have not developed a conception of the Black community as both master and clientele of the agency. They approach the Black community for clients, sometimes for advisors, and for social workers to carry out the policies designed by the white community. One of the public agencies that has taken the Black community seriously is the Los Angeles County Department of Adoptions. The establishment of the Compton office is an example of a serious attempt to serve the Black community better. However, the Black community must have distinct influence on and control over the agency's function before it can begin to approximate a Black agency. In New York City, the appointment of an Advisory Committee on Adoptions on which Blacks and Puerto Ricans constitute a majority is a step in the right direction, but it is a long way from control of an agency.

Pressures are exerted on public agencies specifically to keep them from becoming Black agencies, even though the Black community is where the greatest public need is. There is a lingering, negative conception of Blackness which seeks to legitimize these agencies by making sure that they serve significant numbers of white children too. The conflict between the philosophy and structure needed to serve white children and those needed to serve Black children is often severe. It needs to be recognized and dealt with by creating whatever is necessary in the way of different structures and different philosophies for the placement of children of different ethnic groups. The single color-blind standard for adoptive or foster parents is often ridiculous. One standard, for example, is that parents should be able to speak proper English. This works to the obvious disadvantage of Spanish-speaking couples in Los Angeles and New York. The requirement is not less dysfunctional when applied to the Black community. One result is that Black and Spanish-speaking children are sometimes placed with white families rather than with those of their own ethnic group whose English is not so proper. The underlying rationale for this procedure has nothing to do with the welfare of the children. The agency staff are often able to communicate only with people who speak proper English, and therefore have easily convinced themselves that this is in the best interest of the children too.

Public agencies that wish to make a maximum contribution to Black children must become less white in their conception and operation, and more Black. The Black community must no longer surrender its children to the white system, with minimum say about what happens to them. The major decisions about the children must be made by the Black community, and the public agency must become an enabling mechanism for carrying out these decisions. The agency must also have substantial numbers of Black people on its board and its staff, and must make these Black partners responsible for the total agency operation, and specifically for the portion devoted to Black children. The agency that wishes to serve must also abandon its strain for whiteness in clientele. The proportion of children served who are Black may range from fifty to ninety-five percent, depending on the community. It is imperative, however, that the agency's conception, as well as its structure and function, adequately reflect a commitment to the service of Black children.

Black System

However committed and professional the private white agencies may be, their major concern must remain white children. However large the public agencies may be, their major concern must be for *all* the children in need, and they must operate within certain universalistic principles which are in the final analysis subject to the white majority. Clearly, the public agencies cannot have the flexibility and particularistic character needed to create new ways of serving Black children. There is, therefore, a crying need for specifically Black-conceived, -designed, -managed, and -staffed agencies to serve in a specific way the needs of the Black children in the context of Black families and the Black community. This third system of child welfare agencies, which might appropriately take the title Afro-American Child Care Association, might indeed take in a few white children who lived in the community and could benefit from its service. It might indeed employ some white staff with special skills and commitment. It might even have some white board members. The important thing about these Black agencies—the thing which makes them Black—is that the community would conceive them, design them, and make the important policy decisions about their structure, functions, staff, and services to children.

This Black system of child welfare should be voluntary or private, just as the first system is private. It would therefore have greater autonomy and flexibility than the public agencies. It would be in an excellent position to innovate in meeting the needs of Black children. It could set its own standards. We cannot anticipate exactly how the Black system would differ from the white system or the public system, but we do not need to. The importance of the Black agencies would not lie in their distinctiveness but in their usefulness. In some respects they would be just like other agencies and in some respects different, depending on *what benefits the children*—not on the standards and procedures of white agencies. It is unlikely, for example, that these Black agencies would conclude, as the white ones now do, that Black children are hard to place because Black families are not generally qualified to be adoptive or foster parents.

While the structure and services of the Black system would depend on the given city and its people, some general outlines can be identified.

First, the conception of the service, the design of the service, and the policymaking and administration should all be essentially Black and indigenous to the Black community. This means a wide cross section of the Black community. Participation in this association should not be limited to any one segment or social class of the community. The Board of Directors, for example, should be composed of men and women from the Black upper class, middle class, working class, and under class. It should include the "respectables" and the "nonrespectables," the "church folk" and the "street folk."

Second, the association might well grow out of some existing organization in the Black community, although it should have its own independent governing board. But the association should be tied to some existing community structure, so as to provide legitimation, to help enhance the social fabric of the community, and to contribute to the emerging sense of Black peoplehood. In some communities, the Urban League might be an appropriate agency to initiate the association. In other communities, an existing child welfare council would serve the purpose. So would the Black Ministerial Alliance or the Black United Leadership Group, or some other social, civic, or business organization. In still other communities, a new independent Ad Hoc Committee or Board of Directors might be necessary.

Third, in order to maintain autonomy, the fund raising should be launched within the Black community. A good precedent was established by the Harlem River Cooperative Society in New York City. The very first fund-raising activity was to assess each member of the Board of Directors $100. Thereafter, the Board solicited funds within the neighborhood. Only then did the society turn to more extensive sources outside the Black community.

Fourth, whatever form the agencies might take, it seems unlikely that they should follow the current specialized, segmentalized, bureaucratic forms of organization now characteristic of the white agencies.

Fifth, the role of white people in the agencies should be determined by members of the Black community. This role should be minimal, and at most, supportive and technical. Whites should not play any substantial role in the leadership or policy making. Nor should they participate in any substantial numbers in the activities of the association. Nor, finally, should they reap the financial benefits of designing, constructing, managing, or servicing whatever facilities are involved. Substantial participation of whites in these traditional ways in programs designed for Black people subverts the essential efforts to increase ethnic solidarity and to build up the psychological and social structure of the Black community. For those who would tear down this structure, or fail to build it, because they have some theoretical commitment to racial integration or assimilation, these prescriptions will be anathema. But the question is, Who should decide on the policies, structures, and practices of Black child welfare? There are, of course, a variety of roles for white people who could support these institutions. They might provide technical assistance where invited, give financial assistance through both public and private sources, and educate the general public to the need for, and functions of, the association.

As we have seen, Black agencies are not without precedent. The Black community began developing its own child welfare institutions just after the Civil War, and continued to do so until we entered the period of integrationist ideology which began after World War II. Even at present there are examples of Black initiatives in child welfare agencies.

But only the rudiments of a Black child welfare system exist. This system is the most underdeveloped of the three we advocate. Nowhere in the country are people committed to systematic development of child welfare agencies in and of the Black community. In our view, such a Black system has the greatest potential of all for new and distinctive approaches to Black children. It is a logical outgrowth of the new sense of ethnic identity in the Black community. It is wholly consistent with the past and present activities of other ethnic groups.

As we indicated at the beginning of this chapter, the idea of Black agencies is beginning to take hold, or more properly to reassert itself, among the Black intelligentsia. It is also beginning to take hold in the child welfare field. Black child welfare agencies have been established. Some of these are established by white people who continue to control them. These agencies are obviously not the kind we advocate, although they are a step forward. One agency of this kind was established and funded by the Boston Children's Services in 1969, in the Roxbury section of the city. In many respects the agency was advanced and innovative. It had a Black executive, a Black staff, and a Black advisory committee. But it was not allowed to offer all the services that the downtown agency offered, and the most prestigious service of all—adoption—was not available. Black families had to go downtown to the white agency for a baby. More important, the ultimate control of the agency rested with the downtown executive and board. Community control was not instituted. Still, this agency represents a step in the right direction.

Other Black agencies have been established by white agencies which surrender policy and control of the new agencies to the Black community. When the Spence-Chapin Adoption Service founded Harlem-Dowling as an independent child welfare agency in Harlem, with its own Advisory Council and staff, the parent agency guaranteed funding to the new agency until 1975. Then the new agency will become completely independent. Harlem-Dowling is New York State's first and only voluntary, all-Black adoption and foster-care agency. If the Advisory Council feels that sufficient funds are on hand, independence may come sooner.

A primary function of the thirty-member, all-Black Council is to ensure that the agency is giving the services desired by the community. At present these services include genuine counseling of natural mothers, their families, and the natural fathers and their families where possible. The agencies consciously employ a screening-in policy on both adoptive and foster homes which includes active rendering of services to applicants to surmount obstacles which might impede adoption.

As of October, 1971, Harlem-Dowling had 155 children in foster care; 103 foster homes have been licensed. Between January and September, 40 children had been returned to their natural parents, and 22 children had been placed in adoptive homes. Ten more adoptive placements were expected to occur in November, 1971. About 160 natural mothers and 16 natural fathers had been seen, and 500 foster-home and adoptive applicants. At that time, Joseph H. Smith, Director of the agency, reported that infants under three months were very easily placed—that, in fact, the demand from Black families was greater than the supply of Black babies. Spurred on by this response, the agency is now intensively pursuing placement for children with physical and psychological difficulties.

Some agencies have also sprung directly from the Black community. In August, 1970, Benjamin Finley, the new executive, presided at the inauguration of the Afro-American Family and Community Services Agency of Chicago. It was a new beginning for a Black agency, now funded by the United Community Fund of Chicago, which had begun in 1965. Mr. Finley has described its beginnings:

> In the fall of 1965, I accepted a position as Director of Casework Services in the Children's Section of the largest Mental Health Center in the world. This Center had developed outstanding clinical services for the outpatient treatment of the mentally ill. By 1965 the neighborhood in which the Center was located was totally Black. Because of this fact and the development of new programs by the Illinois Department of Mental Health, which administered the Clinic, most of the staff left the Mental Health Center in the summer of 1965 to go to work in a new Center located on the northwest side of the city, which is an all white neighborhood.

Manuel Jackson, Anne Fredd, Sung Kim, and Don Wata-
nabe were among the non-white staff who joined me in developing programs and writing a grant proposal, based on our experiences in the community. The Center obtained a three and
one-half million dollar grant from NIMH for the development
of the first and only comprehensive community mental health
service for Black neighborhoods in the state of Illinois.

As fate and racism would have it, Dr. Gyarfas, who had
immigrated to the United States from Hungary following
World War II (and free of racist's attitudes so typical of white
America) died in the fall of 1967 and was temporarily replaced by a white administrator who had little knowledge or
capacity for empathy with poor Blacks in the community.

By January 1968, it had become clear to those of us responsible for having developed the comprehensive mental health
plan that we were no longer needed nor wanted at the Mental
Health Center. Being older and more experienced in these
kinds of racist practices, I dealt with the trauma by submitting
a resignation and securing another position, effective June
1968 when my field work students would graduate.

During the later part of February 1968, the union of
Illinois Department of Mental Health employees, consisting
primarily of non-professionals, and at the Mental Health
Center, Blacks went on strike for improved working conditions and increased salaries. Manny, Anne, Don and I were
some of the few professionals who belonged to the union and
supported the strike by walking picket lines. By the end of the
first week of the strike, Brother Martin Luther King was assas-
sinated and the Black Brothers and Sisters initiated their re-
bellion within a block of the Mental Health Center. Those
workers who had been crossing the picket lines "to serve the
needy patients" made haste to get out of the community that
Friday (April 4, 1968) to the safety of their sanctuaries in
white neighborhoods and suburbia. Some of us on strike saw
the need for our presence in the community to offer assistance
to the community during that trying weekend. The Mental
Health Center closed its doors to the community, because the
new administration was more concerned about the safety of
the white workers than the needs of the community. This was
the crowning blow!

This was also the beginning of the Afro-American Family and
Community Services, Inc. Like so many Black developments, this

agency arose in part from disappointed efforts to gain entrance and equal treatment within white organizations. On April 14, 1968, Benjamin Finley called a planning meeting "for a Black social agency" at his home. On August 14 of the same year a small group of professionals and community people held an all-day workshop to plan the agency. In November, 1969, after initial rejection, and after a change in the policies of the Fund, the United Community Fund of Chicago authorized a grant of $50,000 to the new agency. Mr. Finley's account continues:

> By this time we had lost a number of our members who had become impatient and discouraged. Many of the members who had not left had become inactive because the work that went on between August 14, 1968 and November 1969 was mostly highly technical and tedious, with no glamour and excitement. The few of us left were so burdened with rewriting programs, budgets, and doing other kinds of things that white folks had never let us know about, we were unable to design activities and programs to sustain the interest of the others. In June 1970 the Community Fund cautiously remitted $20,000 of their $50,000 grant, enabling us to open our first office on August 1, 1970.

He has also described for us the basic purposes of the agency.

> The purpose of Afro-American Family and Community Services, Inc. (AFCS) is to assist Black Chicagoans in benefitting from the society in which they are oftentimes only partial participants. AFCS is being established by and within the Black community for the purpose of developing a new system of delivering meaningful social welfare services. The program will be geared toward revitalizing, reaffirming, and reconfirming Black people's involvement as members of the Black community.
>   Specifically, AFCS will seek to attain its objectives through:
>
> 1. Assisting individuals, groups, and the Black community in making effective use of particular service systems in metropolitan Chicago.
> 2. Enabling and supporting Black people in their struggle to gain liberation from social institutions that perpetuate and/or promote the subjugated state of Black people.

3. Working with professionals to insist that they are account-able to the Black community as a way of neutralizing and erasing the deleterious effects of past and present racism.
4. Assuming the responsibility for confronting agencies and institutions in relation to their responsibilities to provide meaningful services in the Black community.
5. Providing consultation services and an operational model to other agencies.
6. Creating resources to provide emergency services in time of crises and in those instances where the meeting of needs is obstructed by bureaucratic processes in other agencies.
7. Fostering, maintaining, and enhancing the dignity of Black people.

A major concern of the agency is to deal with and alleviate the effects upon Black people of years of subjugation in a white racist system calculated to destroy their dignity, power, and self-respect. The primary thrust of AFCS will be acting as advocate of Black people—all services, programs, and ac-tivities will be geared toward the SURVIVAL of Black people and the promotion of a climate where EVERY BLACK PER-SON will have optimum opportunity for sustained, creative, self-determined participation in society.

At the inauguration of the agency the new director announced to a surprised audience containing many of Chicago's prominent profes-sional social workers: "We have abolished the principle of confiden-tiality so dear to professional social work. And now I want to introduce to you our first clients." A brief description of these first clients of the agency will indicate something of its catholicity:

CASE #1

Brother James Morton, one of our first clients . . . asked our help in obtaining sick benefits which he felt were due him from his former employer. He had made a number of attempts through the unions and with the employer to resolve the dif-ferences in opinions regarding his eligibility for sick pay, with no success. He really had little hope that we would be effective in assisting him in obtaining the sick pay he felt he was due. He used most of the initial interview primarily to ventilate his angry feelings toward his employer, a large factory employing a number of Blacks and other minority groups in low status jobs.

Brother Morton had worked for twelve years for the Ajax Electric Company prior to November 1969 when he was hospitalized with a heart attack. While recuperating, he had another attack in February 1970, during which he fell and broke three ribs. He had been unable to work since the first heart attack. The Company's insurance was supposed to provide full pay for the first thirteen weeks of disability and one-half pay for the next thirty weeks of disability. For some inexplicable reason, the Company terminated disability pay after twenty-one weeks without any explanation or any positive response to Brother Morton's inquiries. Consequently Brother Morton applied for Social Security benefits. Brother Morton was also concerned that after three months, the Social Security Administration had not made a determination in his case. He felt that the Social Security Administration, just as the former employer, was giving him the run around.

During his initial visit, I telephoned his former employer and I also was given the run around—having to speak to five or six different persons before finally reaching the appropriate person responsible for resolving the situation. During the course of these calls, one employee, who knew Brother Morton personally, candidly stated that she felt that he was not being treated properly. Finally, the Company agreed to review the total situation.

In a telephone call . . . I was able to determine that the Social Security Administration was moving responsibly in making a determination in Brother Morton's case. . . .

Within three weeks Brother Morton had received the additional twenty-one weeks of half-pay due him from his employer and a determination letter granting disability benefits from the Social Security Administration. Brother Morton was so pleased with the promptness of our response to his request for help and the effectiveness of it, that he began to encourage other employees and ex-employees of the Ajax Electric Company to come to us for help in resolving serious problems of discriminatory personnel practices.

CASE #2

The first request for service . . . involved technical assistance to a group of residents of a new housing cooperative.

As a part of the Urban Renewal program in a deteriorated neighborhood populated by Polish Catholic immigrants and their descendants, the city contracted with a private developer to build cooperative housing with federal funding. The residents of the new housing consisted of from 80% to 90% Blacks, who had moved out of a large public housing complex and the surrounding area consisting primarily of dilapidated housing and a typical slum environment.

During the month of August 1970, the real estate firm responsible for the management of the new housing complex was ready to turn the management and control of the new development over to a cooperative board of directors. A slate of five persons, with obvious political connections (four whites and one token Black Sister) were conducting a sophisticated politically oriented campaign. In reaction to that slate, four Black Brothers decided to assume responsibility for running an opposition slate to assure that Blacks obtained control of the board of directors. Their campaign material and speeches highlighted the struggle for Black power. This emphasis on Blackness, unity, and power was unacceptable to many of the Brothers and Sisters living in the cooperative because their new housing epitomized a dream and wish on their part to forget the terrible housing conditions and neighborhood environment they had lived in for so long. They tended to see their new neighborhood as an integrated one and wanted to protect their new relationships with their white neighbors by being as "unmilitant" as possible.

When our help was sought, the Brothers running the opposition slate were discouraged and extremely frustrated. We suggested that they shift the focus of their campaign appeal to concentrate on community control and several other issues that were merely alluded to by the white slate of candidates. Specific advice and guidance were given in terms of campaign material, its distribution, and timing. Consequently, one and one-half weeks later the opposition slate consisting of four Black Brothers and one white man won the election.

Following the first Board meeting, the new President of the Board came to us asking our assistance in reviewing the financial reports of the real estate company . . . and getting suggestions about how to resolve some very serious financial problems, which appeared to be related to mismanagement. In addition, he asked our help in developing a day care center in

the housing development where space has been built-in. We
are currently giving technical assistance in the development of
a program plan and budget for the day care program which
is to be operated by the Board of Directors of the housing development. The President of the Board recognizes that they
are being critically watched by the tenants and others and the
first responsibility of the Board in establishing some credibility
would be to implement as quickly as possible a much needed
service like the day care program.

Afro-American Family and Community Services encompasses the essential elements of a relevant and innovative Black agency. It has
grown directly out of the experience of Black people. It is conceived,
designed, organized, governed, administered, and staffed by members
of the Black community for the benefit of their neighbors and themselves. It has a carefully controlled set of relationships and resources
from the wider white society. It is an example of the kind of Black
child welfare agency we need. Child welfare services must move beyond placement of children in substitute homes in order to serve the
basic needs of Black children, families, and communities.

But Afro-American Family and Community Services is not yet part
of the community-wide system of childhood and family services that
large urban Black communities need. No such system yet exists in this
country.

The public, white private, and Black private systems will all have
to support and understand one another. The Black system will raise
some money within the Black community, but it must clearly tap the
financial resources of the larger community as well. At the same time,
the other two systems will need the understanding, sanction, and support of the Black community if they are to be viable. All of these
systems will need sustained financial support from the larger community, including both public and private sources. In some cities the
Black system will need to call on the white community for financial
support, technical help, and political assistance. Such resources should,
of course, be provided in high quality and large quantity, but without
the elements of white control which now obtain in child welfare.

The need for Black agencies should not be interpreted as a mandate
for white people to design and impose them on the Black community.
These agencies must be developed by Black people, and the role of

white agencies is to encourage and support them in a variety of ways. The decisions and design must come from the Black community.

Let us be clear that the large metropolitan cities, with large Black communities and large numbers of Black children, need all three types of agencies to meet the needs of the children. Any one or two of these systems alone cannot do the job. But the three diversified systems we advocate seem to offer great hope.

9
Beyond placement: social policy and the welfare of black children

Throughout this book, we have been critical of the prevailing child welfare system as a major solution to the problems of Black children. The residual conception of child welfare—the view that the American system works fairly well and that only a few children whose families have failed them are in need of special care—coupled with the predominant emphasis on placement—the removal of children from their own homes when their families cannot meet their needs—has limited the scope and usefulness of child welfare as a system. An institutional conception of child welfare—resources from the total society harnessed to meet the needs of children as an ordinary permanent feature of society and available to all children—makes more sense. Further, a comprehensive view of the complex problems faced by children seems to offer more promise of help. Thus, we have urged the creation of a system of policies, programs, agencies, and services that is based on an appreciation of the history of Black people and of the larger social context within which Black communities are embedded, and based on the premise that these Black children are the critical focus of concern.

In Chapter 8 we outlined an approach to agency structures that seems to us consistent with this general conception. Thus, a system of agencies which allows for private, white-controlled agencies; public agencies controlled by the public at large; and private, Black-controlled agencies seems to offer an equitable place for Black children. In this final chapter we wish to consider the limitations of agencies, particularly agencies at the community level. However they may be conceived, designed, and administered, they will be inadequate to meet the needs of Black children fully. The institutional network of the largely white society must be reformed in order that the functioning of Black families and the well-being of their children may be enhanced. In this chapter, then, we take a brief look at some of the national social policies which must be reformed if we are to serve Black children properly. Such policies are conceived within and administered by the institutional framework of the larger society—including the political system, the economic system, and the systems of education, health, welfare, law enforcement, communications, and religion. These systems operate with a high degree of interaction. The policies they generate and administer have both direct and indirect impact on the lives of Black children, and have both positive and negative consequences. These institutions and the policies which flow through them are deeply afflicted by the forces of racism that are such a central part of American life, by bureaucratic rigidity and professional and conceptional dysfunctions, and sometimes by sectarianism.

In a moment we shall set forth some of the major social policies that seem to have promise for dealing more effectively with Black children. In order to establish a basis for this discussion, however, let us consider the conditions of life facing Black children in two specific locations in 1971: Washington, D.C., and the Brownsville section of Brooklyn, New York.

In Washington, D.C., according to the 1970 Census, the Black population reached 71 percent of the city total. As Table 9–1 shows, the population of the city had been dropping for twenty years, while the population of Blacks continued to rise. In terms of population, then, Washington, D.C., is among the nation's Blackest large urban areas. However, the city is almost completey controlled by the influence and interests of the surrounding white suburbanites.

This disparity has adverse consequences for Black children. It must

TABLE 9-1

Population of the District of Columbia and Surrounding Suburban Areas by Decades, 1920–1970

	District of Columbia		Maryland-Virginia Suburbs		Total (Washington Metropolitan Area)	
	Total Population	Percent Blacks	Total Population	Percent Blacks	Total Population	Percent Blacks
1970	756,510	71.1	2,104,613	7.9	2,861,123	24.6
1960	763,956	53.9	1,312,654	6.4	2,076,610	23.9
1950	802,178	35.0	905,690	9.0	1,707,868	22.8
1940	663,091	28.2	342,923	14.3	1,006,014	23.4
1930	486,869	27.1	217,132	19.2	704,001	24.7
1920	437,571	25.1	168,548	22.6	606,119	24.6

SOURCE: U.S. Department of Commerce, Bureau of the Census.

be emphasized that life for these children in the inner city is not all bleak by any means. Washington has many parks and other amenities that enhance the quality of life. But these Black children do not have nearly the same access to the resources of the larger society that white children have, and they face more than their fair share of hazards. Let us consider a situation which came to public attention toward the middle of 1971.

Washington health officials began testing children in a section of the inner city for lead poisoning, which is contracted by eating tiny flakes of lead-based paint, usually found peeling from the walls and woodwork in old houses. If untreated, lead poisoning can cause severe mental retardation or even death. The officials found that one child in ten showed an unsafe concentration of lead. The children, 1–6 years old, live in a model cities area of 2.3 square miles. The total population is estimated to be 80,000. Although lead-based paint is sold for exterior use, it is illegal for interior use in the Washington area.

The Brownsville section of Brooklyn is a community of 100,000 that has been described as 99 percent Black and Puerto Rican. As Robert Maynard observed in the *Washington Post* (May 31, 1971), most of the housing is substandard, unemployment hovers around 60 percent, and poverty is overwhelming. This community, like inner Washington, is controlled by forces outside of its own boundaries. One resident remarked, "Look at what people are being put through; welfare has been cut to the point where you are allotted 88 cents a day to feed a child. Our housing is being taken away. There are more people out of work than have jobs and the drugs just pour into the community. What are people to think of all this?" (Maynard, 1971 p. A-14) A community leader observed, "They are driving us off the land just the way they did the Indians." One mother said to Maynard, "The other night I set five traps and caught 13 mice in my apartment in two hours. The rats in the alley are as big as squirrels. My children see the mousetraps; they look outside and see the rats and they watch the firetrucks go by. That's their world, mice, rats, and firetrucks."

The drug problem in Brownsville, Washington, D.C., and hundreds of other Black communities around the country is far from peripheral in the lives of the children. Nor does Daniel P. Moynihan's recommendation to strengthen Black families by drafting Black youth into the armed forces make any positive contribution to the problem. One mother said, "After my oldest son got hooked on drugs, my next son asked me to sign for him to join the army. He was upset with all the drugs on the street. A year later he went AWOL . . . he said that he joined the army to get away from drugs and ran right back into it, only worse. The big shots were selling it and arranging to have it taken out of his pay." (Maynard, 1971 p. A-14)

What is to be done with and for the millions of Black children growing up in Brownsville and a hundred other American cities in conditions such as these? What is to be done with and for the families that struggle to help their children survive and protect their welfare? What is to be done with and for the Black communities that surround these families and children? The most pressing need is for a radical reformation of the social policies and institutions which cause these conditions. Among the chief reforms needed are a commitment to a full-employment economy and a guaranteed minimum income for all families and individuals, and a doctrine of reparations and preferential treatment for Black people.

These reforms will occur only if the Black community is empowered to express its own will and interests in matters which are paramount to it. For that to happen, the political and economic systems must be profoundly reexamined. It is clearly the responsibility of the government to provide for the general welfare of all its citizens, and it is clearly in the realm of economics that the Black community's greatest needs lie. It is in the interaction between the government and the economic system (in which Black people as a group are largely powerless) that the greatest promise for enhancing the well-being of Black children lies. For it is the interaction between these two giant systems that determines social policy and programs in housing, education, health, communication, law enforcement, social welfare, and even religion. In this country, at this point in history, the national government and the national economic system hold the key to the survival of Black children.

We do not ignore the various other levels and types of government. But it is the national government, through its taxing and regulating functions, that holds the greatest promise. History does not allow us to be overoptimistic about the response of the federal government to the needs of Black people. Until shortly after World War II the federal government showed no appreciable interest in the rights or the well-being of Black citizens, and until 1960 only one branch of the federal government—the judiciary—showed any active concern. Furthermore, even in the judiciary it was primarily the U.S. Supreme Court that reflected this commitment. Moreover, even the U.S. Supreme

Court limited its activities to selected areas of life such as education and public accommodations. Finally, the U.S. Supreme Court responded only when private litigation was initiated by Black people, a most burdensome, expensive, and slow mechanism for social change. Since the 1960's, largely on the initiative of Black people, the executive and finally the legislative branches of the national government have begun to respond to the special needs of Black people. Even here, it must be observed, however, that the various executive orders issued and laws passed have been faulty in conception, piecemeal in application, and halting in enforcement. The U.S. Commission on Civil Rights, in the most ambitious report on the subject that has ever been undertaken, found in 1970 that the legislation, executive orders, and court rulings designed ostensibly to enhance the welfare of Black people have been very poorly enforced. The report concluded, "In many areas in which civil rights laws afford pervasive legal participation—employment, housing, education—the discrimination persists and the goal of equal opportunity is far from achievement. The plain fact is that some of these laws are not working well." (*Federal Civil Rights Enforcement Efforts,* 1970, p. xvi) In those areas specifically covered by federal policy, areas where the government has a direct responsibility, Black people are still subjected to the forces of racist discrimination and economic insecurity.

Despite the provisions of the Civil Rights Act of 1964, the federal government, which is the nation's largest employer, continues to be a major cause of the poverty, the poor health, and the inadequate education and substandard housing that present major hazards to the lives of Black children. The Commission found that

> In the area of federal employment where the degree of federal control is absolute, minority group representation has increased substantially but Negro and Spanish surnamed Americans still are grossly underrepresented in the higher salary brackets. One example is the Federal Aviation Administration, which employed more than 20,000 Air Traffic Controllers as of June 30, 1969, only 547 of whom are minority employees. Furthermore there were only 13 minority group supervisors and administrators among the 16,000 employees at Grade GS14 or above. [Federal Civil Rights Enforcement Efforts, 1970, p. 69]

In state and local job programs funded by the federal government and specifically required to offer equal opportunities in employment, the record is even worse. It is disquieting that the enforcement of these policies is lodged with the Justice Department, for its commitment to Black liberation has not been outstanding. In the field of private employment, where companies with government contracts are sworn to follow equal hiring practices, many have flagrantly violated this commitment, not only with impunity but with rewards in the form of more and larger government contracts. In health, education, and housing the federal government has been equally halfhearted. Despite this record, however, we believe that the potential of the federal government for enhancing the welfare of its Black citizens is considerable. What is needed is a new set of priorities, enlightened and strong leadership, and a recognition of the pluralistic nature of our society.

The concepts of Black power and Black reparations provide the new impetus to such a reordering of national priorities. A national commitment to a safe and sanitary home for every American family and to comprehensive health care from birth to death, combined with a commitment to education to the individual's fullest capability, would do far more than attempts to enhance the first five years of life by government policies which are not followed by programs. Only this commitment can set into motion the kind of economic reconstruction of society which will lead to full employment and to the kind of community services that are indispensable for childhood and family life. At the same time, if the commitment is to meet the needs of the Black community, its families and children, the very conception of government policy, as well as the design and execution of the programs, must include a major input from the Black community. In order to be recompensed for centuries of neglect and mistreatment, Black people must be given priority and preferential treatment in the form of guaranteed and indisputable access to the housing, health facilities, educational programs, and other resources of their society which they have had a major hand in designing.

The problems faced by Black children in Washington, D.C., or Brownsville cannot be solved by removing them from their homes, nor by sending social workers into the homes to provide counseling and advice. The hard realities faced by these children must be attacked at their source—not the families or the communities, but the larger society in which the children live. Our present national policies and institutions were designed by white people to meet white needs and are therefore infested with the forces of racism, bureaucratic dysfunction, and professional misconception, as well as a generous portion of personal and cultural avarice and greed. Children cannot change this situation; it is the situation itself which must be changed.

The following, then, are the ideas which must be translated into social policy and comprehensive programs at the national level, with substantial Black initiative and Black control, if the welfare of Black children is to be significantly enhanced during the decade of the 1970's.

1. Commitment to a full-employment economy with a diversified pattern of skill requirements accompanied by on-the-job training.

During the 1960's the solution to unemployment was too often considered a matter of job training and various mechanisms to force poor people to find nonexistent jobs. Instead of exhorting people to work and providing limited job training, the nation must embark on a massive program of job creation. Such a comprehensive policy was called for by the Congressional Black Caucus of all thirteen Black members of the House of Representatives in their Statement to the President in March, 1971. They urged the creation of 500,000 productive jobs during the first six months of operation and 600,000 during the second six months in the public sector alone. (p. H2190) This recommendation, while limited in scope, more closely defines the real needs of Black people than the program later presented by the administration which called for 150,000 new jobs in the public sector. However, a public job-creating program has enormous promise for the years ahead. It does not yet have the kind of powerful support it needs. Just after the urban uprisings of 1967–69, a number of industries, including the insurance industry, announced a commitment to full employment. Even these industries have been very halfhearted and limited in outlook.

2. Commitment to a guaranteed minimum income for each family and individual.

This program should include subsidies for all not able to work or engaged in socially critical pursuits such as education and child rearing. The Congressional Black Caucus has joined the National Welfare Rights Organization in recommending that the income guarantee for a family of four should be a minimum of $6,500 a year, to be reached by a combination of wages and cash assistance, or cash assistance alone where necessary. The assumption is that families require economic self-sufficiency if they are to function properly. The present piecemeal programs of welfare and public assistance have proven grossly inadequate to this need. The administration's proposal in 1970 to guarantee $2,400 for a family of four is little better. We advocate the abolition of the patchwork assistance programs generated in the 1930's and the poverty programs generated in the 1960's. These programs should be removed from the residual category of society to the institutional category, and all of the major systems of the society should be committed to the abolition of poverty and the enhancement of the general welfare.

3. *Commitment to a national comprehensive program of child development.*

The Congressional Black Caucus has urged that the present limited child-development programs, stimulated by the Office of Economic Opportunity, should be significantly expanded. Our view is that such services should be national, comprehensive, and at least as accessible to all children and families as public school education now is.

The Caucus has also urged that such programs be developmental in character rather than simply custodial. The national system of child-development centers and programs should provide comprehensive health services, education, recreation, and cultural enrichment for three- and four-year-olds.

Closely related to the idea of child development is the idea that day-care centers should be available at the neighborhood level where families can take their infants and children for comprehensive care during the day, bringing them home again at night. For children with specialized physical and emotional needs, corresponding night-care facilities should be available in every community.

4. *Reconsideration of Child Placement.*

In some situations both families and children would be better off under a permanent or long-term separation. But this decision must be made not by outsiders, but from the standpoint of the families and children themselves.

The whole conception of placement in child welfare has been

generated without special regard to the history, the present situation, the needs, or the promises of Black people. The spirit of Black communalism has waxed and waned according to the circumstances, but has never died. Consequently, caring for others' children on a temporary, long-range, or permanent basis is a well-established feature of the Black community. Still, it has never made sense to Black people that a family who takes in a child on a temporary basis may be compensated for part of the cost of supporting that child, while the same family who takes in the same child on a permanent basis could not be compensated at all. However this practice might have suited the needs of white people and made sense to them, it has seemed as ironic, even as ridiculous, to Black people as it has been dysfunctional for them. The idea of subsidized adoption needs to be translated into public social policy. Senator Mervyn Dymally of the California State Senate and former Senator Basil Patterson of the New York State Senate have been among the first legislators approaching this idea on a state level. What is clearly needed is a national commitment to this idea and a set of programs to carry it out.

5. *The Necessity for Meaningful Education.*

It is our view that each Black family should be guaranteed that all of its children will have access to a comprehensive and diversified system of educational facilities at least from age three until they have finished benefiting from full-time or part-time education. This requires the development of major alternatives to the present system of education. Some have suggested a national Planning and Development Center, supported by the federal government and controlled by Black people, that could draw on all of the resources of the nation in planning educational facilities. The idea that some Black children should continue to be denied access to meaningful educational opportunities must be effectively abandoned.

6. *Restructuring of the Health-Care System.*

Here there is need for a restructuring of the national health-care system simultaneously with an empowerment of Black people to influence and use health care according to their needs. None of the health-care programs advanced to date comes close to meeting this need. We should start with the people. We should provide a voucher system that would entitle each American family to the best medical care available, on a preventive or curative basis, anywhere in the country. And at the same time there should be a massive federal commitment to the expansion of health-care facilities, with a significant degree of local citizen control.

7. Commitment to Decent Housing.

Finally, no effort to ensure the well-being of Black children can be successful without a commitment to decent, safe, and sanitary homes for all American families. The idea advanced by President Nixon in 1971 that a distinction be made between racial discrimination and socioeconomic discrimination in federal housing policies with the government keeping hands off socioeconomic discrimination seems mischievous at best. At worst, it is a sanction for racism in housing. We urge that as a start toward adequate housing we begin with Black people, then move to a housing program embracing all poor people, and then (and only then) return to the housing needs of the expanding middle-income American population. We urge, in short, a reversal of the traditional pattern of priorities. A national commitment on the part of the national government and private industry can enable this nation to take giant strides during the decade of the 1970's—strides away from its present path toward oblivion.

Bibliography

Abbott, Grace. *The Child and the State*. Vol. I: *Legal Status in the Family, Apprenticeship and Child Labor* (1938a). Vol. II: *The Dependent and the Delinquent Child; the Child of Unmarried Parents* (1938b). Chicago: The University of Chicago Press, 1938.

Adoptions in 1967: Supplement to Child Welfare Statistics—1967. U.S. Department of Health, Education and Welfare, Welfare Administration, Social and Rehabilitation Service, Children's Bureau Statistical Series, 92, 1968.

Bennett, Lerone, Jr. "A Challenge of Blackness." Atlanta, 1971. Manuscript.

——— *Beyond the Mayflower: A History of the Negro in America*. Chicago: Johnson Publishing Co., 1964.

——— "Liberation." *Ebony*, vol. 25 (August, 1970), pp. 36–43.

Billingsley, Andrew. *Black Families in White America*. Englewood Cliffs, N.J.: Prentice-Hall, 1968.

——— and Jeanne M. Giovannoni. "Black Children in Need of Parents." Study conducted under the joint auspices of the Metropolitan Applied Research Center in New York and the National Urban League, 1968. Manuscript.

Black Caucus: Journal of the National Association of Black Social Workers, vol. 3, no. 1 (Fall, 1970).

Brace, Charles L. *The Dangerous Classes of New York: and Twenty Years Work Among Them.* New York: Wynkop and Hallenbeck, 1872.

Bradley, Trudy. "An Exploration of Caseworkers' Perceptions of Adoptive Applicants." *Child Welfare,* vol. 45 (October, 1966), pp. 433–443.

Branham, Ethel. "One-Parent Adoptive Families—After Twenty-Five Months." Los Angeles, 1970. Manuscript.

Child Care Facilities for Dependent and Neglected Negro Children in Three Cities: New York City, Philadelphia, Cleveland. Howard W. Hopkirk, ed. New York: Child Welfare League of America, 1954.

Child Welfare Statistics, N.C.S.S. Report CW-1 (68), 1968, and N.C.S.S. Report CW-1 (69), 1969. U.S. Department of Health, Education and Welfare, Social and Rehabilitation Service, National Center for Social Statistics.

Children Under Institutional Care, 1923. U.S. Department of Commerce, Bureau of the Census, 1927.

Children Under Institutional Care and in Foster Homes, 1933. U.S. Department of Commerce, Bureau of the Census, 1935.

Conference of Black Child Development, Proceedings of the National. "Child Development from a Black Perspective." Washington, D.C., June 10–13, 1970. Mimeograph.

"Congressional Black Caucus' Recommendations to President Nixon." *Congressional Record,* vol. 117, no. 45 (March 30, 1971), pp. H2190–H2194.

Du Bois, W. E. B. *Black Reconstruction: An Essay Toward A History of the Part Which Black Folk Played in the Attempt to Reconstruct Democracy in America, 1860–1880.* 1935. Reprint. New York: Russell & Russell, 1956.

———, ed. *Efforts for Social Betterment Among Negro Americans* (Atlanta University Publication No. 14). Atlanta, Ga.: The Atlanta University Press, 1909. Reprint. New York: Russell & Russell, 1969.

——— *Some Efforts of Negroes for Social Betterment* (Atlanta University Publication No. 3). Atlanta, Ga.: The Atlanta University Press, 1898. Reprint. Russell & Russell, 1969.

——— *The Philadelphia Negro: A Social Study.* New York: Schocken Books, 1967.

——— *The Souls of Black Folk.* Chicago: A. C. McClurg & Co., 1903.

Fanshel, David. *A Study in Negro Adoption.* New York: Child Welfare League of America, 1957.

Federal Civil Rights Enforcement Efforts. Report on the U.S. Commission on Civil Rights. Washington, D.C.: U.S. Government Printing Office, 1970.

Folks, Homer. *The Care of Destitute, Neglected, and Delinquent Children.* New York: The Macmillan Co., 1907.

Gordon, Milton. *Assimilation in American Life.* New York: Oxford University Press, 1964.

Hill, Robert. "Strengths of Black Families." Study presented at the annual conference of the National Urban League, Detroit, July, 1971. Manuscript.

Hunger, U.S.A.: A Report of the Citizens' Board of Inquiry into Hunger and Malnutrition in the United States. Washington, D.C.: New Community Press, 1968.

Hunt, Eleanor P. "Infant Mortality and Poverty Areas." *Welfare in Review,* vol. 5, no. 7 (August–September, 1967), pp. 1–12. U.S. Department of Health, Education and Welfare.

Hylton, Lydia. "Trends in Adoption." *Child Welfare,* vol. 44 (February, 1966), pp. 377–86.

Jacoby, George P. *Catholic Church Care in Nineteenth Century New York.* Washington, D.C.: The Catholic University of America Press, 1941.

Jeter, Helen R. *Children, Problems, and Services in Child Welfare Programs.* U.S. Department of Health, Education and Welfare, Welfare Administration, Children's Bureau Publication No. 403-1963, 1963.

Kadushin, Alfred. *Child Welfare Services.* New York: The Macmillan Co., 1967.

Leonard, Elizabeth. "A History of the Riverdale Children's Association." New York, 1956. Manuscript.

Low, Seth. *America's Children and Youth in Institutions: 1950-1960-1964. A Demographic Analysis.* U.S. Department of Health, Education and Welfare, Welfare Administration, Children's Bureau Publication No. 435-1965, 1965.

Maas, Henry S., and Richard E. Engler, Jr. *Children in Need of Parents.* New York: Columbia University Press, 1959.

MARCH. *Adoptive Placement of Minority Group Children in the San Francisco Bay Area—A Study by MARCH.* San Francisco, 1959.

Maynard, Robert. "Bitter Brownsville." *Washington Post,* May 31, 1971, pp. 1, A-14.

Monthly Vital Statistics, vol. 18, no. 4 (June, 1969). U.S. Department of Health, Education and Welfare, National Center for Health Statistics.

National Urban League records, 1953–60. Washington, D.C.: Library of Congress, Manuscript Division.

Proceedings of the Conference on the Care of Dependent Children Held at Washington, D.C., January, 1909. 60th Congress, 2nd session, Senate Document No. 721 Washington, D.C.: U.S. Government Printing Office, 1909.

Proceedings of the First International Congress of African Peoples, Atlanta, Ga., September, 1970. Manuscript. Mimeographed.

Richmond, Mary, and Fred Hall. *A Study of Nine Hundred and Eighty-Five Widows Known to Certain Charity Organizations in 1910.* New

York: Charity Organization Department of the Russell Sage Foundation, 1913.

Senate of Maryland, No. 567. Annotated Code of Maryland (1966 Replacement Volume), Sec. 67; Article 16—An Act to Repeal and reenact with amendments.

Shireman, Joan Foster. *Subsidized Adoption: A Study of Use and Need in Four Agencies.* Springfield, Ill.: Child Care Association of Illinois, 1969.

Smyth, Albert H. *The Writings of Benjamin Franklin.* New York: The Macmillan Co., 1906.

State of California, Welfare and Institutions Code, Sec. 16117–16118.

State of Michigan, 75th Legislature Enrolled House Bill No. 2117, Amendment Chap. 10 of Act No. 288 of the Public Acts of 1939, Sec. 13a (1).

State of New York, Laws of 1968, Chap. 320, Par. K, Subdiv. 6, Sec. 398 of Social Service Law.

State of South Dakota Senate Bill No. 26 (Barton). 45th Session, Legislative Assembly 1970 (SDCL 25-6-13).

The Negro Family: The Case for National Action, Office of Policy Planning and Research, U.S. Department of Labor. Washington, D.C.: U.S. Government Printing Office, 1965.

Thurston, Henry W. *The Dependent Child: A Story of Changing Aims and Methods in the Care of Dependent Children.* New York: Columbia University Press, 1930.

Turitz, Zitha. "Issues in the Conceptualization of Social Work Services for Children in Their Own Homes." *Child Welfare,* vol. 47 (February, 1968), pp. 66–75.

United Nations Demographic Yearbook, Issue 18 (1966).

U.S. Department of Commerce, Bureau of the Census, *U.S. Census of Population, Population Characteristics,* 1920–1970.

Washington, Booker T. "The Claim of the Colored Child." In *The Child in the City: A Series of Papers Presented at the Conferences Held During the Chicago Child Welfare Exhibit.* Chicago: Chicago School of Civics and Philanthropy, Department of Social Investigation, 1912.

Watson, Kenneth W. "Adoption Practices and Changing Times." Paper presented to the 95th Annual Forum of The National Conference on Social Welfare, San Francisco, May, 1968. Manuscript.

White House Conference on Child Health and Protection of Dependent and Neglected Children. New York: D. Appleton-Century Co., 1930. See especially Ira De A. Reid, "The Negro in the United States," in the *Report of the Committee on Socially Handicapped—Dependency and Neglect,* pp. 279–312.

White House Conference on Children: A Report to the President. Washington, D.C.: U.S. Government Printing Office, 1971.

INDEX

Index

Abbott, Grace, 24, 26, 35, 39
Abolitionist Movement, 27, 29
Adoption: among Black people, 46; extended to Black children in 1950's, 139–73; extended to Black children in 1960's, 175–209; fees, 165, 194–95; infertility requirement, 165, 195–96; as legal institution, 35–36; professional standards for, 66–67; racial distribution of, 94–96; satellite agencies, 183–85; single parent, 197; subsidized, 199–201; transracial, 197–99
African Methodist Episcopal Zion Church, 47–48
Afro-American Child Care Association, 229
Afro-American Family and Community Services Agency, Inc., 232–38

Aid to Families with Dependent Children, 63–64
Allen A.M.E. Church, 116, 177
Almshouse, 25–33
Anglo conformity, 22–25
Atlanta Baptist College, 49
Atlanta University, 43, 49, 81, 159

BABY, 183
Bennett, Lerone, Jr., 87, 217
Birtwell, Charles, 70
Black adoptive applicants: characteristics of in California, 196–97; dropout rates, 192–94; myths about, 142, 150; recruitment of, 161–63, 189–91; screening in, 164–67, 191–97; single, 197